For Michael,

Good discovery

Christine Lamarche

TOQUÉ!
Creators of a New Quebec Gastronomy

Eat and be merry!

Normand Laprise

T!

© les éditions du passage
1115 Laurier Avenue West
Outremont, Québec H2V 2L3
Tel.:   514.273.1687
Fax :   514.908.1354

Distributed in Canada by
PROLOGUE
1650 Lionel-Bertrand Boulevard
Boisbriand, Québec J7E 4H4
Tel.:   450.434.0306
Fax :   450.434.2627

Photography
© Dominique Malaterre

Thank you to the following for their financial
support:
Gouvernement du Québec – Programme
de crédit d'impôt pour l'édition de livres –
Gestion SODEC
Canada Council for the Arts

We acknowledge the financial support of the
Government of Canada through the Canada
Book Fund for our publishing activities.

**Bibliothèque et Archives nationales
du Québec and Library and Archives Canada
cataloguing in publication**

Laprise, Normand, 1961-
Toqué! : Creators of a New Quebec Gastronomy
Translation of: Toqué !: les artisans
d'une gastronomie québécoise.
Includes index.
ISBN 978-2-922892-69-7

1. Gastronomy - Quebec (Province).   2. Laprise, Normand, 1961- .
3. Toqué! Restaurant (Montréal, Québec).   4. Cooking.
5. Cookbooks.

I. Malaterre, Dominique.   II. Title.

TX637.L36 2012   641.01'309714
C2012-941523-5

Legal deposit :
Bibliothèque nationale du Québec
Library and Archives Canada
4th quarter, 2012

NORMAND LAPRISE

TOQUÉ!

Creators of a New Quebec Gastronomy

Photography
Dominique Malaterre

les éditions du passage

GENESIS

*Given that yesterday's generations
were required to clear, build and develop,
I hope that today's generation will
diversify and take a more responsible
approach, without bowing to fashion
or compromise.*

NORMAND LAPRISE

At the heart of *Toqué!* is the desire for a flourishing Quebec gastronomy. It is essential to highlight the origins of our cooking and to pay tribute to our precursors and peers. For us, cooking in Montreal means developing techniques around local food, mainly from the Saint Lawrence Valley, Maritime provinces, Laurentians, Ottawa Valley, Eastern Townships, Ontario and beyond.

The originality of Quebec cuisine rests first of all on its hybrid heritage. The first settlers of the 16th century and First Nation communities shared not only squash, corn, Jerusalem artichokes and a plethora of wild herbs, but also many traditional preservation techniques adapted to Quebec's unforgiving climate. One of the clearest examples of this is the smoking of meat and certain fish like sturgeon, eel and salmon. We still share these traditions today. We go blueberry picking and have corn roasts, for example. These events are an integral part of our seasonal customs. The first settlers here even learned to make corn bloom, otherwise known as popcorn.

Besides the cultural heritage of the First Nations, the newcomers that arrived on these shores over the past few centuries—be they French, English, Irish, Italian or Eastern European Jew—all brought their own traditions with them that have since co-evolved with local specialties. They have participated in building a rich and colourful hybrid culinary heritage. Be it bagels with lox, cheddar, whiskey or canned tomatoes for "spaghetti sauce", traditions, cultures and recipes have been shared between our peoples for generations.

Before the Quiet Revolution, the microwave oven and the emergence of a middle class, it was the women, often without a penny to spare, who preserved our culinary heritage. These women, often known as *bonnes femmes (*a derogatory French-Canadian term meaning *mother hen)*, needed to be ingenious to feed their often large families. To save money, they would never throw away a single item, canning the summer's harvest, preparing soups with poultry carcasses and reusing stale bread. Traditions that required a good dose of ingenuity and sensitivity: darning a sock by inserting a bulb in its heel, rolling dough with an old bottle instead of a rolling pin, keeping the string used for tying up roasts until you had enough to make a dish mop… Today, restaurants don't take the time to think about recycling and reusing, but our traditional culinary knowledge still exists on Quebec farms as well as in the kitchens of an increasingly cosmopolitan Montreal.

Thankfully, a few individuals have swum against the tide and highlighted these traditions still preserved by our artisans. Politicians, artists, actors, sports stars and filmmakers have all laid claim to their Quebec identity, and have stirred the hearts of Quebeckers of all stripes. Among them, René Levesque, Maurice Richard, Gilles Vigneault, Paul-Émile Borduas, Claude Jutra, Jean-Paul Riopelle… And then there are those who have fired their ovens with this same idea in mind: Renaud Cyr, for example, who refused to use products imported from Europe or the United States. In the 1970s, he included local plants, fish and meat in his menu. A remarkable stand at a time when Quebec's food could be defined as plagiarised French cuisine, ill-adapted to local practices and resources. Mr. Cyr's approach was an inspiration for us. The door had been unlocked, but it was not yet wide open!

Building rare and precious relationships with our suppliers over the past twenty years has allowed us at *Toqué!* to develop a gastronomy rooted in Quebecois traditions. Inspired by the ingenuity of our mothers and grandmothers, reusing scraps and trimmings has become a guiding principle. Now, not only do we cook locally sourced products with zero waste, but this creative process, pushed to the extreme, has become our top priority. Our know-how and techniques ensure we completely use every product. After all, a quality ingredient will necessarily produce quality trimmings. Today, this commitment to second-use is part of our everyday cooking. We take this so far that sometimes we even run out of scraps!

I like the idea that the restaurant I opened with Christine twenty years ago has kept its original philosophy: to work with the best possible ingredients. If we are where we are today, it's thanks to quite a few people—most of them behind the scenes. I wanted to give them a voice in this book, since they have all played important roles in the development of Toqué!.

NORMAND LAPRISE

Toqué! opened its doors in 1993 on St-Denis Street in Montreal. A restaurant founded by two passionate people who'd made a daring bet in a city beset by economic woes: to be both chefs and owners at a time when this model was still rare. Normand Laprise and Christine Lamarche sought to develop a local gastronomy without compromise. It would take many years to see the project through, since the two restaurateurs needed to develop trust and respect with the breed of farmers, ranchers, pickers and gardeners who preserve local know-how.

Toqué!'s success allowed Christine and Normand to expand their restaurant and always offer more to their customers. They dug out a basement and extended the kitchen to add a space devoted to baking. Normand's experimenting gradually allowed him to start offering a tasting menu. Alongside all this, the dining room capacity grew from fifty-five to sixty-five, and then to ninety-five seats today. In January 2004, the restaurant moved to Jean-Paul Riopelle Plaza, at the heart of the downtown business core, and in 2006 became a member of the prestigious international network *Relais & Châteaux*.

One year later, the public at large discovered Normand Laprise's cooking thanks to Guillaume Sylvestre's documentary film *Well Done*. Following the chefs and sous-chefs of *Toqué!* and *Au Pied de Cochon* in their daily routine highlighted the friendship and friendly competition between the two restaurants. In 2010, *Toqué!* gave birth to *Brasserie T!,* located in Montreal's *Quartier des spectacles*.

Over the course of twenty years, *Toqué!* has become an incontrovertible place of learning for young cooks. Like a laboratory, the *Toqué!* kitchens are a forum for experimentation that seeks to better every dish. The tasting menu, changed daily, makes *Toqué!* a place where unique and inventive cuisine takes centre stage, a singular voice that resounds throughout Quebec and North America.

Today, chef Normand Laprise and his executive chef Charles-Antoine Crête are among Quebec's top culinary stars. Every day, they work to develop and enhance a culinary identity made of multiple influences, which they strive ever more to promote across borders and cultures.

Normand Laprise
Grand Chef Relais & Chateaux, co-owner

Originally from a region with an aboriginal name, Normand Laprise is particularly fond of his birthplace, located on the south shore of the Saint Lawrence. For him, the magical quality of Kamouraska is due to the subtle play of light and colour that evolves with the passage of every hour. Since childhood, this light has inspired the chef and continues to nourish him in everything he does. Born in the midst of the Quiet Revolution, in a Quebec where the middle class was still very young, Normand Laprise was only two years old when he was sent to live in a foster home. His mother had developed serious health problems and his father wasn't able to take care of their seven children alone. Normand grew up in a farmer's house in Saint-Pâcome, not far from Kamouraska. There, he participated in the daily chores and learned the notion of hard work that is at the centre of farm life. These lessons shaped his dynamic and enterprising personality. The cozy family meals prepared by Madame Lavoie, the farmer's wife, helped him develop his taste for seasonal products and learn the techniques necessary for transforming the summer's harvest into food to feed a large family for an entire winter.

Normand turned twelve before finally reuniting with his family in Quebec City. There, he worked as a caddy at the Boischâtel Royal Quebec Golf Club, where he got his first taste of refinement and travel. As he likes to reminisce today, golf, his second passion, has remained his favourite pastime over the years.

As a teenager, he worked in a kitchen for the first time, in a Greek restaurant on Saint-Jean Street, where he started as a dishwasher before being promoted to assistant. When Normand turned eighteen, encouraged by his friend Daniel Vézina, he decided to sign up at Charlebourg's hotel management institute. He then moved on to work in a restaurant recommended to him by one of his teachers. "I can still see them putting a frozen duck in an oven with a can of orange juice telling me, 'That, son, is duck à l'orange; one day you'll learn!' I didn't know much at the time, but I knew I didn't want to do that!"

He would leave that job and join *Café de la Paix*, a much more rigorous establishment specialized in French gastronomy. There, he would meet Chef Jean Abraham, who would teach him the importance of organization and consistency. At the same time, he tried out for *Marie-Clarisse*, another famous restaurant, where Chef Jacques Le Pluart was developing a more modern and creative cuisine. Full of life and determined to succeed, Normand worked two jobs at once for over a year, serving lunch at *Café de la Paix* and dinner at *Marie-Clarisse*. Between shifts, the young man would sit on the rocks by Quebec's old port and unwind before the Saint Lawrence River. Four years later, with his mentor Jacques Le Pluart's departure from the *Marie-Clarisse*, Normand decided to move to Montreal where he gained experience and met new people.

Motivated by a desire to travel and see the world, Normand left to work in Dijon, Burgundy. "Travel is essential and formative for the young cook. In France, I saw the perfect counter-example of how to lead your kitchen staff: bouts of anger, overblown egos and co-workers sometimes refusing to help each other just to get a leg up, even if the customer ultimately was the one who suffered most." Shocked by the violent clashes he encountered in French kitchens at the time, he was still able to recognize how important it is to value and respect the products you use, as well as maintain friendly relations between chefs and producers.

Barely back in Montreal, he accepted an offer by Mr. Beausoleil, a well-known epicurean, who wanted to open a restaurant—*Citrus*—inspired by California cuisine, which would later become quite popular in Montreal. "At first, everyone wanted to label what I was doing: French cuisine, California, fusion. Personally, I never identified myself with any specific category. I never even felt the need

to qualify my cuisine: I work, and always have worked, on instinct and with the utmost care." Normand was now a chef and surrounded himself with a talented team. Among them was a young Ryad Nasr, today chef at *Balthazar*, and Martin Picard, now chef and owner of the gargantuan *Au Pied de Cochon*. He would also meet Christine Lamarche, who was finishing her training at a hotel management school and wanted to join his team. By straying from the norm and practicing an intense style of cooking focused on vegetables, the new chef made his mark and created a success story, quickly becoming a reference for Montreal's finer palates. When *Citrus* closed, a number of friends and customers encouraged him to open his own restaurant, an idea that Christine was willing to follow up with him. Within a month, the two came together and, with the help of their friends, found a place on St-Denis: *Toqué!* was born.

At the time, Normand took on a hefty challenge: to create a gastronomy that was Quebecois in essence, and to work with quality, locally sourced ingredients. He continued on the path he'd first walked at *Citrus*, waking up every morning at dawn to explore Montreal's markets, searching for the tastiest meat or fish sourced from ethical professional farmers and fishermen. As owner and chef, Normand refused to compromise on quality. In the kitchen, he chose a capable team able to adapt to the daily finds and changing menus. "At first, I was completely obsessed with culinary challenges I wanted to set myself, discovering new products or creating a network of local producers, farmers, growers, pickers and fishermen who understood and shared my concerns and priorities. My top priority was to offer my customers consistent quality and diversity, despite our short seasons. Soon, I needed to increase the size of our kitchen and serving staff to flesh out the menu. That was yet another adjustment, a major evolution from our early and quite modest beginnings."

Normand's humility is an opportunity for aspiring chefs to express their creativity. Under his direction, young chefs have consistently given their best and dared to reinvent themselves daily. His many collaborators include Alexandre Loiseau, Lionel Piraux, Alexandra Shandling and Mehdi Brunet.

For many Montrealers, the St-Denis Street location is fondly remembered as a place of discovery. At a time when the city's main markets offered the same old veggies, *Toqué!* aimed for greater diversity in every dish. Thanks to daily conversations with producers, Normand began to add mushrooms, wild herbs, little known vegetables and countless species of flowers to his menu. He also encouraged the production of certain types of animals like red deer and pigeon and expanded his access to a large number of species of fish and shellfish from the waters of the Saint Lawrence River and Gulf. Normand and his team set the foundations for seasonal Quebecois cooking.

Rapidly, the restaurant enjoyed enormous success. The kitchen staff grew and Normand left to travel abroad once again. Having charmed the palates of guests at an event at Zoe restaurant in New York's Soho, he became a consultant at the famous *Cena*, where he introduced New Yorkers to Quebecois producers and their products. Traceability, variety, freshness and quality have served *Toqué!* well, becoming the restaurant's trademark, and setting the standard for other Quebecois institutions. A legacy and process at the foundation of a Quebec culinary identity which Normand Laprise, with characteristic generosity, wishes to share. "My first thought is to do everything I can to offer an unforgettable experience to my customers. I want them to relish the experience and leave with good memories. I've always considered myself as an artisan, surrounded by other artisans. With the amount of time we spend in the kitchen, it's important to find pleasure in what we do. We cooks are propelled by our passion. Day after day, it's what lets us take up new challenges with the same satisfaction." To walk through the doors of *Toqué!* is to meet passionate people who are trying to offer an authentic gastronomic experience.

Christine Lamarche
Co-owner

Born in Montreal, Christine Lamarche was raised in Saint-Donat in the Lanaudière region. The youngest of a family of five, she learned about wild plants and mushrooms and developed her interest for cooking through her mother. "At our house, we used to eat the mushrooms my mother picked. I remember spending entire evenings helping her clean the mushrooms that she'd dry. Over the course of our long winters, she would use them in everything and even make ice cream with miller mushrooms." Today, from her office next to the kitchen, Christine carefully monitors how forest products are transformed and prepared by the cooks.

The world of restaurants was not necessarily a first choice for the young woman who began her studies in geography. While travelling with her mother, she discovered France's great restaurants. Deeply impressed by this experience, she changed directions and decided to learn the culinary trade at a hotel management school. She earned her first stripes in the kitchen at *Citrus*, where she met Normand Laprise, with whom she shared a love of wild plants and seasonal vegetables. Drawn together by their common desire to develop a subtle cuisine rooted in local know-how, Christine and Normand slowly began building a strong friendship. This special relationship made Normand want to pursue their collaboration following *Citrus's* closure. She followed her instinct and accepted the offer on the spot. "Normand came to see me to say he was thinking of opening a restaurant. I immediately told him, 'If you need help, just tell me. I'm with you on this adventure.' I still remember his reply: 'Put your coat on, let's find ourselves a kitchen!'" Building a restaurant that could rival Europe's greatest institutions was what got her into this trade, and the table was set to face that challenge.

Back in the kitchen, after her daughter's birth, she started off on the lunch menu, with Normand taking responsibility for the evening's fare. Little by little, she migrated to the administrative part of the restaurant to allow her teammate greater creative control of a culinary universe that had first seen the light of day in the *Citrus* kitchens. A task she took to heart by seeing it as an adventure in itself: a way of life reflected in the way she managed her staff and served her clients. *Toqué!* has become an important institution in Montreal, thanks to both Normand's outstanding abilities and Christine's determination.

As the benevolent owner she is, Christine makes sure that everything is running smoothly on the service side of things. She shares her rigorous approach with every new arrival on the staff. Since 2004, she's been seconded by Fabien Novert, her right hand man and *Maître d'hôtel* at *Toqué!*, and Olivier Germain, the manager at *Brasserie T!*. The restaurant on Place Riopelle has become a rite of passage for young people wishing to start their own restaurant, work as managers or become chefs. "*Toqué!* is first and foremost a lifestyle. We want our employees to share this experience with us. That includes communicating our passion and know-how to customers, so when they take a bite, or a sip, or simply walk through the door, they immediately feel the idea behind our restaurant. You can't have one philosophy in the kitchen and another on the floor. Ours is also an art of understanding customers' desires and adapting to their particularities." Gastronomy not only consists of cooking a great meal but also includes hosting your customers with distinction. Customer satisfaction remains the first objective of all those working in the restaurant business. You don't choose that career for its creature comforts, but to ensure that every person who sits down at one of your tables goes home happy.

With her characteristic elegance and discretion, Christine is always there to fulfil her customers' expectations, which, according to her, have evolved in tandem with the scope of Quebec's gastronomy. "One thing is for certain: at *Toqué!,* we do what we do because we believe in it."

Charles-Antoine Crête
Executive chef de cuisine

A native of Saint-Augustin near Mirabel, Charles-Antoine Crête is the executive chef de cuisine at *Toqué!* An absolute live wire, he's responsible for developing new dishes and devising menus at both *Toqué!* and *Brasserie T!* and much, much more...

From his father—a carpenter and sculptor—he learned the importance of patience and rigour at a young age, both essential qualities of the craftsman. His mother, more of a dreamer, led him to discover the effervescence of the kitchen, which she saw as a laboratory. "When I was about nine years old, I loved to spend time with my mother in the kitchen. I thought time went by faster there than with my father in his studio. We'd go into the garden, hunting for ideas. She tried things; sometimes it worked, sometimes it didn't, but she always had such style." Inspired by this, as a teenager he used to experiment with techniques, trying different flavour associations that led him to develop his particular palate and culinary intuition. "To understand taste, you've got to eat. As a boy, I'd put a spoonful of salt in my mouth, followed by a spoonful of sugar. Then I'd put another spoonful of salt in my mouth, and take a sip of sweet wine, just to see the effect. I was very experimental."

His first experiences were also shaped by the teachings of Chef Jean-Paul Giroux, who, at the time, had a restaurant near the family home. "With Jean-Paul we mucked around a lot. He had such a creative vision. I had a wheelbarrow in which I'd drag around a bunch of stuff I picked up in the fields. I'd steal all my mothers' raspberries and run out the back door so she wouldn't see me. Half her kitchen utensils ended up in Jean-Paul's kitchen." Today, Charles still approaches every new dish with as much exuberance. His creative process is fundamentally anchored in Quebec's cultural heritage, that of a people who adapted to a harsh climate and relied on true ingenuity to survive. "If I'd become an architect, I'd be one of those who recycles old materials to build houses. If I'd become a storyteller, I'd

pick up stories from everywhere to tell them. I'm a cook, so I'm inspired by all sorts of ingredients and tools in the kitchen." A vision close to Christine and Normand's, who opened their doors to him after he was kicked out of the ITHQ, Montreal's premier cooking school, for his nonconformist conception of the culinary arts.

After years spent with *Toqué!,* Normand encouraged Charles to finish his training outside Canada. In 2003-2004, during an internship at the Catalan restaurant *El Bulli,* with the famous chef Ferran Adrià, he discovered a process close to his own: "Over there, I met people like me, people who left in the morning with a shovel to unearth a cactus they'd serve at supper! We let ourselves be inspired by what surrounded us. Over there, I learned how to organize my chaotic creativity! " A process he made more effective while working as chef de cuisine for Orio Castro, for whom discipline is the fundamental ingredient of the creative process. There, he understood that his father's methodical approach in the carpenter's studio wasn't so different from that of the great chefs he met. After four years abroad, Charles-Antoine returned to Montreal to continue developing a process that he sees as a series of experimentations. An approach that he transmits today to his co-workers at *Toqué!* who follow him on his daily quests for new discoveries. For Charles, it's essential that cooks participate in every step of the creation of a new recipe in order to understand how each contribution is essential to the final product. It's also a way of managing a team that he sees as one of the keys for a truly creative kitchen.

At *Toqué!,* he also learned about the importance of building relationships with suppliers, and met his right-hand woman and best friend, Cheryl Johnson. "When I'd start experimenting on a new project, I'd leave her with it, and go off to work on something else. I'd come back later and we'd talk about it. Not only was she a leader in the kitchen, but she followed me when I fell off my rocker

Without Normand, no Charles-Antoine. I owe
him a lot. After all these years, we're like an old
couple. The secret behind such a long relationship?
We don't sleep together!

Working with Christine is like going downhill
on cross-country skis; there's no effort behind it!

CHARLES-ANTOINE CRÊTE

and began working on some new twisted invention." By
grounding their work on taste, diversity and quality ingredients, the two young cooks, accompanied by Normand,
gave a talk in New York where they developed *Cooking from*
Scraps: techniques that pushed Normand's creative process even further. A know-how developed in the kitchen
that maximizes, in the most creative way possible, the
complete use of every ingredient. Little by little, they began
to fry asparagus peels, make chips from squash trimmings
or reuse strawberry hulls to make water for cocktails.

Charles-Antoine stands out of the crowd with his unique
style, seen in every dish he prepares. Spontaneous and
playful but never pedantic, his presentations are symbolic
of his simple cuisine that fits perfectly with the *Toqué!*
philosophy. Refusing stylish effects, garish decoration and
overbearing stiffness, Charles-Antoine sets out his dishes
like a canvas painted in the style of Riopelle, playing with
colours and the irregularity of materials. "We like to play
around by throwing liquids and powders that spill over the
edge of our plates. It's simultaneously elegant, wild and
very precise. It's a bit disconcerting, really, but it reflects
who we are." An extravagance which has become a signature
for *Toqué!*'s youngest son.

A Cooking School,
a Place of Inspiration

THE KITCHEN AS WORKPLACE

As chef and co-founder of *Toqué!,* Normand Laprise created an environment in which talent could be expressed in the kitchen. After preparing thousands of meals in the basement kitchen of *Toqué!,* back when it was located on Saint-Denis Street, he wished to create a pleasant working environment for his cooks. This was one of the reasons that led him to the restaurant's new location.

To create an improved environment, Normand conceived and drew up the initial plans for the kitchen, which he saw as spacious, bright and open. Equipped with large bay windows and top quality appliances, the kitchens are an exceptional workspace for apprentice cooks.

In the words of one young vegetable chef, Tony: "The kitchen itself is one of the reasons why I wanted to come and work here. It's an incredible space. The placing of each station makes sense: cold storage, warm storage, entremets, pastry... Even the floors make sense! " By allowing curious customers to visit the kitchen, Normand and Christine establish a link between front and backstage. A stimulating idea that warm station chef Raphy particularly enjoys. "Clearly this adds additional pressure since we have to be that much more rigorous, but it's totally worth it when we see the awe and pleasure showing on our customers' faces. This interplay is crucial since, for us, customer satisfaction needs to be our first priority."

KITCHEN PILLARS

Normand and Charles-Antoine share responsibilities. The latter's role is to keep an eye on everything. He leads his six sous-chefs, whom he calls his pillars, split between *Toqué!* and *Brasserie T!* The first among them is Jean-Sébastien, one of the oldest, since he's been with *Toqué!* since 2005. "My role is to second Charles. I filter his ideas before transmitting them to the rest of the staff, and when he isn't there, I represent him. In fact, I'm his

projection in the kitchen." The tasks of a sous-chef require full investment: checking with the lunch service manager that lunchtime runs smoothly, organizing the evening's service, changing the à la carte menus, organizing wine tastings and all of the *mise en place*... To manage these tasks, Jean-Sébastien is ably supported by Amin, a sous-chef. It was as a dishwasher that Amin first discovered the kitchen. His curiosity and willingness to learn were noticed by Charles, who encouraged him to go for a culinary career. "Little by little, Charles started giving me little tasks in the kitchen. Once he showed me how to debone a pigeon. It's rare you see a chef showing kitchen techniques to a dishwasher!"

Being flexible is a difficult test that every member of the staff knows well, since working at *Toqué!* requires constant flexibility. As Amin says, "Here, in this restaurant, routine doesn't exist." Lunch service sous-chef Valérie, a young cook who joined Normand Laprise's team in 2009, is a real pedagogue. On a daily basis, she teaches fundamental culinary rules to her team. "When you work a station, you have to be able to do it with your eyes closed. You can't waste time looking for something during a service. When you have a meal, you know where your utensils are; when you're working, it should be the same thing. Everything should be in its place: the fork on the left, the knife and the spoon on the right."

At *Brasserie T!,* the same rigorous method applies: François is the chef there, seconded by André and Aaron, his sous-chefs. For François, the *Toqué!* philosophy has always been the same: "Do well today, do better tomorrow." At his side, André, the lunch service sous-chef, sees this process as a stimulating one that leads cooks to experiment with a variety of techniques and presentations. "It's a signature, a style that is found nowhere else. There's a freedom in the way we cook that remains very spontaneous, 'on the spot.'"

*The tasting menu is our beating heart.
It brings together all the new techniques
and development work done in the
kitchen. It's also the final test for a new
dish: if it passes the taste test, then it
has a chance of making its way onto our
à la carte menu.*

CHARLES-ANTOINE CRÊTE

THE *TOQUÉ!* WAY

The *Toqué!* style is defined in opposition to European and French kitchens, as Jean-Philippe, a French cook, observes: "I see some pretty daring things here, more 'funky,' Charles would say. In Quebec, chefs can really let their imaginations run wild. When Charles systematically invents or develops something, he comes and gets us to taste it. We participate in the taste test, it's very interesting." At *Toqué!* and *Brasserie T!,* more than thirty young men and women give their very best every day. An approach that Cheryl, former sous-chef at the restaurant, sees as unique: "I think the word honesty best qualifies *Toqué!*" She first experienced the restaurant's philosophy after finishing culinary school in the United States. She came here to discover Quebec and Normand Laprise's cooking. "I had heard really great things about their method and the pedagogical approach they take with young apprentice cooks. During my internship, I had the opportunity to discover the way every station worked and to develop my techniques, as well as rigour and speed." Quickly becoming Charles-Antoine's right hand, she became sous-chef and left behind an indelible mark in the *Toqué!* kitchen.

THE TASTING MENU: A LABORATORY

The tasting menu is our laboratory. Every new technique and idea is expressed there. It's also a way for us to use our extremely perishable products quickly. As opposed to our à la carte menu, the tasting menu is the result of a last-minute whim. For example, if we receive nasturtium flowers one morning, instead of cooking a little bit every day we prefer to build a dish around the flower and serve it that same night. Composed of seven dishes, the tasting menu is a risky adventure. The menu is never fixed, and can evolve over the course of the evening as new items arrive or new ideas are born in the kitchen; this is why we never write it down. However, we have a very strict process to ensure balance between dishes.

This balance is strengthened by our wine pairings, concocted each week by Samuel Chevalier-Savaria, the restaurant's sommelier since 2009. He sees his job like a game, always keeping in mind the importance of trying new things: "I've decided to remember what tastes good, what I feel like drinking." At *Toqué!,* since the dishes are remarkably sophisticated and balanced, the sommelier's role consists in finding the perfect pairing that will highlight the dish's flavours while letting the wine express itself. "There is a two-fold adaptation here: one to the season, meaning that I try to find what's most pleasant to drink at any given time; and the other to the dish, the goal being to diversify pairings and go beyond preconceived notions." While a sommelier's vocabulary is often very technical, Samuel likes to use metaphors. It's a way for him to share and communicate his passion to as many people as possible. "To help people understand, I use all sorts of images and adjectives when talking about Beaujolais wines, like an *autumn* flavour, or a taste of *dead leaves*, since granite soils usually express that characteristic."

AWAKENING

Dianne Duquet

DUNHAM, EASTERN TOWNSHIPS

My grandmother was a horticulturist by trade. It's thanks to her that I'm drawn to the earth. At a very young age, I used to follow her around the garden, where she would let me touch and taste everything. I remember how meticulously she wiped down her tools at the end of every day and hung them in her tiny shed. I loved watching her hands, always admiring her slow, precise movements. I'll never forget that smell of geraniums and damp earth that welcomed you whenever you walked into her house.

It wasn't long before Dianne got noticed at Toqué! Why? She would bring her own chopsticks! She preferred them to silverware because they made it easier for her to take her time and savour each item on her plate individually.

NORMAND LAPRISE

GROUNDWORK

My garden is on the outskirts of Dunham in the Eastern Townships. It's nothing like your everyday, rectangular garden—it winds and follows the contours of its natural setting. At first I cultivated a tiny patch, but I immediately sensed what my garden could become. Two years later, after I had taken time to really soak up my surroundings, I started drawing up plans. Someone once told me it's hard to see where my garden ends and the hills and wilderness begin... I think that's a wonderful compliment.

My specialty is growing wild plants. Normand says I pick them with the delicacy of a lace-maker. Once you start cultivating a garden like mine, you learn to taste, to wait, to observe. It's more an experimental research lab than a production garden. You need to have a certain degree of know-how.

PASSION AND SIMPLICITY

I've been working with Normand since 2002. I first started going to his restaurant when it was on St. Denis Street. Over time our friendship blossomed, and one day he asked me if I would grow products for his restaurant. We did a trial run with garlic, herbs and my grandmother's beans. In the early days, production was pretty limited, but we cooperated more as time went by. Normand prefers collaborating with people who work with the same passion and simplicity that he does. His main criterion for selection is taste. For instance, he'll favour a leaf with imperfections due to cold weather over a prettier, less tasty one. What I enjoy most about the *Toqué!* team is that everyone takes a keen interest in the testing stages. When Normand and Charles-Antoine come over, they remind me of young goats because they're constantly looking everywhere and sampling everything. They're willing to try some pretty crazy things. Their experiments don't always work, but when something does, it's a keeper!

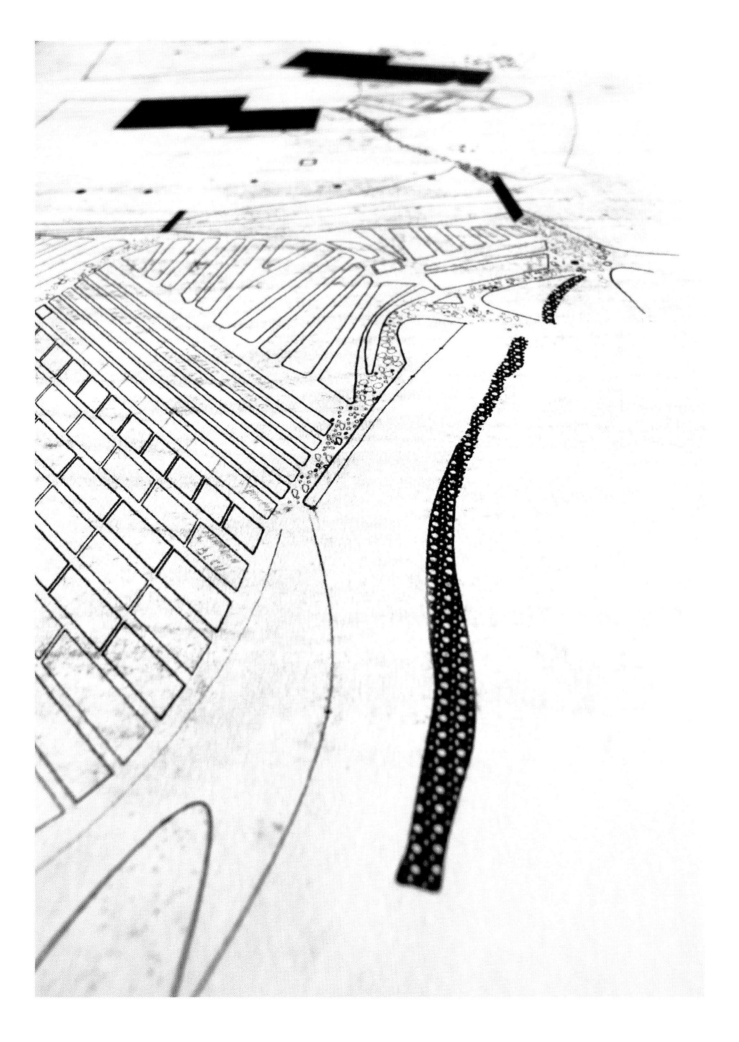

Modern Day Gatherers

At Toqué!, Dianne is queen. When she sets foot in the kitchen, the entire crew gathers around to open her boxes and see what she has picked. What's remarkable about Dianne is that all her products are beautiful and carefully presented. Her attention to detail and aesthetic sense are highly developed, which is something that can be seen in her garden. For example, she has taken to collecting our princess scallop shells which, in addition to adding natural and essential minerals to the soil, delineate where we can walk within the rows. Our collaboration with Dianne gives us quick and regular access to first-rate, exceptionally fresh garden and wild herbs, vegetables, plants and flowers.

Having such a tireless, disciplined gardener is a real motivation for a kitchen crew. When you know how demanding her work is, you almost feel obliged to use the greatest care in the way you prepare her produce, since every crate she brings in is a treasure chest. This kind of trust is built over an extended period of time; for Normand, the process began in the 1990s. Back then, he would make his way to Jean Talon Market, Montreal's most venerable farmer's market, several times a week. That's where he met, among others, Ms. Bougie, a celeriac grower, Mr. Lauzon, an herb vendor, and François

Brouillard, a master of wild forest plants. By working closely with the latter and encouraging him to expand his business, the chef was able to infuse his dishes with a local signature and authentic flavours. As a result, our Quebecois dishes often feature fruits and berries, daylily and orpine shoots as well as wild ginger. While some chefs saw François as a fool who sold weeds, Normand always trusted him. The picker would drop by *Toqué!* unannounced, arms filled with produce he had picked the day before. Unreachable, always on the road, he lived in his trailer, moving between forests and restaurants. François eventually expanded his operations to picking seaside plants in the Kamouraska region. Thanks to François, Normand rediscovered dog rose hips, which he used to eat like candy as a boy.

François was the first in a long line of "woodsmen" who make their way to *Toqué!* every summer. Guy Lacoste is another. We met him through the Desteredjian family, who are pioneers in the mushroom distribution business in Quebec. From Montreal to Yukon and down the west coast of Canada and the US, Guy criss-crosses the territory hunting for mushrooms, which he learned to identify in California in the 1970s. His business involves a great deal of research. First, he seeks

out trees that will guide him to the mushrooms. Then he learns about soil types and their drainage capacity, which helps him find different species. He also watches for squirrels that will show him where to find particular mushrooms such as the matsutake, which they guard and feast on. Guy Lacoste, the Desteredjian family, François Brouillard, Gérard Mathar on the Gaspé Peninsula, Claudie Gagné in Kamouraska… All passionate and environmentally conscious people who, every summer, present the *Toqué!* cooks with the very best of their harvest.

DANDELIONS

NETTLES

While most people think of dandelions as nothing but weeds to be ripped out of the ground, Dianne disagrees. As soon as the snow has melted, she's in her garden, diligently picking them. The first batch, which has survived the cold, is the tastiest since frost heightens the plant's sweet, mild taste. The dandelions she collects are curled and turned toward the ground. Early every spring, they herald the start of the season in our kitchens.

Nettles have been found in kitchens since the Middle Ages. Most people are afraid to eat them until they know that it's the stems that sting, not the leaves. Dianne keeps a healthy crop of wild nettles growing in the borders of her garden. Our cooks use them to make wild nettle chips grilled à la plancha with a drizzle of oil and coarse salt. You can also make nettle milk, a popular concoction in Europe during World War II because of its rich, nutritional value.

BARBERRY

From the genus *berberis*, the barberry is a shrub that yields small, oblong fruit rich in vitamin C. The shrub itself is extremely thorny, reason why our ancestors used it to close off pastures. First Nation communities used barberry for its various therapeutic qualities. The berries themselves resemble cranberries, though smaller and more acidic. Before the first frosts, the fruit is inedible. It needs to be picked while there's still snow on the ground, since the cold reduces its acidity and intensifies its taste. Since the branch is very prickly, it requires a great deal of patience to manipulate. At the restaurant, we initially cooked it as a jelly with foie gras, then gradually integrated it into our desserts and smoked fat.

SEA BUCKTHORN

This berry has a unique life. Since picking the fruit from the prickly shrub is a difficult task, major growers cut off whole branches and freeze them, allowing the berries to be easily shaken off. Dianne, however, picks them by hand, so she can only bring us a few hundred grams worth per week. *At Toque!,* we steep the branches and use the sea buckthorn infusion as a base for cocktails. As for the fruit, we make powders, juices, mousses, sorbets, fruit pastes and, more recently, chips—a fun addition to our desserts and dry salads.

FIDDLEHEADS

ASPARAGUS

Fiddleheads are the fronds of the ostrich fern, which grows in Quebec forests. François Brouillard was our official supplier for a long time. Fiddleheads are best at the start of the season, at the end of April or in early May, as they grow too bitter with the summer heat and, ultimately, uncurl into fully grown ferns. The plant can be dangerous if eaten uncooked. Blanching the fiddleheads, while taking care to throw out the stock, makes them safe for consumption. Most of the time, we pan-fry our fiddleheads and serve them as a garnish.

At *Toqué!*, in May and June, we cook green, white, and purple asparagus. Green asparagus is known to be heavy and gorged with water. The larger they are, the better they will be, since the juices make them tastier. The white asparagus we use are actually albino green asparagus grown underground. The original white asparagus, a plump and bitter Belgian variety, oxidizes very quickly and has a unique taste and texture. It's difficult to find it in Quebec, since its culture is extremely time-consuming. Normand discovered the Belgian variety at Café de la Paix under Chef Jean Abraham who came from the Portneuf region, where the soil conditions are favourable to optimal growth. Normand continued to use them in the kitchen when he became chef at *Citrus*, and all the way to the early days of *Toqué!*

DAYLILY

The daylily is an escaped plant present throughout Quebec. Like the dandelion, it sprouts as soon as the snow begins to melt. Every part is edible: the leaves, flower, pistil, etc.

Back when *Toqué!* started, François Brouillard brought us fresh flower buds that we marinated and served with a *grenobloise* sauce as a side dish to lobster. With Dianne, we learned to use the entire plant.

If daylilies grow near enough to the surface, their small shoots remain very tender and white. They're quite crunchy, with a pronounced vegetable flavour similar to that of young leeks. They can be served raw or cooked, in a salad with vinaigrette.

The most tender leaves grow at the base of the stem in a "v" shape. We thought to use this "v" as a container, as in our daylily with caviar and whipped cream recipe. When the daylily stem is still young, the scape is soft enough to eat. We prepare it like asparagus, blanching it, pan-frying it whole, or serving it with a vinaigrette. We use the base of the stem, which is drier, as a straw for cocktails.

When buds begin to grow more plentiful on the plant, we collect them when they're still small, firm and hard, and marinate them like capers. When they're bigger, we pan-fry them for use in vegetable salads.

The flower is similar to an orange lily and is very pretty. Its petals and pistils lend colour to our salads, and its mild coconut flavour is perfect for awakening the palate in early spring. When the flowers start to fade, we make chips with them, which we serve as a snack or side dish.

BALSAM FIR

In Dunham, Dianne has balsam firs growing everywhere. In spring, she brings us their vibrant, distinctively flavoured buds. When cooking, we use the small needles to complete salty dishes (other types of conifers can also do).

The fir tree is present in many of our current dishes. Initially, we steeped its branches to make water for cocktails or to flavour the butter we use in certain meat confits such as pigeon. We christened this butter *Beurre de l'amour* in honour of the herb-infused butter mixture Charles made for his family during lobster season. He'd gather the aromatic herbs from his mother's garden and put them through the blender to produce a powder that he mixed with melted butter.

Starting in 2011, we decided to look for ways to cook with foods in their purest form. We tried making fir sugar; the result had a rosemary flavour which brought back memories of the rosemary and grapefruit vinaigrette we used to make in the early days of *Toqué!* We made a discovery as we cleaned a coffee grinder (in which we had previously blended whole fir) with coarse salt. The salt we used to clean our machine was infused with a coniferous taste and the salt itself had turned into a fine, floury powder that was ideal for seasoning the endive salads we serve with pressed foie gras. We have been using this salt ever since in many of our seasonings—recycling at its best! Nowadays, fir is as important to *Toqué!* as sage or rosemary and it is available year round.

Once every five years, fir trees regenerate themselves, resulting in the growth of reddish buds, which release a white powder. Despite their rarity, Dianne manages to provide us with a small quantity of these sweet and tasty buds every year. We use them to make a very pink, nearly fuchsia infusion.

TOQUÉ! GROWERS AND COOKS SHARE A VERY CLOSE CONNECTION. THE LAST TIME WE PAID DIANNE A VISIT, WE GATHERED ROCKS FROM HER BACKYARD. BACK IN THE KITCHEN, WE USE THEM TO BOTH COOK AND AS DECORATION. ANOTHER TIME, WE PRUNED HER NETTLES SO THEY WOULD GROW TALLER AND FULLER. THAT INSPIRED US TO MAKE NETTLE CHIPS. IDEAS LIKE THESE COME TO US EVERY SO OFTEN. "I HATE TO THROW ANYTHING OUT, SO I LIKE TO REUSE, WHICH IS ONE OF THE THINGS THAT FUELS MY CREATIVITY," CHARLES-ANTOINE EXPLAINS. "IT REALLY MOTIVATES ME. WHEN I THINK I CAN REUSE SOMETHING, I'LL TRY A BUNCH OF DIFFERENT TECHNIQUES UNTIL I FIND A WAY TO PUT IT TO GOOD USE."

CREATIVITY REQUIRES DISCIPLINE. YOU HAVE TO BE AN ASSIDUOUS NOTE TAKER BUT ALSO FOLLOW UP ON YOUR IDEAS. CHARLES-ANTOINE HAS HIS OWN REFERENCE POINTS: HIS DRAWINGS AND OLD OBJECTS, ITEMS HE ACCUMULATES AND KEEPS ON HIS DESK FOR YEARS ON END.

COCKTAILS

FIR MOUSSE AND SEA BUCKTHORN COCKTAIL

GIVES 8 × 90 ML GLASSES (3 OZ)
PREPARATION: 1 HR
REST: 6 HRS

Fir Mousse

· 3 gelatin sheets
· 375 ml (1½ cups) water
· 55 g (1 cup) balsam fir needles
· 80 g (⅓ cup) white sugar

Sea Buckthorn Water

· 750 ml (3 cups) sea buckthorn berries
· 375 ml (1½ cups) water
· Simple syrup, to taste [P. 448]

Finishing Touches

· 240 ml (8 oz) vodka

Fir Mousse

1 Bloom the gelatin sheets in a bowl of cold water. Bring the water, fir needles and sugar to a boil in a pot. Remove from heat and steep for approximately 15 minutes (be careful: if you let the water boil for too long, the mixture will turn bitter). Strain in a conical strainer and whisk in the drained gelatin. Let cool in the refrigerator. Pour the liquid into a small whipped cream dispenser, and load the dispenser with two N_2O chargers. Place the dispenser head down in a large bowl of ice water, and refrigerate for 6 hours. [P. 451]

Sea Buckthorn Water

2 In a pot over medium high heat, heat the sea buckthorn berries and water until the berries start to burst. Remove immediately from heat, and strain with a conical strainer. Let the liquid drain slowly, pressing the fruit as little as possible to minimize the amount of pulp. Strain the mixture with a coffee filter. Sweeten to taste with the simple syrup.

Finishing Touches

3 In each glass, stir 60 ml (2 oz) of sea buckthorn water with 30 ml (1 oz) of vodka, and then top with a burst of fir mousse.

FLOWERS

The Spoonful of flowers idea was a spontaneous creation for one of our restaurant's good customers. That day, Dianne had delivered a cargo of flowers. Instead of dividing them among several different dishes, we thought, "Why not offer him the entire garden in one bite?" It's like an explosion of flavours, all going off at once in your mouth.

SPOONFUL OF FLOWERS

SERVES 4 TO 6
PREPARATION: 15 MIN

· 4 to 6 small, washed, edible flowers (of at least 4 varieties: begonia, calendula, lovage flowers, carnation, clary sage, etc.)
· A few seasonal berries (strawberry, raspberry, black currant, red currant)
· Organic sugar, to taste
· 1 pinch fleur de sel

1 This recipe should be served in individual tablespoons. Cut the larger berries into small pieces. Break the petals down if the flowers are too big. Place the fruit and flowers in the spoon, building from the smallest to the largest pieces. Sprinkle with sugar, and finish with a pinch of salt.

TIP
+ Serve with a glass of ice water with a splash of lemon to bring the flavours to the fore. You can vary the combination of flowers over the course of the summer.

WASABI MOUSSE BEGONIAS

SERVES 4 PEOPLE
PREPARATION: 15 MIN
REST: 6 HRS

· 3 gelatin sheets
· 375 ml (1½ cups) water
· 3 tbsp lime juice
· 30 g (1 oz) wasabi paste (from a tube)
· A few small begonias (or some large petals)

1 Bloom the gelatin sheets in a bowl of cold water. Mix together the water, lime juice and wasabi in a pot and heat over medium heat. Strain the gelatin, and whisk it into the mixture until dissolved.

2 Pour the mixture into a small whipped cream dispenser loaded with two N_2O chargers. Place the dispenser head down in a large bowl of ice water and refrigerate for 6 hours. [P. 451]

Finishing Touches
3 Pick the begonia petals and garnish with wasabi mousse.

CRISPY APPETIZERS

The *Toqué!* team is always looking for new ways to cook readily available ingredients. This was the inspiration behind our dandelions grilled à la plancha. Perhaps it's not the most beautiful-looking dish, but it's really delicious! The leaves are crispy while the stems and shoots remain soft and juicy. Nettle leaves can be sautéed in the same way, and both variations pair well with dry salads.

SAUTÉED DANDELIONS OR NETTLES

SERVES 2 TO 4
PREPARATION: 30 MIN

· 20 nettle stems or young spring dandelion shoots
· 2 tbsp olive oil
· Salt and freshly ground black pepper

1 Remove the nettle stems (wearing gloves), and keep the leaves whole. Remove all the dandelion roots from the shoots, and arrange the flowers in a bouquet.

2 Preheat the oven to 200°C (400°F). Spread the nettles or dandelions on a large baking sheet lined with parchment paper. Brush them with oil and cook until they become nice and crispy.

TIP
+ You can also grill horns of plenty or wild salsify shoots in the same manner. The key to this recipe is to chose ingredients that contain little water.

FRIED FIDDLEHEADS AND POPCORN

SERVES 4 PEOPLE
PREPARATION: 30 MIN

· 10 g (1 cup) plain popcorn
· 250 g (8 oz) fiddleheads
· 1 L (4 cups) canola oil
· Salt and freshly ground black pepper

1 In a coffee grinder, grind the popcorn to a fine powder and set aside.

2 Meanwhile, soak the fiddleheads in cold water for 10 minutes, stirring occasionally to completely remove their brown skins. In a pot of boiling salted water, blanch the fiddleheads for 2 minutes. Remove and place in a bowl of ice water to cool.

3 In a deep fryer, heat the canola oil to 180°C (350°F). Remove any oxidized portions of the stems, then cut the remaining fiddleheads in half width-wise and pat dry. Fry for approximately 30 seconds, and drip dry on paper towels. Add salt and pepper to taste.

4 Dust with popcorn powder and serve with poultry or game.

WILTED DAYLILY CHIPS

MAKES 8 TO 12 CHIPS
PREPARATION: 30 MIN
DRY 24 HRS

· 250 ml (1 cup) simple syrup [P. 448]
· 8 to 12 wilted daylily blossoms

1 Preheat the oven to 210°C (410°F).

2 In a bowl, dip the flowers one by one in the syrup. Remove any excess syrup and lay the flowers flat on a silicone baking mat. Bake for 10 minutes, then rotate the mat, and cook for another 10 minutes. Flip the flowers over with a metal spatula and bake for 5 more minutes. Finally, turn off the heat and switch on the oven light, and let the flowers dry for at least 24 hours until very crispy.

TIP
+ Once picked, daylilies only remain open for a short time. Wilted flowers or those collected at the end of the season work best for daylily chips.

ANOTHER ROUND
FOR SAMUEL...

ANGIOLINO MAULE
Garganega, Trebbiano
VENETO

We use the term *vegetable wines* for wines that comple-
ment the chlorophyll taste of our spring dishes. These
are sharp, crisp wines with a mineral edge that pair well
with vegetables and chlorophyll. Mediterranean wines
have all these characteristics. The varieties we work
with most at *Toqué!* are Vermentino (Corsica), Rolle
(Provence), Assyrtico (Greece) and Maccabeu (from
Languedoc-Roussillon to Spain).

DAYLILIES

The idea of associating a noble ingredient such as caviar with the leaves of a common plant makes us very happy. Ever since Charles-Antoine learned that daylilies were edible, his mother has been dreading the destruction of her flowerbed every time summer rolls around!

DAYLILIES STUFFED WITH CAVIAR AND WHIPPED CREAM

SERVES 4 TO 6
PREPARATION: 20 MIN

· 4 to 6 young daylily shoots
· 60 ml (¼ cup) 35 % cream
· 2 tbsp smoked arctic char roe, sturgeon caviar or other roe
· Freshly ground black pepper

1 Wash the daylily shoots. Cut them into 12 to 15 cm pieces (5 in to 6 in). Whip the cream until soft peaks form. Carefully stuff the daylilies with the smoked roe. Add a little whipped cream, and pepper to taste.

DAYLILY ASPARAGUS WITH SUGAR, SALT AND SPICES

SERVES 4 PEOPLE
PREPARATION: 5 MIN

· 3 tbsp sugar
· 1 tbsp salt
· 1 tbsp *ras el hanout* or ground curry
· Daylily shoots

1 Blend the sugar, salt and spices in a bowl. In a pot filled with boiling water, blanch the daylily shoots for 10 to 15 seconds. Remove and cool in ice water. Strain and season with the spice mix.

TIP
+ Daylily asparagus is the name usually given to young daylily shoots because of their resemblance to asparagus.

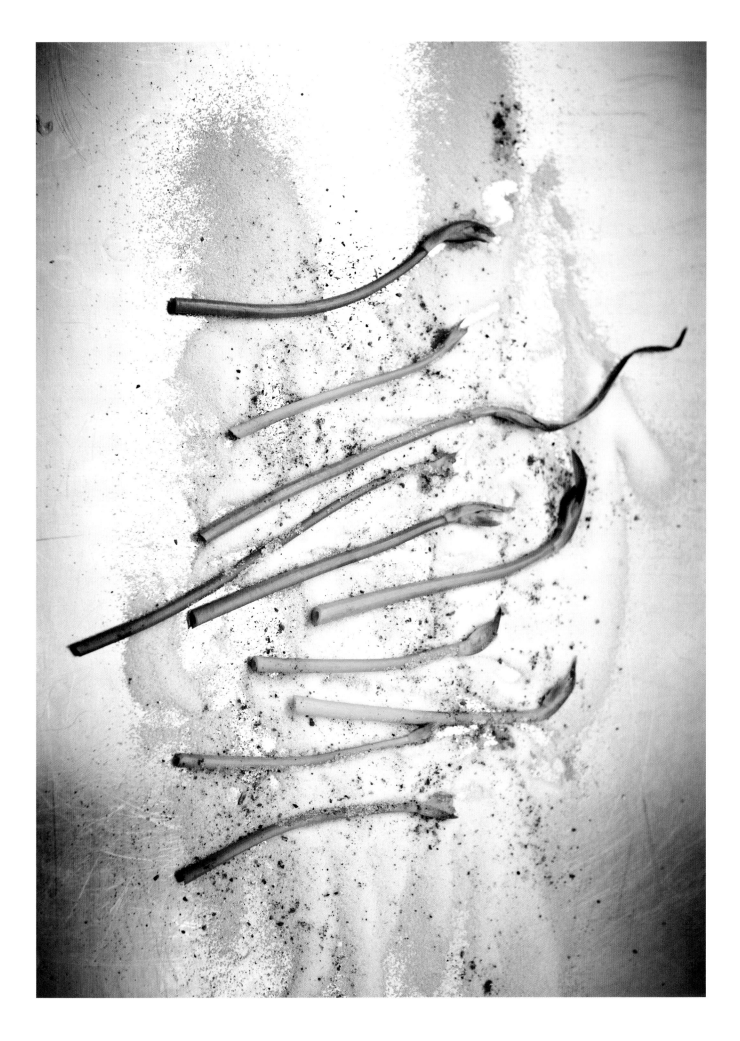

ASPARAGUS

ASPARAGUS WITH GRIBICHE SAUCE

SERVES 4
PREPARATION: 45 MIN

· 8 room temperature eggs
· 5 tbsp chardonnay vinegar
· 125 ml (½ cup) olive oil
· 180 ml (¾ cup) grape seed oil
· 2 tbsp mustard
· Salt and freshly ground black pepper
· 2 tbsp marinated daylily buds, minced
· 2 tbsp tarragon, minced
· 2 tbsp marinated wild leek, minced
· 2 tbsp parsley, minced
· 24 asparagus

1 In a pot of boiling water, add the eggs and cook for 7 minutes. Let cool in a bowl of cold water before shelling.

2 Separate the egg yolks from the whites. Use the yolks to whisk up a mayonnaise [P. 448], using the vinegar, oils, mustard, salt and pepper. Add the minced egg whites, daylily buds, tarragon, wild leek and parsley.

3 Break off the stems and peel the asparagus. Cook in a pot of salted boiling water for 1 to 2 minutes. Serve hot covered with the cold sauce.

GARBAGE ASPARAGUS: FRIED ASPARAGUS PEELS

· Canola oil (for frying)
· Green asparagus peels
· Salt

1 In a deep fryer, heat the oil to 190°C (375°F) and fry a few peels at a time for a few seconds, until lightly coloured. Let strain on paper towels. Salt to taste, and serve as a garnish with cheese, for example.

ASPARAGUS

ASPARAGUS MOUSSE
WITH BURNT BUTTER

SERVES 4
PREPARATION: 1 HR

· 250 g (1 cup) asparagus peels
  and trimmings, roughly chopped
· 375 ml (1½ cups) 3.25 % milk
· Fine salt
· 125 ml (½ cup) 35 % cream
· 75 g (⅓ cup) butter
· Maldon salt

1 In a pot, cook the asparagus peels
  and trimmings, milk and fine salt
  over low heat for 20 minutes, or
  until the asparagus start resembling
  a purée. Purée the mixture further
  in a food processor before passing
  it through a conical strainer. Add
  the cream and let cool on ice.

2 Pour 400 ml (1⅔ cups) of the
  preparation into a whipped cream
  dispenser and add two N_2O chargers,
  mixing well after each addition.
  Store in the refrigerator until ready
  to use [P. 451].

3 In a small pot, over medium-high
  heat, brown—even burn—the
  butter. Pour through a coffee filter
  and set aside.

4 Divide the asparagus mousse
  in bowls or cups. Add a spoonful
  of warm burnt butter and a pinch
  of Maldon salt.

MAPLE SYRUP CARAMELIZED
WHITE ASPARAGUS

SERVES 4
PREPARATION: 20 MIN

· 12 medium white asparagus
· 1 tbsp butter
· 5 tbsp maple syrup
· Salt and freshly ground black pepper
· Young fir or spruce shoots (optional)

1 Break off the stems and delicately
  peel the asparagus. Blanch in salted
  boiling water for about 2 minutes,
  depending on the size of the
  asparagus.

2 In a frying pan, over medium-high
  heat, simmer the butter and maple
  syrup for a few seconds. Add the
  asparagus and caramelize lightly.
  Remove from heat, season to taste
  and add the young shoots. Serve as
  an entrée or side dish.

ASPARAGUS

STUFFED MORELS WITH
ASPARAGUS AND WHIPPED
GARLIC CREAM

SERVES 4
PREPARATION: 1:30 HRS

Morels
· 400 g (4 cups) morels

Croutons
· Bread
· Olive oil
· Salt

Asparagus
· 4 green asparagus spears
· 4 white asparagus spears

Garlic Cream
· 125 ml (½ cup) 35 % cream
· 2 cloves garlic, fine-cut
· Salt and freshly ground black pepper

Red pepper Glaze
· 6 red peppers, hollowed
· 1 tbsp honey

Pepper Compote
· 5 ml (1 tsp) spicy oil
· 1 tbsp garlic oil
· 1 tbsp soy sauce
· 7 tbsp olive oil

Finishing Touches
· 200 g (7 oz) fresh goat cheese
  (Tournevent), at room temperature
· 2 tbsp olive oil
· 2 tbsp butter
· A few strawberries, quartered
· 150 g (5 oz) Laiterie Charlevoix
  1608 cheese, thinly sliced
· Fresh herbs
· 60 ml (¼ cup) green onion oil [P. 445]

Morels
1 Wash the morels thoroughly in cold water and blanch in a pot of salted boiling water for 15 seconds. Dry well on paper towels.

Croutons
2 Preheat the oven to 180°C (350°F). Cut the bread into 1 cm (½ in) cubes and coat lightly with olive oil and salt. Place on a baking sheet and dry in the oven until crispy.

Asparagus
3 Remove the woody part of the asparagus stems before peeling the rest of the spears. Blanch in salted boiling water until slightly crunchy. Cool in a bowl of ice water. Drain and cut into sections.

Garlic Cream

4 Whip the cream until firm, and then add garlic. Add salt and pepper to taste.

Red Pepper Glaze

5 Juice the peppers in a juicer. Separate the juice and the pulp. Heat the pepper juice in a pot over medium heat. After skimming the surface, add the honey and reduce to a syrupy consistency. Remove from heat and let the glaze sit at room temperature. Reserve the pulp to make pepper compote.

Red Pepper Compote

6 In a pot, mix all the ingredients with the reserved pepper pulp. Cook over low heat until the preparation starts sticking to the sides. Filter through a sieve to remove the skins and set the compote aside.

Finishing Touches

7 In a bowl, mix the goat cheese and pepper compote. Stuff the morels using a pastry bag fitted with a tip the same size as the hole at the base of the mushrooms.

8 In a pan over high heat, sear the stuffed morels in half of the olive oil and butter, gently flipping them with tongs to brown them on every side. In another frying pan, stir-fry the asparagus in the remaining olive oil and butter.

9 Preheat the oven on broil. Place the morels, asparagus, croutons, strawberries and garlic cream in a large ovenproof dish. Cover with thin slices of cheese and melt under the grill. Remove before the cheese browns. Arrange on a serving dish and garnish with the pepper glaze, herbs and green onion oil.

TIP

+ You can also serve all these ingredients raclette style.

MUSHROOMS

Every year, one of our best customers picks mushrooms for us in northern Quebec. One year, he brought us pholiotas. While cooking them, Charles-Antoine left them on the stove a little too long, and the mushrooms turned into a gum with a rather distinct taste. Since then, we have been reducing our mushroom trimmings to produce this very same savoury gum.

MUSHROOM GUM

SERVES 4
PREPARATION: 30 MIN
REST: 24 HRS

· 1 kg (2 lbs) Portobello mushrooms or mushroom trimmings
· 500 g (1 lb) melted butter

1 Finely mince the mushrooms and dry them in the refrigerator overnight.

2 In a pot, melt the butter over low heat and lightly sauté the mushrooms. Keep the pot in the refrigerator overnight.

3 The following day, place the pot over low heat. The mushrooms will start to soften and a black gum will start forming at the bottom of the pan. Stir regularly to keep the mushrooms from burning; they'll eventually turn into a sticky black purée. Refrigerate in a sealed container. Before you use the gum, let it warm to room temperature. This will give it a spreadable texture.

CRISPY BLACK TRUMPETS

SERVES 4
PREPARATION: 30 MIN
COOKING: 1 HR

· 150 g (5 oz) black trumpets (also known as black chanterelles or trumpets of the dead), carefully cleaned
· 2 tbsp olive oil
· Salt and freshly ground black pepper

1 Preheat the oven to 150°C (300°F).

2 Split the mushrooms in two length-wise with your fingers to make sure there are no insects inside.

3 In a round-bottom bowl, mix the mushrooms with the other ingredients. Spread a single layer of mushrooms on a baking sheet lined with parchment paper. Cook for at least 1 hour, tossing after 30 minutes. The mushrooms are ready when they become crispy. Serve at room temperature with meat or fish. Black trumpets will keep for 2 days.

MUSHROOMS

COCO BEAN SALAD WITH BLACK TRUMPETS AND BASIL

SERVES 4
PREPARATION: 1 HR
SOAK 12 HRS

Beans

· 150 g (1½ cup) fresh coco beans
· ½ onion, cut into chunks
· 1 small carrot, cut into chunks
· 2 tbsp olive oil
· 30 g (1 oz) large cubes of salted pork lard
· 1 whole clove garlic
· Salt
· 1 tbsp butter

Finishing Touches

· A few leaves of basil
· A few sprigs of chive
· A few leaves of mint
· 200 g (7 oz) black trumpets, cooked [P. 70]
· Zest of 1 lemon

Beans

1 The day before, hull the beans and soak and refrigerate them overnight in a bowl of cold water.

2 The following day, in a pot over low heat, lightly brown the onion and carrots in olive oil and lard. Add the strained beans, stir gently, and cook for 1 minute. Pour water (approximately 2½ cm / 1 in) on the beans, add garlic, and let simmer over low heat for approximately 40 minutes or until the beans are tender. Salt only at the very end so that the skin of the beans will not harden. Set aside in the cooking water.

3 In a food processor, reduce 180 g (1 cup) of warm beans into a smooth purée. Add 250 ml (1 cup) of cooking water and the butter. Strain through a sieve and set aside.

Finishing Touches

4 Heat the bean purée and spoon it onto the plates. Heat the whole beans in the cooking liquid, adding basil, chives and mint. Strain and put the whole beans on top of or next to the purée. Add the black trumpets and garnish with basil, chives and lemon zest.

5 Serve with poultry, fish or alone as an appetizer.

MUSHROOMS

SERVES 4
PREPARATION: 1 HR
REST: 2 HRS

Beef

· 8 slices of rib eye steak, about 25 g (¾ oz) each
· 1 tbsp grape seed oil

Vinaigrette for Beef

· 1 tbsp miso
· 1 tbsp water
· 5 ml (1 tsp) mirin
· 5 ml (1 tsp) lime juice
· 5 ml (1 tsp) wasabi paste
· 1 tbsp organic soy sauce

Mushroom Preparation

· 12 morels, washed thoroughly with plenty of water
· 1 tbsp olive oil
· 1 tbsp butter
· Salt and freshly ground black pepper
· 350 g (2 cups) green beans, cooked and cut into sections
· 15 g (2 cups) popcorn (popped)
· 2 tbsp white wine vinegar
· Mix of herbs, minced

Sauce

· 60 ml (¼ cup) vegetable glaze [P. 450]
· 2 tbsp green onion oil [P. 445]

Beef

1 Ask the butcher for 8 individually wrapped slices of rib eye steak of about 25 g (¾ oz) each.

Vinaigrette for Beef

2 Whisk all the ingredients together.

3 Brush grape seed oil on 4 sheets of parchment paper. Place 2 steaks on each sheet. Brush vinaigrette on both sides of the meat and marinate in the refrigerator for 2 hours.

Mushroom Preparation

4 Stir-fry the morels in a very hot frying pan with the olive oil, butter, salt and pepper until nice and soft. Add the cooked green beans. Place in a bowl and mix with the popcorn, white wine vinegar and herbs.

Sauce

5 Warm the vegetable glaze over medium heat. Remove from heat and add the green onion oil.

Finishing Touches

6 Preheat the oven on broil. Place two slices of beef and two lines of the mushroom mixture on each plate. Grill each one for 10 to 15 seconds until the meat turns a little pale. Add a spoonful of sauce, and serve immediately.

ANOTHER ROUND
FOR SAMUEL...

GUY BRETON
Gamay
BEAUJOLAIS

MARK KREYDENWEISS
Riesling
ALSACE

In the recipe for Beef Sashimi with Morels the beef is served almost raw. We pair it with supple wines with minimal tannins. This dish is perfect with Beaujolais, especially Morgon or Moulin-à-Vent, because the morels draw out the earthy, almost "dead leaf" taste present in this region's wines. However, if you decide to add asparagus spears and more greens to the recipe, it's best to move toward what we call *vegetable wines*. An Alsatian white or a dry, full-bodied Riesling works well.

Produce of France

2 0 0 8

MORGON

APPELLATION CONTRÔLÉE

"VIEILLES VIGNES"

Mis en bouteille à la propriété

ALC. 12,5% BY VOL   CONTENTS 750 ML

GUY BRETON VILLÉ MORGON 69910

ALSACE GRAND CRU

2007

A.S TSCHLECC

La Dame

WIEBELSBERG RIESLING

APPELLATION ALSACE GRAND CRU CONTROLÉE

MIS EN BOUTEILLE AU DOMAINE - PRODUIT DE FRANCE #15

MARC KREYDENWEISS

VIGNERONS EN BIODYNAMIE A ANDLAU 67140 FRANCE

MUSHROOMS

CHANTERELLES AND GLASSWORT SALAD WITH BLUEBERRY VINAIGRETTE

SERVES 4
PREPARATION: 45 MIN

Vinaigrette
· 125 ml (½ cup) red wine vinegar
· 1 tbsp honey
· 75 g (¼ cup) small blueberries
· 60 ml (¼ cup) tarragon oil [P. 449]

Salad
· 500 g (1 lb) chanterelles
· 2 tbsp olive oil
· 2 tbsp butter
· 60 g (2 oz) finely chopped glasswort
· 60 g (½ cup) fresh almonds, peeled

Finishing Touches
· A few leaves of tarragon

Vinaigrette
1 In a pot over low heat, reduce the vinegar and honey by half until slightly syrupy in consistency. Remove from heat and add the blueberries and tarragon oil.

Salad
2 In a frying pan, lightly brown the chanterelles in olive oil and butter. Add the glasswort and almonds.

Finishing Touches
3 Place a handful of salad on each plate, drizzle with vinaigrette and garnish with a few leaves of tarragon.

4 Serve as an appetizer or a garnish.

TIP
+ Chanterelles are among the most common and best known mushrooms in Quebec. Our pickers deliver them in July and August, when they are abundant. To remove the dirt and sand, rather than wash the chanterelles, we cut off their stems and use a brush or wipe them with a cloth to preserve their earthy, woody taste.

MUSHROOMS

We were looking to create a new kind of tiramisu. As we began creating it, what appeared before us resembled a small forest: the coffee mousse was like a mushroom, the spices like pebbles, and the begonia petals like a field in bloom. Although our inspiration was Italian, our new creation is more evocative of a stroll through a Gaspé forest.

MOCK MUSHROOMS

SERVES 6
PREPARATION: 2 HRS
REFRIGERATE: 6 HRS

Coffee Mousse
· 2½ gelatin sheets
· 125 ml (½ cup) simple syrup [P. 448]
· 250 ml (1 cup) espresso

Iced Rowan Milk
· 750 ml (3 cups) 3.25 % milk
· 180 g (¾ cup) sugar
· 25 g (½ cup) young rowan shoots

Sugar and Spice
· 6 g (1 tsp) vanilla powder
· 6 g (1 tsp) cinnamon
· 3 g (½ tsp) Guinea pepper
· 6 g (1 tsp) anise
· 1 egg white
· 120 g (½ cup) sugar
· 60 ml (¼ cup) water

Tiramisu Cream
· 3 gelatin sheets
· 3 tbsp espresso
· 3 tbsp Tia Maria
· 150 g (5 oz) mascarpone
· 60 ml (¼ cup) water
· 60 g (¼ cup) sugar
· 4 egg yolks at room temperature
· 60 ml (¼ cup) 35 % cream

Coffee Mousse

1 Place a baking sheet or marble slab in the freezer.

2 Meanwhile, bloom the gelatin in a bowl of ice water. Heat the simple syrup in a small pot. Add the strained gelatin to the syrup and dissolve it with a whisk. Add the coffee. Let the mixture cool to room temperature and pour it into a whipped cream dispenser. Add the N_2O chargers and place the dispenser in the refrigerator for 6 hours [P. 451].

3 Cover the frozen baking sheet with parchment paper and quickly dot it with dollops of coffee mousse the size of mushroom heads. Return to the freezer immediately so the mock mushrooms retain their shape. Do not freeze for longer than 12 hours. Take them out just before serving.

Iced Rowan Milk

4 In a pot over low heat, warm the milk and sugar. Add the rowan shoots, and let them steep for 15 minutes. Filter the mixture in a conical strainer. Once cooled, process in an ice cream maker and freeze.

Sugar and Spice

5 Pulse the spices together in a coffee grinder. Add the egg white and mix well. In a pot, cook the sugar and water until the mixture reaches 135°C (275°F). Set the pot on a damp cloth and add the spices to the cooked sugar, stirring vigorously with a wooden spoon until the preparation becomes granular.

Tiramisu Cream

6 Bloom the gelatin in a bowl of ice water. Meanwhile, in a pot over low heat, warm up the coffee without letting it boil. Add the strained gelatin and mix thoroughly. Remove from the heat and cool to room temperature. Pour in the Tia Maria and add the mascarpone, mixing well.

7 In a separate pot, heat the water and sugar to 121°C (250°F) to make a syrup.

8 Meanwhile, whisk the egg yolks using a stand mixer. Pour the syrup in little by little, whisking constantly and vigorously until the mixture has cooled down. When the mixture has reached room temperature, incorporate into the mascarpone. Whip the cream and fold into the mascarpone preparation.

Finishing Touches

9 Pour the tiramisu cream into a pastry bag fitted with a 1 cm (½ in) tip. On each plate, pipe some cream to create stems for the mushrooms. Place a frozen mock mushroom on each stem to complete the effect. Drizzle with sugar and spice and complete the dish with a scoop of iced rowan milk.

TIP

+ Use an offset spatula to pick up the frozen mock mushroom heads from the baking sheet.

GLOSSARY

Rowan The rowan, or American Mountain Ash, is a tree from the Rosaceae family that blooms in spring. Its shoots taste like amaretto.

SEA BUCKTHORNS

SERVES 4
PREPARATION: 2 HRS
COOKING: 1:15 HRS

Wafers

· 3 egg whites
· 80 g (⅓ cup) sugar
· 60 g (¼ cup) sea buckthorn berry
  or cranberry purée

Cranberry Purée

· 250 ml (1 cup) water
· 60 g (¼ cup) sugar
· 250 g (8 oz) cranberries

Finishing Touches

· 2 g (1 tsp) cumin seeds
· 5 g (1 tsp) salt
· 1 tbsp citric acid
· 120 g (4 oz) pressed foie gras [P. 354]

Wafers

1 Whisk the egg whites in a stand mixer until stiff. When they start to rise, gradually add the sugar in 3 steps, whisking continuously.

2 Preheat the convection oven to 110°C (225°F) [TIP].

3 Use a spatula to mix a quarter of the meringue with the fruit purée. Gently fold with the remaining meringue. Use an offset spatula to lay it on a silicone pastry mat, 5 mm (¼ in) thick. With the tip of a wooden spoon, make a cross-shape, dividing the preparation into four equal parts to help it cook evenly. Bake. After 25 minutes, rotate 180°, and leave in for another 25 minutes.

4 Flip the mat onto a baking sheet lined with parchment paper. Pull the mat off, and put the preparation back in the oven for about 25 minutes (depending on its texture). Let it sit for 5 minutes at room temperature (if the preparation is still not crispy, put it back in the oven). Cut each rectangle in half with a serrated knife. In all, you should get 8 rectangles of about 4 cm × 8 cm (1 ½ in × 3 in).

Cranberry Purée

5 In a pot over low heat, cook the water, sugar and cranberries for 10 to 15 minutes, until the fruit bursts and starts to purée. Add water if needed; however the mixture should remain pretty thick.

Finishing Touches

6 Grind the cumin, salt and citric acid in a coffee grinder. Dip a very sharp knife in hot water, and cut the pressed foie gras into thin slices approximately 5 mm (¼ in) thick.

7 Spread a little cranberry purée on the wafers. Make a sandwich with the foie gras in the middle. Sprinkle the cumin powder, and serve right away.

TIP
+ You can also make this dish in a regular oven; however, it will cook less evenly.

RHUBARB

RHUBARB FOR TOTS

· 3 rhubarb stalks
· 60 g (¼ cup) organic sugar

1 Peel the rhubarb with a vegetable peeler, and refrigerate the peels for the next recipe. Then peel the stalks, making long strips. Add sugar and serve.

FRIED RHUBARB TRIMS

· Canola oil (for frying)
· Rhubarb peels
· Sugar

1 In a deep fryer or large pot, heat canola oil to 180°C (350°F). Fry the rhubarb peels for a few seconds, until lightly coloured. Drain on paper towels, and sprinkle with sugar.

2 Serve with cheese, foie gras or as *petits-fours*.

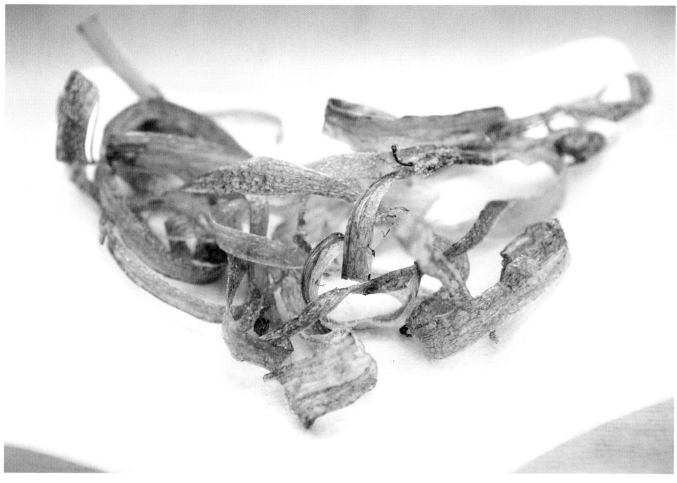

RHUBARB

Visually, the rhubarb cannoli resembles the traditional Sicilian dessert. The pastry is made with rhubarb and strawberry, an easy pairing. Once it's ready, we serve our cannoli with ice cream, compote and sugar all made out of rhubarb. Three great ideas for our trims.

RHUBARB CANNOLI

SERVES 4
PREPARATION: 2 HRS
REST: 24 HRS (CANNOLI)

Cannoli Shells
· 120 g (1 cup) icing sugar
· 35 g (¼ cup) organic, unbleached all-purpose flour
· 1 pinch ground Guinea pepper
· 60 ml (¼ cup) orange juice
· 1 tbsp butter, melted

Thyme Custard Filling
· 375 ml (1½ cups) 2 % milk
· 1 vanilla pod
· 5 g (2 tsp) lemon thyme + a few leaves
· 80 g (⅓ cup) sugar
· 4 egg yolks
· 35 g (¼ cup) cornstarch
· 2 gelatin sheets
· 250 g (1 cup) 10 % Mediterranean yogurt
· 160 ml (⅔ cup) 35 % cream

Rhubarb Sorbet
· 1 kg (2 lbs) rhubarb stalks, peeled and sliced thinly
· 300 g (1¼ cup) sugar
· 60 ml (¼ cup) lemon juice
· 125 ml (½ cup) water

Sweet Strawberries
· 300 g (1¼ cup) sugar
· 60 ml (¼ cup) water
· 80 g (¼ cup) strawberry purée
· 1 tbsp dried albumen powder

Cooked Rhubarb
· 4 rhubarb stalks
· 60 g (¼ cup) sugar

Finishing Touches
· 8 strawberries, diced

Cannoli Shells
1 Whisk the icing sugar, flour and Guinea pepper together. Add the orange juice and butter. Stir well and refrigerate for 24 hours (refrigeration is a must).

2 The next day, preheat the oven to 180°C (350°F). On a baking mat, spread the preparation thinly with an offset spatula, making 4 rectangles of 15 cm × 10 cm (6 in × 4 in). Bake 6 to 10 minutes, rotating the mat halfway through. The preparation is ready when it turns clear. Take it out of the oven and immediately shape using a 2½ cm (1 in) cylinder to get a 15 cm (6 in) long tube with a 2½ cm (1 in) diameter. Let it cool so the shells harden and keep their shape.

Thyme Custard Filling

3 Bloom the gelatin in cold water. In a pot over low heat, warm the milk, vanilla, thyme and half the sugar, and cook until the sugar has melted. Run the mixture through a sieve. In a bowl, beat the egg yolks with the remaining sugar and the corn starch until pale. Temper the yolks with a little hot milk, and pour this new mixture into the remaining milk. Keep warm over low heat, and stir until the mixture coats the back of a spoon. Add the strained gelatin, and mix well. Let it cool to room temperature, and refrigerate. Gently stir in the yogurt, and fold in the whipped cream. Add a few leaves of lemon thyme.

Rhubarb Sorbet

4 Mix the ingredients together, and cook over medium heat until the rhubarb is done. Purée the mixture in a blender, and run it through a conical strainer. Process the liquid in the ice cream maker, and freeze. Refrigerate the stewed fruit left in the sieve.

Sweet Strawberries

5 Mix the strawberry purée with the albumen. In a pot over medium heat, cook the sugar and water until it reaches 135°C (275°F). Remove from heat. Stir in the strawberry purée mixture. Place it back on the burner for 1 minute. Remove from heat, and mix vigorously with a wooden spoon (the mixture will start to crystallize; continue to mix well to crush the crystallized pieces that form). Spread the preparation on parchment paper and crush the remaining too-large pieces (the texture should be fairly fine). Let this mixture dry out for a few minutes. Store in a sealed container at room temperature.

Cooked Rhubarb

6 Preheat the oven to 180°C (350°F). Use a vegetable peeler to cut long strips of rhubarb lengthwise, and lay them out on parchment paper. Make squares of about 15 cm × 15 cm (6 in × 6 in) that straddle each other slightly. Sprinkle with sugar. Cover with parchment paper, and bake until the rhubarb becomes soft. Refrigerate.

Finishing Touches

7 Using a pastry bag, fill the cannoli halfway with the custard filling. Place the strawberry cubes in the centre, before adding the rest of the filling. Using parchment paper, roll a baked rhubarb square around the cannoli (as if rolling a sushi). Prepare the other cannoli in a similar fashion. Put a bit of rhubarb purée on each plate, and place a cannoli on top. Add a ball of sorbet, and garnish with sweet strawberries.

TIP

+ It's always best to practice the method with a single cannoli before preparing a full serving.

MAPLE

EXPLOSIVE
SPONGE TOFFEE

- 450 g (2 cups + 2 tbsp) organic brown sugar
- 6 tbsp maple syrup
- 310 ml (1¼ cups) water
- 10 g (2 tsp) baking soda, sifted

1 In a pot, over low heat, cook the sugar, maple sugar and water until the temperature reaches 150°C (300°F). Remove from heat.

2 Once off the heat, add the baking soda and whisk vigorously for 5 seconds. Quickly pour into a 20 cm × 20 cm (8 in × 8 in) stainless steel baking pan lined with parchment paper and let cool. Break the toffee into pieces or cut into cubes before serving.

CREAM FUDGE
WITH EXTRA CREAM

MAKES 30 PORTIONS
COOKING: 35 MIN

- 480 g (2 cups) sugar
- 340 g (2 cups) brown sugar
- 500 ml (2 cups) 35 % cream
- 60 ml (¼ cup) maple syrup
- 60 g (¼ cup) butter
- 125 ml (½ cup) whipped cream

1 In a pot, bring the sugar, brown sugar, 35 % cream and maple syrup to a boil. Lower the heat, stir and bring the internal temperature of the mixture to 113°C (235°F). Immediately turn off the heat, add the butter, and mix well.

2 With a whisk, continue mixing for 10 to 15 minutes in order to temper the preparation, or until it crystallizes and changes colour. Pour 1 to 2 cm (½ to ¾ in) thick of the preparation on a baking sheet lined with parchment paper. Set aside at room temperature until the fudge has completely set. Cut into cubes and serve with whipped cream.

FROM THE RIVER
TO THE GULF

Ghislain Cyr

MAGDALENE ISLANDS

I'm a coastal fisherman who works on a small scale. Deep down, I'm really a trawler, looking for cod and halibut. Trawling is a controversial technique. I practice it in a traditional way, placing my hooks very precisely. Trawling is done on the open water and requires a high degree of knowledge about the habits of the species you're fishing. You need to place your line based on what you're trying to catch and account for its clutching period. With recent catch limits and changes imposed on the industry, I've now turned mostly to crab fishing with cages, line fishing for mackerel, and using mesh nets to catch herring and plaice, which all require careful methods to avoid wasting resources.

Ronny, a fisherman from the Magdalene Islands, first introduced me to Ghislain fifteen years ago. When we sailed out together, he taught me fishing techniques and told me about the limits imposed by regulations. He often calls me from his boat to tell me about his most recent catch. Back in the kitchen, we immediately start changing the menu.

NORMAND LAPRISE

RETHINKING FISHING

We're privileged to be able to extract this precious resource. A fisherman needs to constantly rethink his habits since he's the first one to observe changes in our marine environment. In 1990, I witnessed drops in the cod stock that led to a moratorium. Despite the scientific infrastructure put in place during that period, we can still observe similar situations with other species today. I think the solution isn't to ban fishing, but instead to renew our methods. If we continue to scour the ocean floor without any selection, we're going to be in serious trouble. We should be working towards using more eco-sensitive methods to avoid draining the entire reproductive biomass in a single go, and destroying the habitat. Species protection must also include restrictions on fish discards. Many fish, like herring or rays, are currently bountiful but have limited markets, and are often thrown back dead into the sea.

AN INCREASINGLY COMPLEX ACTIVITY

The transmission of our know-how is threatened. I'm lucky to have had a helper at my side for the past nine years. He's curious and works well. I think he's hooked! Fishing has become a very competitive activity in the Gulf of St. Lawrence. Today, quotas limit not only the number of fish we can catch, but also the amount of time we have on open water. Some of the government's measures aren't always in tune with what we know to be effective in terms of protecting the maritime environment.

Before, when I sailed beyond the jetty, I would tell myself: "Forget the land." I always loved the idea of leaving land and its problems behind. Today, when I sail out of port, the checklist I need to go through to follow the rules is so long that some of the pleasure is gone.

AWARENESS THROUGH COOKING

On the Magdalene Islands and all along the Gaspé coast, fish have been part of our diets since time immemorial. In the old days, during the winter, we used to eat the preserves we prepared in summer. The paradox is that, today, fishmongers all sell imported fish: tilapia, salmon and aquaculture trout, while our best resources are exported by large food companies. And yet, without spending too much, you could eat fish from the Gulf of St. Lawrence all year long. All you need are basic conservation tricks and a bit of time to cook. If we learned to better use what we already have, we wouldn't need to fish in such quantities.

A Network of Traditional Fishermen

At *Toqué!,* we've made the choice to know the source of every fish we serve. As restaurant owners, we promote responsible fishing by always trying to purchase fish that have been hooked, not trawled, and by serving in-season products. We are convinced that instead of stigmatizing the fishing of certain species, emphasis should be on the regulation of industrial techniques. This advocacy has to come from chefs, grocers, exporters and especially consumers who ultimately have the power to change habits through responsible purchasing.

Europe has a number of laws that cover traceability of ocean products. The restaurant owner knows where and when the fish he's purchasing was caught, ensuring its freshness. This is something we don't have in Canada: it's always difficult to trace a fish's travels before it reaches our kitchen. As a young cook, Normand learned to recognise freshness by the colour of the gills and the lustre of the eye. For example, if the eyes are glossy, firm and bulging, the fish is fresh, probably part of the day's catch. However, a fish with brown gills has been dead for quite a few days. Normand was forced to develop these and a myriad other techniques when he started in the kitchen to survive in a business in which quality and freshness are not always the first priority.

To ensure the highest quality possible, we've attempted to limit the number of middlemen between cooks and fishermen. To get what we need, we work with fishmongers who receive their stock directly from fishermen. John is one of these fishmongers. We've been working with him for years now. Through him, we met Richard Saint-Pierre who delivers our fish and seafood every week. In the early days of our collaboration, Normand shared the importance he put on fresh products with Richard. More than once, Normand returned merchandise that didn't meet his expectations. By integrating the *Toqué!* values of consistency and freshness into his work, Richard has become our main fish supplier. He comes down from the Gaspé penninsula to Montreal every week, and is responsible for keeping channels open between fishermen and the restaurant. Everything comes in fresh at *Toqué!;* shrimp and crab are cooked directly on the boat or on shore factories due to conservation concerns. Thanks to people like Richard, we've been able to build a network of fishermen who supply us with crustaceans, shellfish and fish.

In winter, even if it isn't always easy, we avoid cooking with imported fish. Aquaculture is something we accept if it's done as naturally as possible, in a controlled and respectful manner. For many years now, we've collaborated with Maison Pec Nord, which practices small-scale eco-friendly aquaculture. In the mid-90s, when they were barely starting to experiment with scallop farming off the coast of the Magdalene Islands, they came to us with their products. After making sure our quality standards were met, we began putting in orders regularly. Since then, we've been receiving and serving fresh Princess scallops year-round, changing the garnish with the seasons.

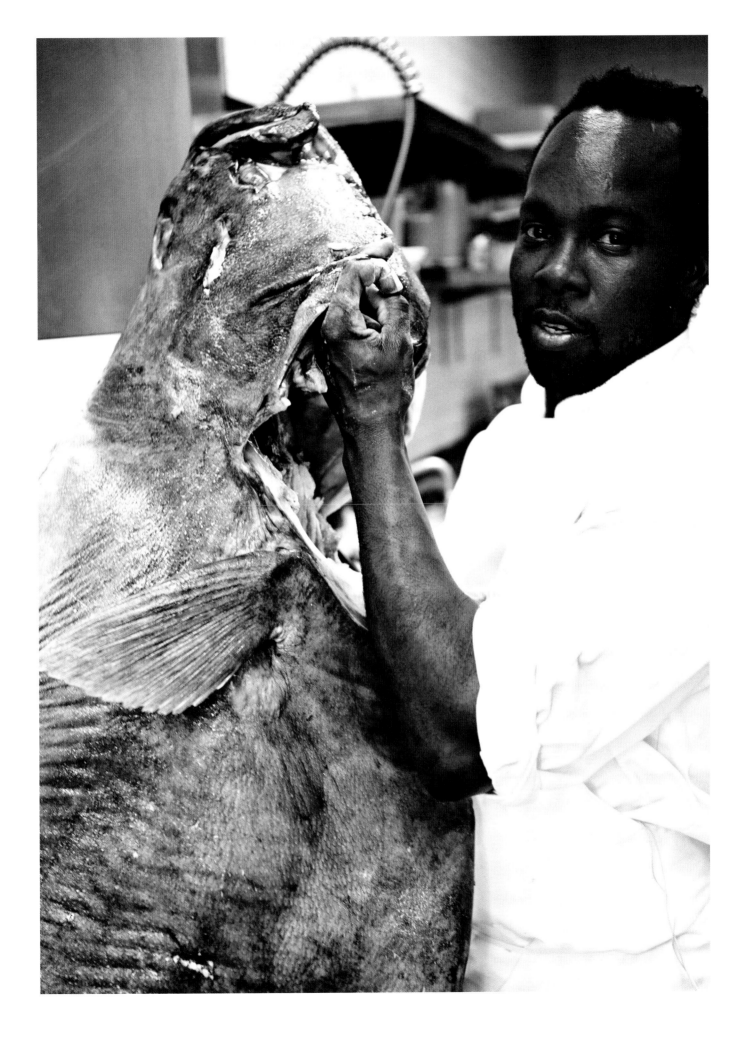

EELS

RAZOR CLAMS

There are only half a dozen eel fishermen on the St. Lawrence River, including the Lauzier and Lizotte families. Georges-Henry Lizotte is one of them. Seventy-two years old and fourth generation of eel-fishers—a tradition he's passing on to his son. Eels live in freshwater, but make their way to salt water to spawn. In Kamouraska, eel fishing is done twice a day, in September and October. At high tide, eels are caught in nets held up by wooden structures, and collected at low tide with the help of a tractor. Once caught, they're transferred into basins with oxygen pumps, a method that keeps the eel alive until it reaches the point of sale. At the end of October, the structures are removed, dried and stored to be used again the the following year. For Normand, who grew up in Kamouraska, the memory of those structures remains vivid. Today, in the restaurant's dining room, a sculpture by ceramist Pascale Girardin conjures up the shapes and landscape of his childhood. It's a way for him to add his roots to the *Toqué!* environment.

Some fishermen dig razor clams with a tool that lets them suck the clams straight from the sand. It's an interesting technique, since it preserves the shell; however, it also fills them with sand. We're forced to soak the clams before cooking them. Some fishermen clean them with seawater by installing clam pots at the back of their boats when they're sailing to and from port. This ingenious technique preserves the iodized and saline taste of the shellfish while cleaning them and readying them for the kitchen.

SEA URCHINS

TUNA

In Quebec, it is First Nations from the Rimouski area, close to the Gaspé peninsula, that gather sea urchins. Divers collect these "hedgehogs of the sea" by hand near rock formations. In spring and autumn, sea urchins acquire a slightly sweet and very iodized taste. It's the type of product that everyone dreads a little due to its milky texture. Sea urchins are particularly rich, and should be enjoyed in small quantities to really be appreciated. At *Toqué!,* we serve them in their shell as a whipped cream.

Every year in August, the tuna sport-fishing season begins off New Brunswick and Nova Scotia. It's regulated the same way hunting is: the number of fish each fisherman is allowed to catch is drawn in a lottery. Be it red tuna, salmon or trout, the technique is always the same: angling. It's very hard to get a hold of them, as they're usually sold off the pier, and most of the merchandises sent to the United States and Japan. Every year, at *Toqué!,* we usually get our hands on five or six tuna of a few hundred pounds each, which we usually share with other restaurants like *Le Pied de Cochon.*

MACKEREL

Mackerel is a migratory species, preferring cold water in summer, and making its way to warmer climes in autumn. Unlike a number of other fish, mackerel doesn't have an air bladder, a sort of air pocket located directly under the backbone. This forces mackerel to swim constantly. Like urchins, the best mackerel are caught in May, June, September, October and November when the water is still cold.

A difference of two or three degrees will be felt in the firmness of the flesh.

Mackerel is a fatty fish that cannot be kept. At the restaurant, we're lucky to get some nice specimens thanks to Ghislain, among others. Since they're so cheap, lobster fishermen often use them as bait. A method, Ghislain likes to remind us, that has led to a drop in the mackerel population in the Gulf of St. Lawrence.

LOBSTER

In Quebec, lobster season begins in May and lasts some nine to twelve weeks—a relatively short period given the constantly increasing demand. On the Magdalene Islands, there are only a few hundred lobster permits left that are transferred from father to son, since the government no longer hands them out. Lobsters are caught in traps dropped to the bottom of the sea. Each fisherman can deposit a maximum of 325 traps, which they drag back up to the surface once a day. This type of fishing is random: you can bring up six or eight lobsters, or come up empty. To protect their resource, not to mention their jobs, for future generations, Magdalene Islands fishermen have decided to reduce the number of traps per boat per day. This seemingly insignificant gesture has led to a noticeable reduction in the number of lobsters caught every season. However, to really have an effect, the initiative needs to be extended throughout the East Coast, since the crustacean migrates when it overpopulates.

The most tender, most succulent, sweetest lobsters are found off the coast of the Magdalene and Anticosti Islands. The quality of the meat is directly related to the environment: very cold waters with sandy bottoms make the flesh firmer and tastier. In the kitchen, lobster always comes in alive. It's possible to keep them for two days in cool temperatures, covered with a humid cloth. We cook lobster in two steps to avoid making them rubbery.

WHEN NORMAND IS INVITED TO SPEAK AT A CONFERENCE IN A FOREIGN COUNTRY, HE TAKES THE TIME TO LEAVE THE KITCHEN AND MEET LOCAL PRODUCERS. WHILE KEEPING THE SAME STANDARDS HE'S ALWAYS HAD, HE VISITS MARKETS AND FISHING PORTS TO FIND WHAT HE'S LOOKING FOR. "WHEN I GO AND COOK IN A FOREIGN COUNTRY, I WANT TO MAKE SURE THAT WHAT I'M COOKING WILL BE OF THE HIGHEST QUALITY POSSIBLE," NORMAND EXPLAINS. "WHEN I WENT TO THE BERMUDAS, WHERE THERE'S FISH EVERYWHERE, SOMEONE OFFERED ME FISH THAT WEREN'T FROM THE AREA. I INSISTED THAT THE FISHERMEN BRING US LOCAL CATCH. IT'S IMPORTANT TO ADAPT AND COOK WITH WHAT YOU HAVE AVAILABLE."

TODAY, AFFILIATION WITH THE RELAIS & CHÂTEAUX GROUP KEEPS US IN CONSTANT CONTACT WITH CHEFS THE WORLD OVER. A TRUE SOURCE OF INSPIRATION, TRAVELLING REMAINS AT THE HEART OF THE *TOQUÉ!* CREATIVE PROCESS. FROM NEW YORK TO HONG KONG VIA DENMARK, NORMAND, CHARLES AND CHRISTINE TRAVEL THE GLOBE TO DEBATE AND DISCUSS ISSUES OF LOCAL CUISINE AND COOK WITH OTHER CHEFS AND RESTAURANT OWNERS. IT HAS BECOME A WAY TO PROMOTE THE RICHNESS OF QUEBEC'S CULINARY TRADITIONS.

SHRIMP

SHRIMP COCKTAIL

SERVES 4
PREPARATION: 1 HR

Shrimp

· 250 g (8 oz) of Gamba shrimp
  or Spot Prawn

Cocktail Sauce

· 8 large fresh tomatoes
  or 500 ml (2 cups) tomato sauce
· 2 tbsp honey
· 1 clove garlic, minced
· 160 g (1 cup) onions, minced
· Juice and zest of 1 lemon
· 1 tbsp rice vinegar
· 5 g (1 tsp) sugar
· 2 tbsp Worcestershire sauce
· 1 tbsp black and/or yellow mustard
  seeds
· Fresh horseradish, finely grated

Whipped Cream

· 60 ml (¼ cup) 35 % cream
· 1 tbsp Worcestershire sauce
· Salt

Finishing Touches

· 1 shallot, diced
· 1 bunch chives, finely chopped
· Salt and freshly ground black pepper
· Olive oil
· 4 green onions sliced diagonally
· 1 lemon, quartered
· Smoked paprika
· A few stalks of chives (garnish)

Shrimp

1 Shell the shrimp and remove the heads. Rinse the heads under cold water and pat dry with paper towels before setting aside for fried shrimp heads with potato mousse [P. 121]. Cut the shrimp across the back and remove the black vein. Rinse and pat dry. Cut the shrimp into pieces.

Cocktail Sauce

2 In a pot of boiling water, blanch the tomatoes for 10 to 15 seconds, or until the skins begin to loosen. Immerse them in ice water. Remove the skin, then quarter and seed the tomatoes. Crush them with a hand blender or in a food processor and reduce by half over medium heat.

3 In a pan over low heat, warm up the honey and sauté the garlic and the onion without browning. Add the tomato sauce. Pulse with a hand blender a few seconds at a time, ensuring a few pieces of crunchy onion are conserved. Pour into a bowl and add the rest of the ingredients.

Whipped Cream

4 Whip the cream until stiff peaks form. Add Worcestershire sauce and salt to taste. Put the cream in a pastry bag equipped with a fluted nozzle.

Finishing Touches

5 Mix the shrimp with the cocktail sauce (a spoonful of sauce for two spoonfuls of shrimp), the shallot and the chives. Add salt and pepper to taste, before adding a drizzle of olive oil. In each martini glass, place a quarter of the shrimp preparation and cover with a rosette of cream. Add the green onion and a lemon quarter. Sprinkle with paprika and garnish with a few chives.

TIP

+ Pre-cooked, cleaned shrimp can also be used in this recipe.

SHRIMP

Matane shrimp don't keep very long, so fishermen cook them in seawater right on their boats (or sometimes in port factories). The result is wonderfully prepared shrimp, since the salt density of the shrimp is the same as that of water.

FRIED SHRIMP HEADS WITH POTATO MOUSSE

SERVES 4
PREPARATION: 1:30 HRS

Potato Mousse
· 2 unpeeled Yukon Gold potatoes
· 250 ml (1 cup) whole milk
· 60 g (¼ cup) butter
· 1 tbsp Dijon mustard
· Salt and freshly ground black pepper

Shrimp Heads
· 100 g (3½ oz) Matane shrimp heads
· 3 litres (12 cups) Canola oil for frying

Finishing Touches
· 5 green onions, sliced diagonally

Potato Mousse
1 Cook the potatoes in a pot of boiling salted water. Peel the potatoes and purée. Pass through a sieve to make it smoother (the purée will be slightly liquid). In a pot, heat the milk and butter, add the potato purée and mustard. Add salt and pepper to taste. Immediately put in a heat-resistant whipped cream dispenser and add 2 N_2O chargers [P. 451]

Shrimp Heads
2 In a fryer or a large pot, heat the canola oil to 190°C (375°F). Fry the heads and the legs for about 20 seconds or until lightly coloured.

Finishing Touches
3 Spoon the warm potato mousse onto four plates. Cover with the fried heads and legs. Garnish with green onions.

SHRIMP

During a stay in Cancun for an event, we ate an incredibly simple omelette made from onions, mushrooms and shrimp. The eggs were cooked directly on a hotplate with the stuffing before being folded over like a crepe. When Normand returned to Montreal, he enthused about it and suggested we try something similar but using crab or lobster. So that the edges remain regular, Charles cooked the omelette in a pastry mould. Finally, shrimp were chosen as the perfect stuffing for this simple appetizer.

MATANE SHRIMP OMELETTE

SERVES 2
PREPARATION: 20 MIN

Lemon Mayonnaise

· 1 egg yolk
· ½ tbsp Dijon mustard
· Salt
· 1 tbsp lemon juice
· 180 ml (¾ cup) grape seed oil
· 60 ml (¼ cup) olive oil
· 1 tbsp warm water (if needed)

Omelette

· 8 egg yolks
· 4 tbsp water
· Salt and freshly ground black pepper
· 20 whole Matane shrimp with their caviar
· 25 g (¼ cup) green onion, thinly sliced
· A few leaves of basil

Finishing Touches

· 4 tbsp green onion oil [P. 445]
· 4 tbsp mix of Kamouraska algae, sesame seeds and Maldon salt [P. 443]

Lemon Mayonnaise

1 Whisk the mayonnaise [P. 448] and set aside.

Omelette

2 Mix the yolks with the water. Add salt and pepper to taste. Pulse with a hand mixer, without incorporating too much air.

3 Shell the shrimp. Set their eggs aside. Fry the shrimp heads and set aside.

4 In a non-stick pan over medium heat, pour in the eggs, and then add the shrimp, green onions, basil and the shrimp eggs.

Finishing Touches

5 Take the omelette off the heat once it's cooked but still slightly runny. Slip it on a plate without flipping it. Garnish with a little lemon mayonnaise, fried shrimp heads, green onion oil and the algae mix. Serve immediately.

TIP

+ If it's too difficult to slip the omelette out of the pan, just eat your meal straight out of it!

GIANT KOHLRABI ROLLS

Tuna rolls were one of sous-chef Jean-Sébastien Giguère's favourite dishes. For him, tuna rolls are a symbol for the Toqué! values of rigour, hard work and meticulousness. With the difficulty we have obtaining responsibly sourced tuna these days, we've adapted this recipe using other fish: rolls made of lobster, marinated salmon, scallops. All of these with Mr. Bertrand's famous giant kohlrabi.

DAIKON ROLLS WITH MARINATED SALMON

SERVES 4
PREPARATION: 1 HR
REST: 24 HRS

Lemon Mayonnaise
· 1 egg yolk
· ½ tbsp Dijon mustard
· Salt
· 1 tbsp lemon juice
· 180 ml (¾ cup) grape seed oil
· 60 ml (¼ cup) olive oil
· 1 tbsp warm water (if needed)

Confit Salmon
· One 200 g (7 oz) salmon filet, with the skin removed
· 120 g (½ cup) sugar
· 120 g (½ cup) salt

Avocado Purée
· 1 avocado
· 1 tbsp lemon juice
· 2 tbsp water
· Salt

Marinated Daikon and Carrots
· 1 litre (4 cups) rice vinegar
· 240 g (1 cup) sugar
· 2 g (1 tsp) pink peppercorns
· 1 bay leaf
· 1 medium carrot, julienned
· 1 medium daikon, julienned

Finishing Touches
· 1 daikon or 1 giant kohlrabi, peeled
· 2 tbsp white and black sesame seeds, roasted
· 5 ml (1 tsp) Dijon mustard
· Salt and freshly ground black pepper

Lemon Mayonnaise
1 Whisk the mayonnaise [P. 448] and set aside.

Confit Salmon
2 Mix the sugar and salt very well and sprinkle half of it on a baking tray. Place the salmon on the tray and dust with the rest of the mixture. Refrigerate for 24 hrs. Rinse with care and pat dry with paper towels.

Avocado Purée
3 Cut the avocado in half. Remove the flesh and pit. With a hand mixer, in a deep and narrow container, blend the flesh into a smooth purée with the lemon juice and water. Salt to taste. Seal the purée immediately with plastic film to prevent oxidation.

Marinated Daikon and Carrots
4 Bring the vinegar, sugar, pink peppercorns and bay leaf to a boil. Allow to cool, then pour over the julienned daikon and carrots.

Finishing Touches
5 With a mandoline, cut the daikon lengthwise in slices a few millimetres thick. Using a spatula, spread a thin layer of very smooth avocado purée on each slice of daikon. Garnish with sesame seeds. Add a large piece of confit salmon, some marinated vegetables, a bit of mayonnaise, mustard, salt and pepper. Form a few rolls and slice in half.

TIP
+ Filter the daikon and carrot marinade to marinate other vegetables or prepare a vinaigrette.

GRISSINI

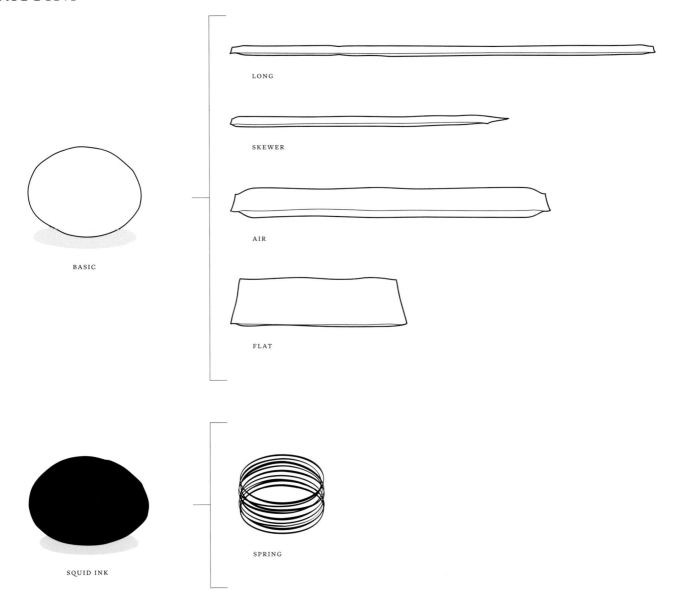

LONG

SKEWER

AIR

FLAT

BASIC

SQUID INK

SPRING

BASIC GRISSINI DOUGH

PREPARATION: 15 MIN
REST: 1 HR

· 250 g (1¾ cups) flour
· 7 g (1½ tsp) salt
· 135 ml (½ cup + 2 tsp) water
· 5 ml (1 tsp) molasses
· 2 tbsp olive oil

1 In a bowl, combine the flour and salt. In another bowl, mix the water, molasses and olive oil. Pour over the dry ingredients.

2 Using a stand mixer at high speed, knead the dough for 7 minutes. Wrap in plastic film and refrigerate for an hour. The dough's shape and cooking time will vary depending on the chosen recipe [SEE BELOW].

VARIATION
+ Grissini dough with squid ink: add 1 tbsp of squid ink before kneading the dough.

GRISSINI

CRAB GRISSINI

SERVES 4
PREPARATION: 1 HR
COOKING: 10 MIN

Grissini
· Basic grissini dough [P. 126]

Lobster Couscous
· 3 room temperature eggs
· 4 tbsp rubber lobster eggs [P. 176]

Garlic Cream
· 125 ml (½ cup) 35% cream
· 1 tbsp garlic powder
  or 1 clove garlic, finely chopped
· Salt and freshly ground black pepper

Finishing Touches
· 200 g (7 oz) fresh crabmeat
· Fresh herbs, to taste
  (lovage, mint, chervil, lemon balm)
· A few drops of hot sauce
· A few radishes, julienned
· 1 Lebanese cucumber, thinly sliced
· 4 tbsp salmon eggs

Grissini
1 Using a rolling pin, roll out the dough into a thin rectangle. Fold the two sides towards the centre, without overlapping them. Flatten the dough a little.

2 Pass the dough a number of times through a pasta machine while coating it with flour to obtain a rectangle about 1 millimetre thick.

3 Preheat the oven to 200°C (400°F). Lightly flour the dough and spread it on a work surface. Cut into 17 cm × 5 cm (7 in × 2 in) strips and place them between two sheets of parchment paper. Place these strips between two baking trays to ensure that they remain quite flat. Bake for 10 minutes. Remove the topmost baking tray, and cook for another 2 to 3 minutes until the grissini are uniform in colour.

Lobster Couscous
4 Cook the (chicken) eggs in boiling water for 10 minutes. Separate the whites from the yolk (while keeping the whites for another use). Pass the yolks and the rubber lobster eggs through a sieve to obtain a texture similar to that of couscous.

Garlic Cream
5 In a bowl, whip the cream until firm peaks form. Add the garlic powder, salt and pepper.

Finishing Touches
6 Spread garlic cream on the grissini. Place the crab uniformly on top. Add the herbs, hot sauce, vegetables and lobster couscous. Finish with salmon eggs.

TIP
+ You can make smaller grissini to serve as an appetizer.

GRISSINI

GRISSINI SKEWERS
WITH SALMON

SERVES 4
PREPARATION: 1 HR
REST: 24 HRS

Grissini

· Basic grissini dough [P. 126]

Marinated Salmon

· Zest of 1 lemon
· Zest of 1 orange
· 300 g (10 oz) salmon with the skin
  (thicker cut)
· 120 g (1 cup) icing sugar
· 120 g (1 cup) salt

Finishing Touches

· 2 red and yellow beets, marinated
· 1 green apple
· 1 bunch green onions
  (only the green part), cut into 1 cm
  (½ in) straight pieces
· 8 whole leaves of pak-choï
· 60 ml (¼ cup) vegetable glaze [P. 450]
· 60 ml (¼ cup) whipped cream
· 1 tbsp green onion oil [P. 445]
· 1 tbsp white sesame seeds, roasted

Grissini

1 Preheat oven to 200°C (400°F).
  Using a rolling pin, roll out the
  dough into a thin rectangle. Fold
  the two sides towards the centre,
  without overlapping them. Flatten
  the dough a little.

2 Pass the dough a number of times
  through a pasta machine while
  coating it with flour to obtain a rectangle about 1 millimetre thick.

3 Cut into eight 25 cm (10 in) by 1 cm
  (½ in) sticks [TIP]. Cut the end of each
  stick into a sharp point, to make it
  easier to skewer the salmon.

4 Place the grissini sticks on a baking
  tray lined with greaseproof paper
  and bake for 4 to 6 minutes.
  Set aside at room temperature for
  a few minutes so the grissini can be
  easily removed from the tray.

Marinated Salmon

5 Dress the salmon with the citrus
  zest. Sprinkle with a mix of icing
  sugar and salt. Cover with plastic
  film and refrigerate for 24 hours.
  Remove the skin and cut the salmon
  into 12 pieces of equal size.

Finishing Touches

6 Using a mandoline, thinly slice
  the beets and apple. Use the grissini to alternately skewer pieces
  of salmon, beet slices, pieces of
  green onion, pak-choï leaves and
  apple slices. Repeat until there
  are three pieces of salmon per
  skewer. Place on plates and drizzle
  with vegetable glaze. Just before
  serving, add the whipped cream
  and green onion oil. Garnish with
  sesame seeds.

TIP

+ We always cook more grissini
  than needed in case they break—
  they're so fragile. You can replace
  pak-choï by young crunchy lettuce
  leaves when in season. A variation is to prepare longer skewers
  wrapped in thin slices of dried duck
  breast, garnished with Espelette
  pepper.

Brochette

GRISSINI

SERVES 4
PREPARATION TIME: 4 HRS
TIME IN THE FREEZER: 1-2 HRS

Tuna
· 150 g (5 oz) tuna belly, chilled
  in the freezer for a few hours
  to make slicing easier.

Grissini
· Basic grissini dough [P. 126]

Spicy Mayonnaise
· 1 egg yolk
· ½ tbsp Dijon mustard
· Salt
· 1 tbsp lemon juice
· 180 ml (¾ cup) grape seed oil
· 60 ml (¼ cup) olive oil
· 1 tbsp water (optional)
· 1 tbsp sesame oil
· 2 tbsp organic soy sauce
· 1 tbsp sriracha
  (Thai hot pepper sauce)
· 1 tbsp sambal oelek
  (Indonesian hot pepper sauce)

Finishing Touches
· Olive oil
· A few leaves of lovage or other herbs
· A few flowers (pansies, sage,
  onion and bronze fennel flowers)
· 2 tbsp chives, minced
· Maldon salt
· 1 tbsp smoked paprika

Grissini
1 Preheat oven to 200°C (400°F).
  With a rolling pin, roll out the
  dough into a thin rectangle. Fold
  the two sides towards the centre,
  without overlapping them. Flatten
  the dough a little.

2 Pass the dough a number of times
  through a pasta machine while
  coating it with flour to obtain a rectangle about 1 millimetre thick.

3 Cut the dough into eight 23 cm
  (9 in) by 3 cm (1¼ in) strips. Place
  on a baking tray lined with parchment paper and bake for about
  10 minutes to get the desired
  colour. The grissini have to rise and
  puff up. Be careful when handling
  them, since they're very fragile.

Spicy Mayonnaise
4 Whisk the mayonnaise [P. 448]
  and set aside.

Finishing Touches
5 Preheat the oven on broil. Using
  a meat slicer, cut the frozen tuna
  belly into 8 thin slices. Wrap each
  grissini in two slices of tuna and
  place on a baking sheet. Place in
  the oven for a few seconds. Sprinkle
  with a few drops of olive oil, and
  then garnish with herbs, flowers
  and chives. Add Maldon salt and
  smoked paprika and serve with the
  spicy mayonnaise.

CONFIT
FISH

CONFIT SALMON

SERVES 4
PREPARATION: 30 MIN
REST: 1:30 HRS
COOKING: 30 MIN

Confit Salmon

· 4 × 150 g (5 oz) salmon filets with the skin, or 2 salmon heads cut in two lengthwise
· 120 g (½ cup) salt
· 120 g (½ cup) sugar
· 2 tbsp maple syrup
· 2 tbsp olive oil

Finishing Touches

· Herbalicious [P. 445] (optional)
· Zest of 1 lemon, finely grated (optional)
· Hot sauce (optional)

1 If using salmon heads, first soak them in cold water for 30 minutes.

2 In a bowl, mix the salt and sugar. Coat the salmon generously on each side, cover and refrigerate for 45 minutes.

3 Rinse the fish under running cold water, pat dry and allow to sit at room temperature for 15 minutes.

4 Preheat the oven to 120°C (250°F). Place the fish, skin down, in a baking dish. Drizzle with the maple syrup and olive oil. Bake for 20 to 30 minutes, basting the fish every 5 minutes until the skin comes off easily.

Finishing Touches

5 Garnish with the herbalicous mixture, lemon zest, and hot sauce.

TIPS

+ After preserving the fish, coat it with maple syrup and burn it with a blowtorch to caramelize it. What's more, this recipe works great with arctic char, mackerel or brook trout. However, you'll need to adjust your cooking time depending on the thickness of the cut: the flesh should remain supple while giving way under a fork.

+ Confit Salmon is a classic at *Brasserie T!*; we serve it with a crunchy fennel salad.

ANOTHER ROUND
FOR SAMUEL...

RICHARD LEROY
Chenin Blanc
LOIRE

Preserving fish raises and sharpens its flavour. In terms of wine, this gives us many more possibilities. With caramelized fish confit, we usually propose elegant yet persistent crackling wines. The goal is to find balance between the fattiness of the fish and the palate of the wine. The fact that preserved fish is caramelized allows us to try wines with more earthy notes. We'll go towards the Chenin Blanc from the Loire region. We also prefer very ripe Chenin, with oxidative notes. The maturity of these wines makes us think of vines or cedar wood. Another potential pairing is with Burgundies like Meursault or other white wines from Côte de Beaune, but these are more classic choices.

Richard Leroy, vigneron à Rablay sur Layon

Les Noëls de Montbenault

ANJOU

APPELLATION ANJOU CONTROIEE

2007

ALC 13 % /VOL   MIS EN BOUTEILLE AU DOMAINE - PRODUIT DE FRANCE   750 ML

SALMON

We were looking to make a smoked salmon dish without smoked salmon. To keep the idea of smoked salmon, we decided to use marinated salmon and smoke sour cream on ice. Potato chips remain the most important part of the dish. Developing them took a lot of trial and error in the kitchen, since they need to be at once translucent, flat and crunchy.

MOCK SMOKED SALMON

SERVES 4
PREPARATION: 1:30 HRS
REST: 24 HRS

· 300 g (10 oz) marinated salmon, with the skin [P. 130]

Smoked Cream
· 60 ml (¼ cup) sour cream
· 125 ml (½ cup) 35 % cream
· Smoker or wood chips

Chips
· 3 Russet potatoes, peeled
· 125 ml (½ cup) clarified butter, very hot [P. 444]

Finishing Touches
· A few sprigs of chives
· Maldon salt

Smoked Cream

1 Spread the sour cream on the sides of a mixing bowl. Place in a slightly larger mixing bowl filled halfway with ice.

2 *Method with a smoker:* Smoke the sour cream over high heat for about 10 minutes. Make sure the cream does not cook. Refrigerate. Whip the 35 % cream until stiff and salt to taste. Fold the whipped cream into the smoked cream using a spatula.

3 *Method without a smoker:* Place the wood chips in a metal container and carefully light them. Control the fire with ice cubes in order to obtain smoke but no flames. In an unlit barbecue, close the lid over the mixing bowls and the smoking wood chips. Smoke the cream for 10 minutes. Refrigerate. Whip the 35 % cream until firm, and salt to taste. Fold the whipped cream into the smoked cream using a spatula.

Chips

4 With a mandoline, thinly slice the potatoes lengthwise to a thickness of about 3 mm (⅛ in) and place in a bowl of warm water. Strain and pat dry. In a mixing bowl, soak the potatoes in the clarified butter. Remove the excess butter and spread a single layer of potatoes on a silicone baking mat. Cover with a piece of parchment paper and a baking sheet to prevent the chips from rippling. Preheat a convection oven to 105°C (220°F). Cook the potatoes for 45 minutes, rotating the baking tray every 15 minutes. Turn the oven fan off and continue cooking for 1 hour to 1 hour 20 minutes, rotating the baking sheet every 15 minutes. Monitor the cooking and remove the chips as they become ready (those on the side of the pan will be ready before those in the middle). The chips shouldn't brown; they should be amber-coloured and crunchy. Store on parchment paper, at room temperature in a cool, dry place.

Finishing Touches

5 Cut the salmon in 5 mm (¼ in) thick slices.

6 Spread some smoked cream on one side of the salmon. Place on a chip and spread cream on the other side. Add a sprig of chive and a pinch of Maldon salt. Cover with another chip to make a sandwich. Repeat and serve immediately.

MACKEREL

SERVES 2
PREPARATION: 30 MIN
COOKING: 45 MIN
REST: 1:15 HR

Mackerel

· 120 g (½ cup) sugar
· 120 g (½ cup) salt
· One 150 g (5 oz) Spanish
  mackerel filet
· 4 tbsp olive oil
· 4 tbsp maple syrup

Finishing Touches

· 2 tbsp maple syrup
· 1 tbsp miso
· 1 tbsp sriracha
  (Thai hot pepper sauce)
· 2 tbsp green onion oil [P. 445]

Mackerel

1 Mix the sugar and salt together in a baking dish or on a baking sheet and coat the mackerel on both sides. Refrigerate for 45 minutes. Rinse well and place the fish on a baking sheet, skin down. Brush with olive oil and maple syrup on both sides and allow to rest at room temperature for 30 minutes.

2 Preheat the oven to 110°C (230°F). Bake the fish for 30 to 45 minutes. The fish is done when the bones come out easily. Allow to cool before slicing into portions.

Finishing Touches

3 Brush the skin with maple syrup, and run the blowtorch over it (as for a crème brûlée). Garnish with miso, sriracha and green onion oil. This dish can be served with fried fiddleheads ferns [P. 56].

TIP

+ This recipe also works well with salmon, arctic char or brook trout.

MACKEREL

U-SHAPED MACKEREL

SERVES 4
PREPARATION: 1:15 HRS
COOKING: 15 MIN

Croutons
· 1 loaf of day-old bread
· Olive oil

Spicy Mayonnaise
· 1 egg yolk
· ½ tbsp Dijon mustard
· Salt
· 1 tbsp lemon juice
· 180 ml (¾ cup) grape seed oil
· 60 ml (¼ cup) olive oil
· 1 tbsp warm water (optional)
· 1 tbsp sesame oil
· 2 tbsp organic soy sauce
· 1 tbsp sriracha
  (Thai hot pepper sauce)
· 1 tbsp sambal oelek
  (Indonesian hot pepper sauce)

Tomato
· 1 large firm-fleshed tomato with few
  seeds (Beefsteak variety)

Coleslaw
· 4 tbsp olive oil
· 2 tbsp honey
· 4 tbsp rice vinegar
· ¼ red cabbage, minced
· ¼ green cabbage, minced

Mackerel
· 4 fresh mackerel filets
  of about 75 g (2½ oz) each
· Salt and freshly ground black pepper

Croutons
1 Preheat the oven to 180°C (350°F). Slice the bread thinly and wrap the slices around clean empty tin cans or beer cans. Brush with olive oil and bake for 10 minutes until golden. Take the bread out of the oven as soon as it's crunchy, leaving it on the container used for baking.

Spicy Mayonnaise
2 Whisk the mayonnaise [P. 448] and set aside.

Tomato
3 With a small knife, score an X on the bottom of the tomato. Blanch in boiling water for 15 seconds and cool immediately in a bowl of ice water. Peel and remove 4 cylinders of flesh from around the core using an apple corer.

Coleslaw
4 In a bowl, combine the olive oil, honey and vinegar. Add salt and pepper to taste. Pour over the cabbage and mix well.

Mackerel
5 Preheat the oven to 180°C (350°F). Debone the mackerel filets. Make small sideways incisions on the skin to help the fish take on the U-shape of the croutons. Add salt and pepper to taste. Place on a baking sheet, skin-side up, and bake for 2 to 3 minutes. Place on the bread.

Finishing Touches
6 Spoon a little spicy mayonnaise onto each plate. Garnish with the coleslaw and a tomato cylinder. Carefully add the bread covered with the mackerel.

HALIBUT

HERRING

ROASTED HALIBUT TAIL WITH GARDEN HERBS

SERVES 2
PREPARATION: 3 HRS
COOKING: 45 MIN
REST: 1:30 HRS

· 1 halibut tail
· 240 g (1 cup) salt
· 3 sprigs thyme
· 3 sprigs sage
· 3 sprigs oregano
· 2 balsam fir branches
· Zest of 1 lemon
· Zest of 1 orange
· 3 cloves garlic, peeled
· 60 ml (¼ cup) olive oil

1 Soak the halibut tail in a bowl for 30 minutes under cold running water. Carefully pat dry.

2 Sprinkle the halibut tail with salt and refrigerate for 1½ hours. Rinse under cold water to remove all the salt.

3 Preheat the oven to 190°C (375°F). Place the halibut tail on a baking sheet. Garnish with the herbs, and then drizzle uniformly with olive oil. Bake for 30 minutes until the flesh detaches easily from the skin. Serve immediately.

TIP
+ You can replace the tail of the halibut with its head. Cooking time will be shorter in that case: remove from the oven as soon as the skin can be removed easily.

SMOKED HERRING CREAM

SERVES 4
PREPARATION: 30 MIN

· 250 ml (1 cup) 35 % whipping cream
· 2 tbsp shallots, minced
· 2 tbsp chives, minced
· Zest of 1 lemon
· 2 tbsp smoked herring eggs or 4 tbsp smoked and dried herring cubes
· A few leaves of lettuce
· Olive oil bread [P. 446]
· Freshly ground black pepper
· A few leaves of basil, minced

1 Using a mixer, whip the cream until soft peaks form. Pour into a bowl, and using a spatula, incorporate the shallots, chives and lemon zest. Add the herring and mix with a spoon. Serve in bowl accompanied with lettuce and croutons. Pepper to taste and garnish with basil.

EEL

VEAL SWEETBREADS AND ENDIVES WITH SMOKED EEL BUTTER

SERVES 4
PREPARATION: 1 HR
COOKING: 30 MIN
REST: 14 HRS

Smoked Eel Butter

· 100 g (3½ oz) smoked eel trimmings, without the skin or bones
· 150 g (5 oz) mackerel trimmings, without the skin
· 240 g (1 cup) unsalted butter, at room temperature
· ½ shallot, minced
· ½ bunch chives, minced
· Zest of 1 lemon
· Zest of 1 orange
· Zest of 1 lime
· A few drops of green Tabasco sauce
· Salt and freshly ground black pepper

Veal Sweetbreads

· 625 g (1¼ lbs) of veal sweetbreads
· Vegetable stock, chilled [P. 450]
· 6 tbsp butter
· Salt and freshly ground black pepper

Finishing Touches

· 1 tbsp butter
· 2 tbsp olive oil
· 4 endives, with leaves separated
· 60 ml (¼ cup) brandy
· 60 ml (¼ cup) maple syrup
· 60 ml (¼ cup) brown stock [P. 444]

Smoked Eel Butter

1 Adjust the quantity of eel and mackerel depending on how much of each you have, in order to obtain a total weight of 250 g (8 oz) of fish.

2 Steam the mackerel trimmings for 1 or 2 minutes. Use a fork to break the trimmings down and cool at room temperature for 2 hours.

3 Pass the smoked eel trimmings through a sieve to remove bones. In a food processor, mix all the ingredients together to obtain a homogenous butter.

4 Dampen a work surface.Roll out a long sheet of plastic film and place half the smoked eel butter on top. Roll into a tight tube of about 3 cm (1¼ in) in diameter and twist the ends into knots. Refrigerate for at least 12 hours before using.

Veal Sweetbreads

5 Soak the veal sweetbreads under running cold water for 15 minutes to eliminate the blood and any impurities. Cover with cold water and refrigerate overnight

6 The next day, soak the veal sweet-breads once again in fresh water for 15 minutes. Place them in a pot of vegetable stock. Bring to a simmer and cook for one minute. Turn off the heat and allow the veal and stock to cool for about 30 minutes. With a small paring knife, remove the fine film of skin covering the sweetbreads. Make 4 portions of 125 g (4 oz) each.

7 Preheat the oven to 200°C (400°F). Foam the butter in an oven-safe pan. Salt and pepper the sweetbreads and cook over medium heat , adding butter until all sides are properly coloured. Place in the oven for 5 minutes until the surface is golden and crunchy. Set aside in a warm place.

Finishing Touches

8 In a frying pan, heat the butter and olive oil. Gently sauté the endives, and add salt and pepper to taste. Turn the heat off and flambé with brandy. Deglaze with maple syrup and remove from the heat.

9 Drizzle the veal sweetbreads with the cooking butter. Pat dry to remove excess fat and arrange on plates. Position the endives both vertically and horizontally to lend volume to the plate. Garnish with dabs of eel butter and top with brown stock.

COD

Recipes always begin with either a story or an accident. With cod, we started making a *brandade*. We then began reusing the cooking water as a base for a cold soup. To make the soup, we use the less attractive pieces of the cod (collar, tail) that we cook in milk. For a few years now, we use the soup as a base for a foam we serve with olive oil bread or grissini.

SOPHIE'S
COLD COD SOUP

SERVES 8
PREPARATION: 45 MIN
REST: 1:15 HRS

Cod Soup
· 625 g (1¼ lbs) fresh cod filets
· 600 g (2 cups) coarse salt
· 2 tbsp olive oil
· 1 Spanish onion, roughly choppped
· 1 leek, white only, roughly chopped
· 2 Yukon gold potatoes, peeled, medium-dice
· 1 clove garlic, minced
· A few sprigs of fresh herbs (thyme, sage, oregano, bay leaf)
· 1.5 litres (6 cups) milk
· 125 g (4 oz) labneh

Confit Cod
· 300 g (1 cup) coarse salt
· 5 or 6 sprigs thyme
· 1 sprig rosemary
· ⅓ bunch parsley
· ½ head garlic
· 1 tbsp juniper berries
· 80 ml (⅓ cup) extra virgin olive oil

Cod Soup
1 Trim the cod keeping a 200 g (7 oz) portion for confit and use the trimmings for the soup.

2 On a baking sheet, cover the cod trimmings with coarse salt and refrigerate for 30 minutes. Rinse under cold water to remove the salt. Pat dry.

3 Warm the olive oil in a saucepan. Sauté the onion until it begins to colour, then add the leek, potatoes, garlic and herbs. Allow to sweat slightly. Pour in the milk and bring to a simmer. Add the cod and continue simmering over low heat for about 1 hour, until the vegetables are completely cooked. Reduce to a smooth purée in a food processor, then filter in a strainer and allow to cool down completely. With a hand mixer, mix in the labneh.

Confit Cod
4 Preheat the oven to 120°C (250°F).

5 In a food processer, roughly mix the salt, thyme, rosemary, parsley, garlic and juniper berries (the mixture should not be too fine). Generously coat the cod with this mixture and refrigerate for 30 to 45 minutes. Remove all the salt by rinsing quickly under running cold water and pat dry.

6 Place the cod on a baking sheet lined with aluminium foil. Brush the whole fish with olive oil and bake for 25 to 35 minutes, depending on the thickness of the cut. Remove from the oven when the fish becomes flaky.

Finishing Touches
7 Serve the soup cold and delicately place a few flakes of confit cod on top.

TIP
+ Don't forget that cod and olive oil are the greatest friends in the world. Feel free to add a dash of oil to your cod soup. You can also serve it with olive oil bread or warm it and omit the labneh.

MONKFISH LIVER

Monkfish liver is large, delicious and looks as if it's related to duck foie gras. For two years, we were regularly ordering some for kitchen tests. Finally, cooking it the traditional Japanese way—a technique taught to us by Kazu, one of our former cooks—seemed to be a great way to prepare it.

TOQUÉ! STYLE
MONKFISH ANKIMO

SERVES 6
PREPARATION: 1 HR
COOKING: 1 HR
REST: 14 HRS

Monkfish Liver

· 1 kg (2 lbs) monkfish liver, with major nerves removed
· 240 g (1 cup) salt
· 240 g (1 cup) sugar
· One 750 ml bottle of sake
· 1 bunch green onions, cut into pieces
· 100 g (3½ oz) ginger, roughly chopped
· 12 gelatin sheets

Soy Vinaigrette

· 160 ml (⅔ cup) soy sauce
· 60 ml (¼ cup) water
· 5 ml (1 tsp) sriracha (Thai hot pepper sauce)

Finishing Touches

· 4 French radishes, thinly sliced
· A few young basil shoots
· 1 lemon, supremed and diced
· Lime juice

Monkfish Liver

1 In a large dish, coat the liver with salt and refrigerate for 45 minutes. Rinse carefully, return to the dish and coat with sugar. Refrigerate for 45 minutes. Rinse well.

2 On a large baking tray, mix 500 ml (2 cups) sake, green onions and ginger. Place the liver in this mixture and refrigerate for 1 hour.

3 Rinse off the liver and tap dry. Place on a sheet of aluminium foil and roll into sausages 8 cm (3 in) in diameter. Twist the ends and tie with elastics. Roll in a maki mat to retain the desired shape.

4 Steam the liver sausages for about 1 hour, or until the temperature at the heart of the sausage reads 85°C (185°F). Allow to cool. Cut into 1 cm (½ in) slices, and then mould them into disks using lightly oiled pastry cutters. Do not remove the cutters.

5 Bloom the gelatin sheets in a bowl of ice water. Meanwhile, flambé the rest of the sake. With a whisk, incorporate the strained gelatin into the sake. Let rest at room temperature and pour on the monkfish liver to obtain a uniform layer of about 4 mm (⅙ in).

Soy Vinaigrette

6 Combine all the ingredients in a bowl.

Finishing Touches

7 Remove the liver from the moulds by heating the molds lightly with a blowtorch. Drizzle a little soy vinaigrette onto the plates. Add a piece of monkfish liver and garnish with radish, basil shoots, a lemon slice and lime juice.

MONKFISH LIVER

We got into the habit of cooking monkfish liver in an herb butter, *Beurre de l'amour*. It was delicious but not very practical. As livers vary in size depending on the fish, it was difficult to obtain consistent results. One day, we began using a poultry liver recipe that Normand had kept in a notebook for thirty years. By following the recipe to the letter using monkfish liver, we obtained a perfect mousse!

MONKFISH LIVER MOUSSE AND VEGETABLE ROLLS

MAKES 1 TERRINE
PREPARATION: 2 HRS
REST: 24 HRS + 4 HRS FOR MARINATING

Monkfish Liver Mousse
· 750 g (1½ lbs) monkfish liver
· 480 g (2 cups) salt
· 480 g (2 cups) sugar
· 360 g (1½ cups) butter
· 8 egg yolks
· 6 tbsp cream, boiled and cooled
· 6 tbsp cognac, flambéed
  (to remove the taste of alcohol)
· Salt and freshly ground black pepper

Soy Jelly
· 4 gelatin sheets
· 180 ml (¾ cup) sake
· 60 ml (¼ cup) mirin
· 20 ml (4 tsp) organic soy sauce

Honey and Rice Vinaigrette
· 1 tbsp honey
· 2 tbsp unseasoned rice vinegar
· 2 tbsp olive oil
· Salt and freshly ground black pepper

Vegetable Rolls
· A few baby carrots, sliced
· 1 Honeycrisp apple, sliced
· 1 fennel bulb, thinly sliced
· A few slivers of radish
· A few slices of rutabaga
· 4 daikon or kohlrabi slices.

Finishing Touches
· 60 ml (¼ cup) green onion oil [P. 445]
· 60 ml (¼ cup) vegetable glaze [P. 450]
· Maldon salt

Monkfish Liver Mousse
1 Place the liver in a bowl of cold water and refrigerate overnight. Rinse under cold water and lightly pat dry with a paper towel. Remove the nerves and make a few small incisions on all sides. Coat in salt and refrigerate for 1 hour. Rinse, coat in sugar, and marinate for 1 hour. Rinse and chop into pieces.

2 In a small pan over low heat, melt the butter until golden. Allow to cool at room temperature.

3 Preheat the oven to 105°C (220°F). Line a terrine mould with plastic film. In a blender, purée the liver with the egg yolks, cream and cognac. Add salt and pepper to taste. Slowly incorporate the butter into the mixture, mixing constantly. Pass through a sieve and pour into the mould. Place the terrine mould in a large baking dish and fill the dish with water about three quarters

up the mould. Cook until the temperature in the middle reaches 72°C (162°F). Refrigerate overnight.

Soy Jelly

4 Bloom the gelatin sheets in a bowl of ice water. In a pot, bring the sake, mirin and soy sauce to a boil. Remove from heat, add the strained gelatin and mix well. Let cool at room temperature, and then pour into a small tray lined with plastic film. Refrigerate for about 2 hours. Turn out the jelly and cut into 5 mm (¼ in) cubes.

Honey and Rice Vinaigrette

5 In a bowl, whisk all the ingredients together and set aside.

Vegetable Rolls

6 Just before serving, mix all the ingredients together (except for the daikon) with the honey and rice vinegar. Divide amongst the daikon slices and make small rolls. (You can also simply mix all the ingredients together and serve as a salad.)

Finishing Touches

7 Place a slice of monkfish liver, about 2 cm (¾ in) thick, on a plate. Add a vegetable roll and a jelly cube. Garnish with green onion oil, vegetable glaze and Maldon salt.

TIP

+ To add a bit of crunch, incorporate fried bread [P. 446] inside the vegetable rolls.

CALAMARI

CALAMARI, SQUID INK AND TOMATOES

SERVES 4
PREPARATION: 45 MINUTES

· 2 or 3 tomatoes, in season
· 125 ml (½ cup) olive oil
· 1 clove garlic, finely minced
· A few leaves of basil
· 250 g (8 oz) fresh calamari
· Salt and freshly ground black pepper
· 1 tbsp squid ink

1 Using a small knife, score an X on the bottom of the tomatoes and blanch them in boiling water for 10 to 15 seconds. Cool immediately in ice water. Peel and cut into 1 cm (½ in) cubes.

2 In a frying pan over medium to high heat, heat 80 ml (⅓ cup) of olive oil and sear the tomatoes. Add the garlic and basil, remove from the heat, and set aside.

3 Separate the calamari heads from the bodies and soak the tentacles under cold running water for 20 minutes to remove any excess ink. Separate the tentacles from the body and remove the cartilage. Also remove the small layer of translucent skin. Turn the calamari inside out. Clean with cold water. Remove the eyes and the horned beak around the mouth at the base of the tentacles. Cut the bodies into thin strips 5 mm (¼ in) thick. Set aside.

4 Season the calamari to taste. In another pan over medium-high heat, heat the remaining olive oil until very hot and sear the calamari for 10 seconds. Place in a bowl and mix with the squid ink. Serve with the tomatoes on a plate.

CALAMARI

PIGEONS AND CALAMARI

SERVES 4
PREPARATION: 1:30 HRS
REST: 12 HRS

Cranberry Beans
- 100 g (1 cup) fresh cranberry beans
- ½ onion, roughly chopped
- 1 clove garlic, crushed
- 1 carrot, roughly sliced
- 2 tbsp olive oil
- 1 piece of salted lard of about 60 g (2 oz), diced in large pieces
- 2 litres (8 cups) water
- Salt

Calamari
- 150 g (5 oz) medium sized calamari (bodies and heads) cleaned and sliced [P. 158]

Garlic Flower with Hot Pepper
- 60 ml (¼ cup) olive oil
- 1 small pepper (Espelette variety), minced
- 1 garlic flower, minced

Meat Jus
- 500 ml (2 cups) meat stock [P. 444]
- 125 ml (½ cup) red wine
- 1 tbsp very cold butter, in small pieces

Zucchinis
- 2 yellow zucchinis, in 5 mm (¼ in) slices

Pigeons
- 1 tbsp butter
- 4 tbsp olive oil
- 4 pigeon supremes, with skins, of about 100 g (3½ oz) each
- Salt and freshly ground black pepper
- Tub o' Duck Fat [P. 449]

Finishing Touches
- 1 tbsp butter
- 4 tbsp olive oil
- 2 sprigs crimson basil, leaves only

Cranberry Beans
1 The night before, shell the beans and soak them overnight in a bowl of cold water in the refrigerator, to ensure they don't burst during cooking.

2 The next day, in a saucepan over medium heat, sauté the onion, garlic, carrot and salted lard in the olive oil until lightly coloured. Add the strained beans, stir and cook for 1 minute. Add the water and simmer over low heat for about 40 minutes, or until the beans are soft and plump. Salt at the very end, or the bean skins will harden. Allow to cool in the cooking liquid.

Garlic Flower with Hot Pepper
3 In a frying pan, heat the olive oil to a high heat. Turn off the burner and add the pepper and garlic flower. Set aside.

Meat Jus

4 In a saucepan, let the meat stock reduce by half. Add the red wine, and gradually whisk in the butter. Remove from heat and set aside.

Zucchinis

5 In a pot of boiling salted water, blanch the zucchini for 30 seconds.

Pigeons

6 In a pan, heat the olive oil and butter over medium heat until golden. Season the pigeon supremes. Place in the pan, skin side down. Place a weight over the supremes to prevent them from curling and to ensure more uniform cooking. Sear over high heat for 30 seconds or until the skin is golden. Immerse the supremes in the tub 'o fat for about 3 minutes. Remove from the tub and allow to rest under aluminium foil for 6 minutes before serving.

Finishing Touches

7 In a pan, over high heat, heat the butter and olive oil. Sear the calamari until lightly coloured. Add the strained beans, meat jus, garlic flower, zucchini and basil.

8 Place some calamari and beans on each plate. Slice the pigeon in half and place in the middle of the plate.

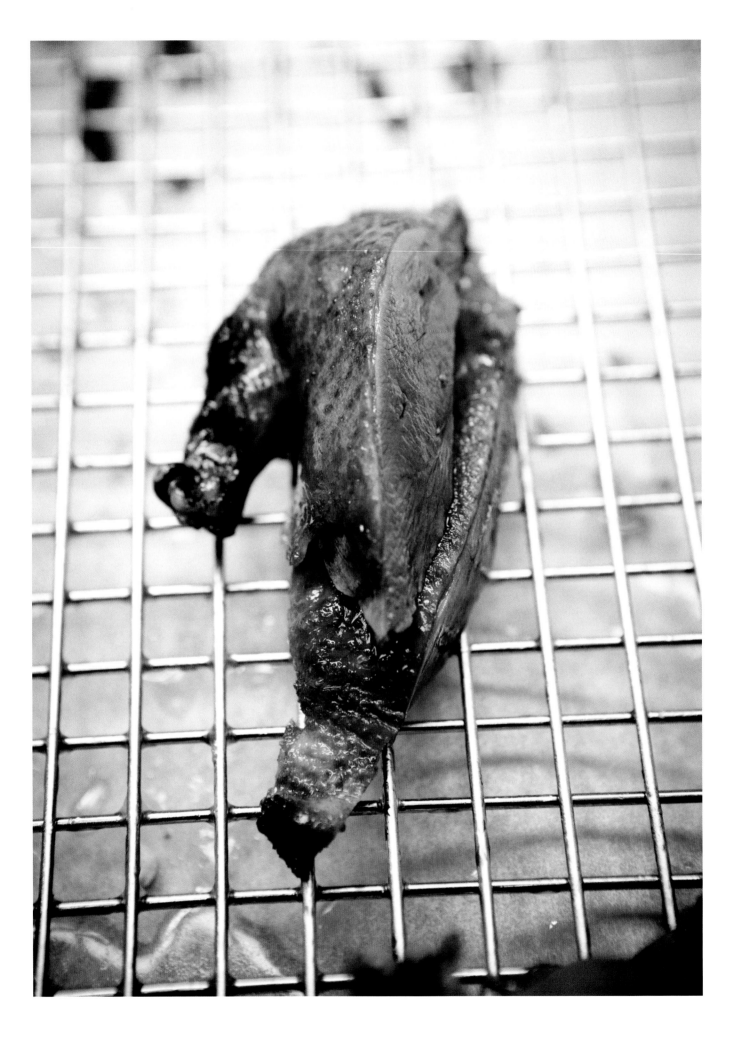

SEA URCHINS

This dish is one of the must-haves from the tasting menu at *Toqué!*. To avoid losing the damaged gonads during opening, we prepare the urchin as a purée. Due to the very iodized taste of the flesh, we mix the purée with whipped cream. It's a very simple way to flavour this product, often considered difficult to prepare.

SIGNATURE SEA URCHINS

SERVES 4
PREPARATION: 1 HR

Urchins
· 8 sea urchins
· 250 ml (1 cup) 35% cream

Ginger Sauce
· 1 tbsp ginger juice, extracted with a juice extractor
· 2 tbsp organic soy sauce
· 1 tbsp daikon, thinly diced
· 1 tbsp shallots, minced
· 1 tbsp chives, minced
· 2 tbsp olive oil

Urchins
1 To clean the urchins, prepare three rinsing bowls by filling each with 1 litre (4 cups) of water, 1 tbsp of rice vinegar and ice.

2 Using sharp scissors, cut around the mouth of the sea urchin and remove the tube feet. With a spoon, delicately scoop out the inside of the urchin by running the spoon around its inner surface. Empty the contents into the first bowl. Separate the gonads (the orangey-beige meatier part) and place them in the second bowl. Rinse one last time in the third bowl, and let drain on a paper towel. Set aside the four nicest shells for serving.

3 Divide the 12 nicest gonads among the 4 shells. With a hand mixer, purée the other gonads. Pass through a strainer, mix with the cream and whisk into soft peaks.

Ginger Sauce
4 Mix all the ingredients in a bowl.

Finishing Touches
5 Pour 1 tbsp ginger sauce into each shell. Add 1 tbsp of the sea urchin cream. Then place the shells on coarse salt or crushed iced on a plate.

TIP
+ A sea urchin's preparation can change with the season. You can add a bit of tomato, sweet corn ice cream, small crunchy vegetables, flower petals or even char caviar.

ANOTHER ROUND
FOR SAMUEL…

PIERRE FRICK
Muscat
ALSACE

Given the fattiness of sea urchins, along with its large volume and bountiful flesh, we looked for a wine that is both fresh and crisp, like, for example, Soave Classico La Rocca by Pieropan. It's our classic pairing, since it helps structure the dish. You can also go in a completely different direction by choosing something like the Muscat Grand Cru Steinert Pierre Frick, a dry wine with a clean finish, more lively than the Soave, very floral, with a powerful aromatic nose.

Alsace Grand Cru
Appellation Alsace Grand Cru Controllée

PIERRE FRICK

Muscat

2007

Grand Cru
Steinert

mis en bouteille par

PIERRE FRICK 68250 PFAFFENHEM - FRANCE

ALC 13% BY VOL *Produce of France* 750 ML

WHELKS

WHELK SALAD

SERVES 4
PREPARATION: 1:30 HRS
COOKING: 45 MINUTES

Whelks
· 30 whelks in their shells

Croutons
· Day old bread
· 4 tbsp olive oil

Salad
· 1 Lebanese cucumber
· A few red radishes
· A few cherry tomatoes
· 1 bunch coriander
· 1 bunch dill
· 250 ml (1 cup) aioli [P. 448]

Finishing Touches
· 20 ml (4 tsp) green onion oil [P. 445]
· 2 tbsp butter
· 2 cloves garlic, minced
· Salt and freshly ground black pepper

Whelks
1 In a large bucket, soak the whelks under cold running water for 45 minutes. Strain and place in a large pot. Cover with water and add 2 tbsp of salt. Bring to a boil and cook for 45 minutes (be careful not to overcook the whelks and make them rubbery). Immerse in cold water.

2 With a fork, remove the whelks from their shells. Remove the blackish part. Rinse the muscle (which is of a lighter colour) and pat dry, and then slice in half. Clean and keep the 4 nicest shells for serving.

Croutons
3 Preheat the oven to 180°C (350°F). Slice the bread into 1 cm (½ in) cubes. Spread on a baking tray, brush with 2 tbsp of olive oil and dry in the oven until the croutons become crunchy (about 5 minutes in a convection oven or 10 minutes in a regular oven).

Salad
4 With a mandoline, thinly slice the cucumber and radishes. Cut the tomatoes in half, and pluck the coriander and dill. Mix the vegetables together, adding the garden herbs to taste.

Finishing Touches
5 Divide the aioli among the clean whelk shells, adding 1 tsp (5 ml) of green onion oil to each shell. In a non-stick pan, heat the butter and the remaining olive oil. Sear the whelk with garlic. Immediately mix in the vegetables. Add salt and pepper to taste.

6 Prepare the salad in bowls or on plates. Serve with an aioli-filled shell so that your guests can add the aioli at the last moment.

WHELKS

Fir Beef and Sautéed Whelk with Chanterelles was inspired by the classic French dish of browned snails that Normand used to make when he worked with Mr. Billoux in Dijon. The snails are replaced by Quebec whelks. It is, in a way, a reinvention of *surf and turf*, since it brings together iodized and earthy flavours.

FIR BEEF AND SAUTÉED WHELKS WITH CHANTERELLES

SERVES 4
PREPARATION: 1 HR
REST: 24 HRS

Beef and Whelks

· 1 tbsp of balsam fir needles
· 1 tbsp long pepper
· 4 prepared beef filets of 150 g (5 oz) each, trimmed
· Tub o' Duck Fat [P. 449]
· 200 g (7 oz) chanterelles
· 3 tbsp unsalted butter
· 90 g (½ cup) broad beans, shelled, blanched, and skins removed
· 60 g (½ cup) fresh almonds, shelled
· A few fresh daylily flowers
· 60 g (¼ cup) glasswort
· 120 g (4 oz) whelks (about 20), cleaned [P. 168]
· 2 cloves garlic, minced
· 3 tbsp olive oil

Finishing Touches

· Raspberry oil [P. 263]
· 125 ml (½ cup) bordelaise sauce [P. 443]

Beef and Whelks

1 The day before, pulverize the fir needles and the long pepper in a coffee grinder and coat the meat on all sides. Wrap in plastic film and refrigerate for 24 hours.

2 The next day, let the meat sit for 20 minutes at room temperature, and cook in the Tub o' Duck Fat for 8 to 10 minutes.

3 Sauté the chanterelles in butter. Remove from heat and add the broad beans, almonds, daylily flowers and glasswort. In another frying pan, sauté the whelks and garlic in olive oil and add the chanterelles.

Finishing Touches

4 On each plate, draw a line of raspberry oil and place a piece of beef cut in half on top. Lightly coat with bordelaise sauce, and then add the whelks and vegetable salad.

RAZOR CLAMS

After a night's work, we cooks often make our way to Montreal's Chinatown to eat at *Beijing's*, as this and other restaurants in the area stay open until two or three in the morning. The Chinatown Razor Clam Salad is a tribute to these restaurants we know so well. There, clams are served in their shells with vinaigrette.

CHINATOWN RAZOR CLAM SALAD

SERVES 4
PREPARATION: 2 HRS
REST: 1:30 HRS

Razor Clams
· 1 kg (2 lbs) raw razor clams (about 25 clams)
· Cooled vegetable stock [P. 450]

Garlic and Hot Pepper Oil
· 60 ml (¼ cup) spicy olive oil
· 2 cloves garlic, minced

Gelled Soy
· 2 gelatin sheets
· 180 ml (¾ cup) sake
· 4 tbsp mirin
· 20 ml (4 tsp) organic soy sauce

Salad
· 1 tbsp green onion, minced
· 1 tbsp coriander leaves
· 1 tbsp lemon supremes, diced
· 1 tbsp olive oil
· 1 tbsp peanuts, crushed
· Salt and freshly ground black pepper

Finishing Touches
· Green onion oil [P. 445]

Razor Clams
1 Let the clams sit under cold running water for about 30 minutes, stirring from time to time, to remove any sand.

2 Place the razor clams in the cooled vegetable stock and bring to a simmer over medium heat. Quickly cook for about 30 to 45 seconds and immediately cool in ice water to stop the cooking process. Remove the razor clams from their shells and cut the muscles in half. Remove the blackish parts. Clean the 8 nicest clam shells and set aside.

Garlic and Hot Pepper Oil
3 In a frying pan over medium-high heat, heat the olive oil. Turn off the heat, add the garlic, and let steep for 5 minutes. Set aside.

Gelled Soy
4 Bloom the gelatin sheets in a bowl of ice water. In a saucepan, bring the sake, mirin and soy sauce to a boil. Whisk in the strained gelatin and cool to room temperature. Refrigerate for about 1 hour and 30 minutes. Mix with a hand mixer and set aside at room temperature.

Salad
5 Combine all the ingredients together in a bowl. Add the razor clams and the garlic and hot pepper oil. Divide into the cleaned shells.

Finishing Touches
6 Pour 1 tbsp gelled soy and 1 tbsp green onion oil into each serving bowl. Add 2 razor clam salads. Guests can pour the razor clam salad into the gelled soy at the table.

RAZOR CLAMS

LEMON BUTTER RAZOR
CLAMS WITH CHANTERELLES
AND BEANS

SERVES 4
PREPARATION: 1 HR

Razor Clams

· 1 kg (2 lbs) raw razor clams
  (about 25 clams)

Lemon Butter

· 5 tbsp 35% cream
· 240 g (1 cup) butter
· 3 tbsp lemon juice
· Salt and sugar

Seasonal Vegetables

· 24 snow peas, stringed
· 50 g (¼ cup) broad beans, shelled
· 200 g (7 oz) chanterelles
· 1 tbsp cold butter, in small pieces

Finishing Touches

· 3 tbsp spicy oil
· 3 tbsp green onion oil [P. 445]
· Garden herbs and shoots, to taste
  (ideally basil)

Razor Clams

1 Soak the clams under cold running
  water for 1 hour stirring from time
  to time to remove any sand.

2 Remove the white muscle from
  the clam and set aside. Set aside
  the eight nicest shells.

Lemon Butter

3 In a frying pan, heat the cream over
  medium heat. As soon as it begins
  to boil, whisk in the butter. Remove
  from heat and add the lemon juice.
  Salt and sugar to taste.

Seasonal Vegetables

4 Blanch the snow peas and broad
  beans separately in salted boiling
  water for about 1 minute each. Cool
  off in a bowl of ice water. When
  the broad beans are cool, remove
  the skins.

5 Clean the chanterelles well. In a hot
  pan, sauté them in butter for 1 to
  2 minutes. Lower to minimum heat
  and pour in 250 ml (1 cup) of lemon
  butter. Add the snow peas, broad
  beans and razor clams. Cook for
  1 minute over low heat.

Finishing Touches

6 Portion the mixture into the empty
  and cleaned razor clam shells. Serve
  two shells per plate. Garnish with
  the aromatic oil and garden herbs.

TIP

+ When glazing the clams, it's important to keep an eye on the cooking
  to make sure the butter doesn't separate and make the clams chewy.
  You can add lobster and/or smoked
  eel to this recipe, and accompany
  it with potato chips, caviar, a bit of
  spicy oil, green onion oil and small
  wildflowers.

LOBSTER

Lobster shells are rich in flavour. We use a number of simple techniques to extract every ounce of goodness. This makes lobster a product that we use to "110%"!

Lobster Butter
- 1 kg (2 lbs) lobster heads (remove the flesh, then crack the shell into large pieces)
- 500 g (1 lb) butter
- 100 g (½ cup) vegetable *mirepoix* (medium diced carrots, leeks, onion and garlic)
- 1 tomato, roughly chopped

Lobster Caramel
- 1 kg (2 lbs) lobster heads (remove the flesh, then crack the shell into large pieces)
- 2 tbsp liquid clover honey
- 1 litre (4 cups) water

Lobster Sabayon
- 6 egg yolks
- ½ egg shell of water for each egg yolk
- 2 tbsp lobster coral
- 2 tbsp 35 % cream, whipped to taste
- Salt

Rubber Lobster Caviar
- 125 ml (½ cup) lobster butter
- 2 tbsp lobster coral

Lobster Couscous
- 8 eggs
- 4 tbsp Rubber Lobster Caviar [ABOVE]

Coral Powder
- 2 tbsp lobster coral
- 2 tbsp water
- 2.5 g (1 tsp) albumen powder

Vinaigrette
- 1 part lobster butter
- 2 parts lobster caramel

Lobster Butter

1 In a pot over high heat, sauté the lobster carcass pieces in 2 tbsp of butter. Add the vegetables and colour lightly. Add the tomato and the remaining butter. Lower the heat to its lowest setting, and let steep for 1 hour. Filter through a sieve, and place the resulting butter in the refrigerator.

Lobster Caramel

2 Preheat the oven to 190°C (375°F). Using a kitchen hammer, crush the carcasses into small pieces. Spread evenly on a baking sheet and roast in the oven for 15 minutes.

3 In a pot over medium heat, bring the honey to a simmer and add the carcasses and water. Simmer for 30 minutes. Filter through a conical strainer and immediately cook over low heat until the mixture has the consistency of caramel. (Drizzle a bit of caramel on a cold plate. If the texture is syrupy, remove the caramel from the heat immediately and allow to cool.)

Lobster Sabayon

Coral is found in the tail and head of female lobsters. It's dark green, almost black. Once cooked, it will give an orange tinge to the sabayon.

4 With a Thermomix, mix the egg yolks, water and coral. Cook at 70°C (158°F) for 14 to 18 minutes. The sabayon is ready when the mixture becomes thick and bright orange. Cool on ice, adding the cream and a pinch of salt.

5 If you don't have a Thermomix, bring a double boiler to a boil. In a large measuring cup, using a hand mixer, beat the egg yolks, water and coral. Pour into a round-bottomed bowl and place on the double boiler. Whisking regularly, cook for ten seconds, then remove it for 5 seconds. Repeat until the mixture becomes thick and bright orange. Then add the cream and a pinch of salt.

Rubber Lobster Caviar

6 In a small pot over medium heat, heat the lobster butter until it begins to simmer. Add the coral and cook until the butter becomes red. Remove the coral and set aside on paper towels.

Lobster Couscous

7 Cook the eggs in boiling water for 10 minutes. Separate the yolks from the whites (keep the whites for another use). Pass the yolks and the Rubber Lobster Caviar through a sieve to obtain a texture similar to couscous.

Coral Powder

8 Preheat the oven to 110°C (230°F). With a hand mixer, mix all the ingredients together and spread evenly on a silicone baking mat placed on a baking sheet. Dry in the oven for 30 minutes, rotating the mat halfway through. Once the coral is dry, let rest at room temperature. Pulverize in a coffee grinder, cover and set aside in a cool, dry place.

Vinaigrette

9 In two pots over low heat, heat the lobster butter and caramel separately. Remove from heat and incorporate the butter into the caramel, stirring constantly. Place in the refrigerator for later use. Serve hot.

TIP

+ If you're having lobster, take the opportunity to make lobster butter and lobster caramel, which you can keep in the freezer. The raw coral can also be frozen.

LOBSTER

Back from a trip to China, we tried to reproduce the taste of a lobster dish we had in a Cantonese restaurant in Hong Kong. The lobster was served in a sort of rice wine custard, very moist and crumbly. By mixing egg whites, milk and sake with a little water, we managed to get a rather interesting texture. While it doesn't perfectly match the dish we'd eaten in Hong Kong, the idea is still there. This recipe illustrates the way we work: the idea for a dish comes from a flash, a taste, a smell, and then evolves over time in the kitchen.

HONG KONG LOBSTER

SERVES 4
PREPARATION: 1:30 HRS

Lobsters
· 2 lobsters of 1 kg (2 lbs) each
· Court-bouillon [P. 445]

Sake Custard
· 5 egg whites
· 125 ml (½ cup) milk
· 3 g (½ tsp) corn starch
· 60 ml (¼ cup) sake
· Salt

Finishing Touches
· 2 tbsp lobster caramel [P. 176]
· 2 tbsp lobster butter [P. 176]
· 4 tbsp lobster couscous [P. 176]
· Mint and lovage, minced

Lobsters
1 Split the lobsters, set the bodies and the empty shells aside to make the lobster butter and caramel [P. 176]. Cook the claws and tails separately in the court-bouillon: 3 minutes for the tails and 5 for the claws. Cool before shelling.

Sake Custard
2 Preheat the oven to 175°C (350°F). Combine all the ingredients using a hand mixer. Divide evenly in 4 ramekins and cover with plastic film. Place in a baking dish and fill three-quarters full with water. Bake between 30 and 40 minutes until set (cook longer if necessary). Allow to cool at room temperature.

Finishing Touches
3 Preheat the oven to 95°C (200°F). Reheat the sake custard on a baking sheet for 2 minutes. Remove from the oven and add a few drops of lobster caramel.

4 In a pan over low heat, heat the lobster claws and tails with lobster butter. Place on the sake custard along with the lobster couscous. Garnish with mint and lovage.

TIP
+ You can replace the water and salt by seawater, which will make a more savoury court-bouillon

PRINCESS SCALLOPS

Today, a large proportion of the scallop catch comes from aquaculture farms around the Magdalene Islands; this is why we have them all year long. At Toqué!, we offer them as appetizers. The garnish changes according to the seasons, but the structure of the recipe stays the same: the sweet taste of the scallops is highlighted by a texturizing foam. The liquid accompanying the scallop needs to be slightly tangy.

Basic Marinated Scallop Recipe
- 16 Princess scallops, category 2
- 2 tbsp shallots, minced
- 1 tbsp lime juice
- 1 tbsp olive oil
- Salt and freshly ground black pepper
- 2 tbsp daikon, diced

Preparation

1 With an offset spatula, open the shells, while holding down the rounded side of the shells. Slip the spatula along the top part of the shell to detach the scallop. Pull sharply on the muscle to avoid damaging it. Slowly lift the top part of the shell. Remove the beard, and then detach the scallop's underside. Rinse under ice-cold water. Pat dry and refrigerate until needed.

Blanching Shells

2 In a pot, bring water to a boil. Blanch the 16 hollow half-shells for 5 minutes. Allow to cool and dry, then set aside.

Basic Marinated Scallop Recipe

3 Cut each scallop horizontally into three equal-sized slices. In a small bowl, combine the scallops with the other ingredients and set aside at room temperature for three minutes. Serve in the shells.

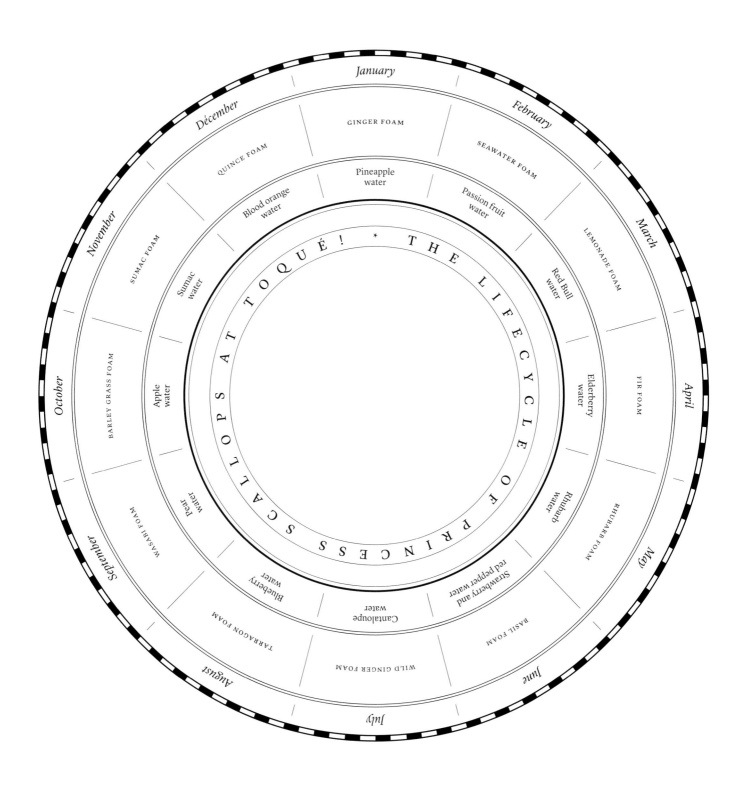

THE LIFECYCLE OF PRINCESS SCALLOPS AT TOQUÉ! *

January — GINGER FOAM — Pineapple water

February — SEAWATER FOAM — Passion fruit water

March — LEMONADE FOAM — Red Bull water

April — FIR FOAM — Elderberry water

May — RHUBARB FOAM — Rhubarb water

June — BASIL FOAM — Strawberry and red pepper water

July — WILD GINGER FOAM — Cantaloupe water

August — TARRAGON FOAM — Blueberry water

September — WASABI FOAM — Pearl water

October — BARLEY GRASS FOAM — Apple water

November — SUMAC FOAM — Sumac water

December — QUINCE FOAM — Blood orange water

PRINCESS
SCALLOPS

SERVES 4
PREPARATION: 1 HR
REST: 6 HRS

*To make this recipe, refer to
the marinated scallop recipe
on the previous page.*

Apple Water
· 4 Honeycrisp apples

Vanilla Grass Foam
· 3 gelatin sheets
· 4 branches of vanilla grass

Finishing Touches
· 16 scallop half shells
· 16 Princess scallops [P. 182]
· 1 Honeycrip apples, diced
· A few radishes, diced
· 2 tbsp basil oil [P. 449]
· A few borage flowers

Apple Water

1 Quarter the apples and extract the
juice in a juice extractor. Bring
to a boil in a pot over medium-high
heat. Skim the surface and filter
through a conical strainer lined
with a coffee filter. Keep 400 ml
(1⅔ cups) to make the vanilla
grass foam and store the rest in the
refrigerator.

Vanilla Grass Foam

2 Bloom the gelatin in a bowl of cold
water. In a small pot, bring 400 ml
(1⅔ cups) of apple water and the
vanilla grass to a simmer. Turn off
the heat, cover and let steep for 10
to 15 minutes. Pass through a conical
strainer and whisk in the gelatin.
Cool at room temperature, then
pour into a whipped cream dispenser. Add the N_2O chargers and
place the dispenser in the refrigerator for 6 hours [P. 451].

Finishing Touches

3 In each half shell, place three
pieces of marinated scallop [P. 182].
Add the apple and radishes, the
remaining apple water and a touch
of basil oil. Garnish with vanilla
grass foam and borage flowers.
Serve immediately.

GLOSSARY
Vanilla grass Also called Indian
grass, vanilla grass grows wild in
the northern regions of the globe.
It has a slight vanilla scent to
it—hence the name—and is usually
used to flavour vodka.

ANOTHER ROUND
FOR SAMUEL...

FERME APICOLE DESROCHERS
Hydromel
UPPER LAURENTIANS, QUEBEC

With these dishes, we avoid aromatic and fruity wines that will produce a pairing with no distinctive flavours. Instead, we look for complexity by increasing the acidity of the dish with a sharp and well-chiselled wine. Muscadet is a good choice since it has strong earthy tones that harmonize well with scallops, natural sweetness and fruit. In summer, you can also use hydromel, a particular type of honeyed mead popular in Quebec, from the Ferme apicole Desrochers. The Envolée is a perfect choice due to its sharpness. Hydromel radiates both a floral and honeyed side, while remaining sharp. The impression of sweetness in hydromel (although it doesn't actually contain artificial sugars) works quite well with scallops and its slight effervescence introduces an interesting freshness.

PROPRIETAIRES
RECOLTANTS
DEPUIS 1978

750 ml

envolée

vin de miel sec | dry honey wine

Produit issu de miel biologique
Certifié par Ecocert Canada

Product made from organic honey
Certified by Ecocert Canada

produit du Québec | product of Quebec

TUNA

GIANT TUNA SASHIMI

SERVES 4
PREPARATION: 30 MIN

Tarragon Mayonnaise
· 1 egg yolk
· 1 tbsp Dijon mustard
· Salt
· 1 tbsp lemon juice
· 180 ml (¾ cup) grape seed oil
· 60 ml (¼ cup) olive oil
· 1 tbsp warm water (if needed)
· 3 g (2 tsp) minced tarragon

Sashimi
· 500 g (1 lb) fresh tuna loin

Finishing Touches
· 2 shallots, sliced thinly
· 4 tbsp organic soy sauce
· 1 tbsp sriracha (hot pepper Thai sauce)
· Maldon salt and freshly ground black pepper
· Fresh herbs (tarragon, basil, etc.) minced

Tarragon Mayonnaise
1 Whisk the mayonnaise [P. 448] and set aside. Consistency should be runny but not too liquid. If it's too thick, adjust with a few drops of water.

Sashimi
2 With a very sharp knife, cut the tuna loin into slices about 2 millimetres thick. Place on the plates without stacking them.

Finishing Touches
3 Brush the tuna with soy sauce and sriracha. Garnish with 4 tbsp of tarragon mayonnaise. Add salt and pepper to taste. Add fresh herbs and the shallots. Serve immediately.

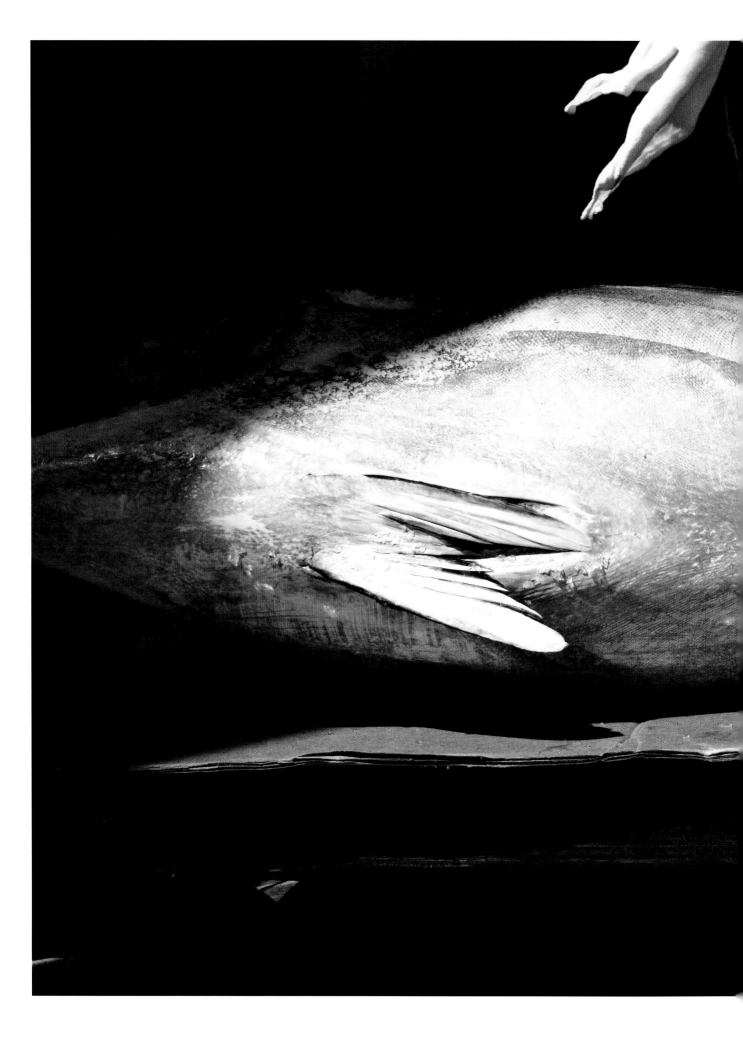

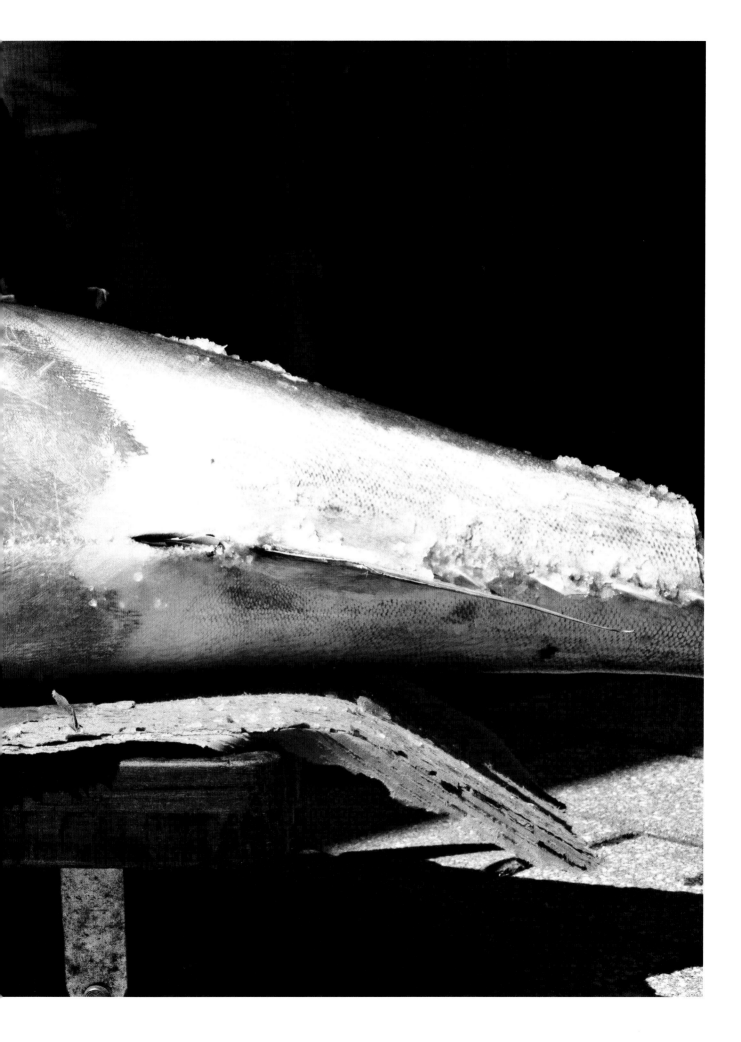

"I met Normand in 1989, during an event organized by *Valrhona* in the Laurentians. His cooking has his character. It's all about risk, but it's not fussy: it's both daring and traditional."

Frédéric Bau, Chocolatier at *Valrhona*

"If I'm a dreamer, she's down to earth. However, she's instinctive, and we've always trusted each other. With the *Toqué!* project, while I might have been the idea man, she made sure that the ideas could be put into practice."

Normand Laprise

"I'll never forget the day I met Normand. It was my first day at the ITHQ's [culinary school] restaurant. He wasn't much older than I was, but he was a real cook. We talked about what we could make that day, and, together, we decided to make lamb loin stuffed with omelette, inspired by the ingredients for a paloise sauce. I love eggs! I feel like we don't cook with them enough. Even today, I still use this dish from time to time at *Balthazar* in New York. For me, meeting Normand was a revelation! After two years in culinary school, it was the first time I ever had such an exchange with an experienced chef."

Riad Nasr, Chef at *Balthazar*

CRAFTING DIVERSITY

Patrice Fortier

I'm originally from Montreal. After a degree in visual arts, I worked in the dance and cabaret world for quite a few years. After turning thirty, I left the city for Kamouraska to become a horticulturist. I've been a gardener for *La Société des Plantes*, the Plant Society, for the past fourteen years. The path that led me here might seem winding, but the study of gardens has always fed my artistic process. My relationship with art has never faded. In 2006, for example, I prepared a series of photographic portraits of a carrot variety for which I produce seeds. Aesthetics play an important role in my world: I like to ensure that everything around me radiates beauty. Even my compost heap is stylish!

I visited Patrice in Kamouraska, and was fascinated by his garden and house—more laboratory than homestead. Everything is organized, but there's simultaneously something wild and wonderful about the place. When we're there, we sleep among the squash and dried beans.

NORMAND LAPRISE

PORTRAIT OF A MODERN DAY FARMER

I grow rare and heirloom vegetables from my own seeds, which I also distribute on a small scale. Besides seeds, I also sell fruits and vegetables to restaurants. When I first came to the Lower St. Lawrence after completing a degree in agriculture, times were tough, since developing the seed market requires a huge investment of time and energy, and very few people actually understood what I was trying to do.

During one of those low points, Normand came to my place unannounced. He tasted a few of my vegetables and found them so savoury that he told me, "If there are any left, I'll take them!" That simple comment made me swell with pride. The seeds of a strong relationship were sown. Today, I remain at the foundation of his production cycle, since I now sell seeds to some of his growers.

SOWING ANGELS

For the past ten years, every summer, I take part in a tradition as old as agriculture itself: that of the sower. I make a crown out of dried *angelica* flowers, filled with seeds. I put it on my head, and stand in the middle of my field. Spinning around, the seeds are scattered to the winds. This production perfectly reflects the spirit of the *Société des Plantes*: one part total art, one part ephemeral poetry, blended into a horticultural gesture.

THE SEEDSMAN'S ROLE

We tend to forget that agriculture begins with harvesting seeds. In general, seeds are at the foundation of commercial agricultural and gastronomical exchange. Unfortunately, real training programs for seedsmen have yet to be developed. Since this part of the process is often not fully understood, gardeners tend to buy the cheapest possible seeds, ending up with varieties poorly adapted to their particular region. Moreover, large seed companies are often more interested in fruits and vegetables that have longer conservation times and can thus travel great distances before sale than varieties with taste and flavour... Fundamentally, it is a battle between ecology and economy.

The seedsman's role is first and foremost that of a geneticist. It's a complex science that requires care and attention in order to avoid crossbreeding different varieties. My job consists in rediscovering heirloom varieties that are often much tastier, and applying a selection process that aims to create breeds of plants adapted to the relatively short, cool summers of our northern climes. If we are relatively free to explore these possibilities here in Quebec, European

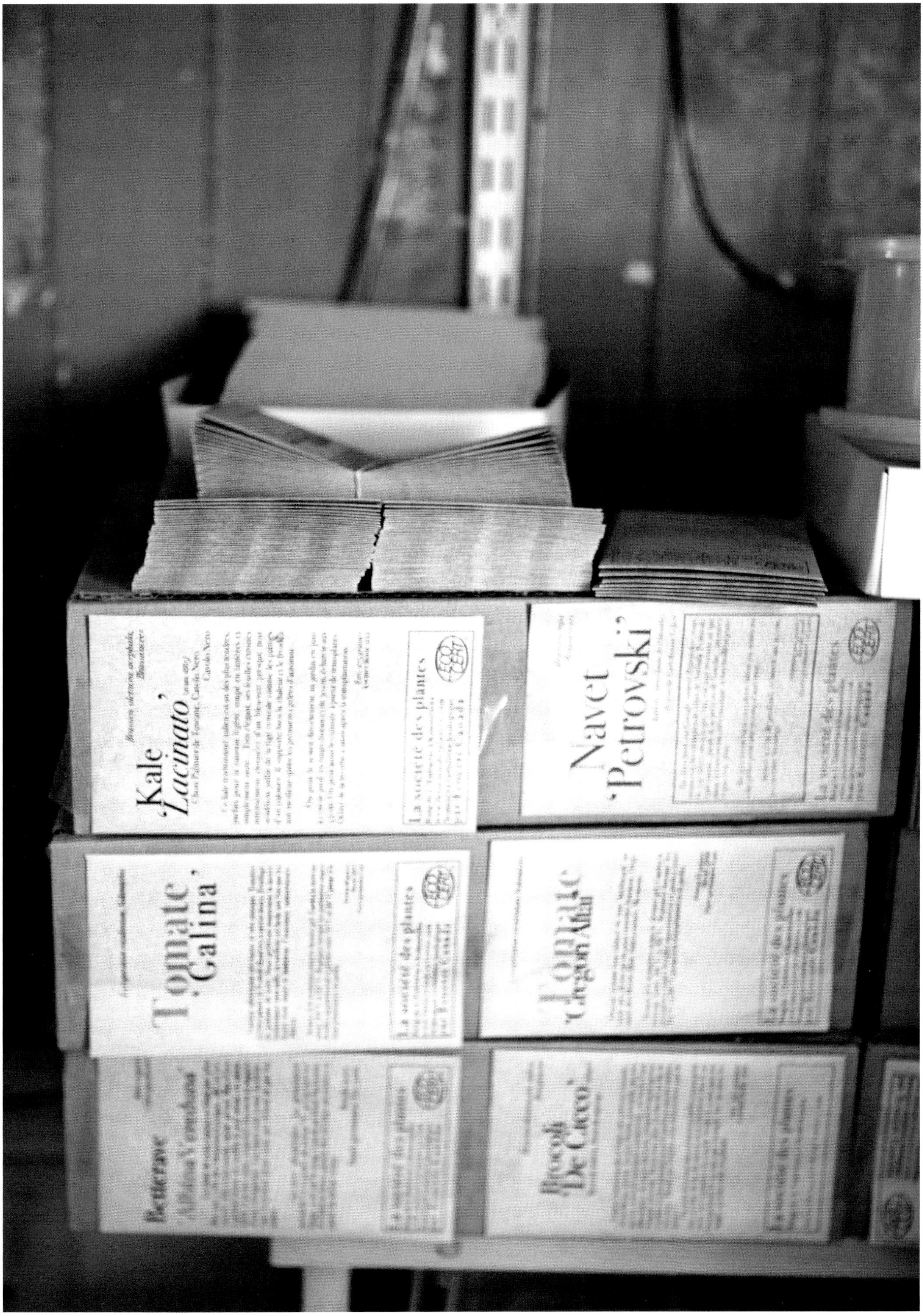
Kale 'Lacinato'
La société des plantes
Navet 'Petrovski'
Tomate 'Galina'
Tomate

legislation is much stricter: in some places, the conservation of seeds from one season to the next—which is the basis of all agriculture—is actually illegal. In the name of profit for a few multinational corporations, farmers are forced to buy new seeds year after year. Moreover, these varieties have a very limited genetic range, since they are perfectly copied in order to protect and renew copyright. It's important to understand that each seed should be the intellectual property of its maker.

WRITING THE CATALOGUE

A seedsman needs to write a catalogue. It's a bit like a lonely hearts column between the farmer and the plants, since the often rather lyrical description is part of what sells the seed. My approach is ethno-botanical without being anthropomorphic: it's important to me that each plant has a personality and can tell its own story. If I wish, I can create varieties with fantastic names. One day, a friend of mine gave me the seed for a type of bean. However, she'd forgotten its name. Since I wasn't sure of the variety, I called it "Jill's Amnesia" and sold it under that name. To facilitate exchange, seedsmen give each species a scientific name in Latin, in reference to binomial nomenclature developed by Swiss naturalist Linné. While a plant has a single scientific name, it can sometimes have a number of common names. That's the case for *Daucus carota*, which is alternatively called wild carrot, bird's nest, bishop's lace or Queen Anne's lace. Older varieties of plants have even more curious names, like the type of lettuce called the "Fat Lazy Blond Lettuce"!

AN ALTERNATIVE WAY TO FARM

As an artisanal seed maker, my work goes far beyond simple knowledge of plants; I'm also interested in the way plants interact with each other. I'm practically a plant sociologist! For example, we often think of self-propagating plants as a curse. However, not only do they not harm production since they participate in a garden's autonomy, but they also add an aesthetically pleasing touch, and, better yet, they can be very tasty. When I weed my garden, I often get a salad to boot!

The Search
for Flavours

To obtain the best possible seeds, Patrice aims to raise the highest quality plants. Like the first geneticists, he uses natural techniques that require vast knowledge, a wheelbarrow full of patience and an interest in cooking—after all, taste is part of his trade. His relationship with chefs contributes to his research, and leads him to be responsive to the needs of consumers and restaurants.

Patrice inspires our growers and gardeners, some of whom purchase and plant his seeds and further his research, experimenting with new crossbreeds and testing different varieties of fruits and vegetables before beginning fully-fledged operations. This is the case of Pierre André Daignault, one of our oldest collaborators, with whom we've been working since the days of Citrus. Here is another passionate man with an atypical path: after studying psychology and organic agriculture, he bought himself a patch of land and began growing organic produce. At first, he limited himself to a few varieties of melons, cucumbers and seasonal lettuces. Seeing Normand's interest—as well as the interest of other chefs—in his work, Mr. Daignault moved his garden to Blainville, just north of Montreal, where he developed expertise in greenhouse agriculture, which helped

him lengthen his production period. Other farmers have followed his lead, which means that restaurant owners can now purchase local products almost year-round.

We are always learning more about the products we eat as well as discovering new varieties, thanks to the passion and expertise of these market gardeners. Jean-Pierre Bertrand, one of the gardeners with whom we work, has always taken the time to explain the particularities of each of the varieties he sells. Normand still has a vivid memory of the day Mr. Bertrand walked through the doors of the kitchen at Toqué when it was still on Saint-Denis, his wicker basket filled with fruits and vegetables. We immediately realized that his products were much more tasty and complex than those we could get at the store. Mr. Bertrand is a researcher; his method is scientific. When he was only twenty years old, he was already interested in horticulture and read specialized journals on the subject. After a career in the medical profession, his passion for horticulture took over and his hobby became his second vocation. His orchard at Saint-Joseph-du-Lac is composed of some hundred different apple varieties, twenty-five pear varieties, plums and all sorts of berries. He's always experimenting and developing new types of fruits. Today, he

delivers his fruits and vegetables twice a week, mainly from July to the end of October. Every year, we drive the crew up to his orchard for the traditional apple picking. It's an important tradition, one that really brings the group together.

Patrice Fortier, Jean-Pierre Bertrand and his partner Lucille, Pierre-André Daignault, Paul Legault, Yves Decelles, Dianne Duquet, Maryel Bousquet, the Birri brothers and many others like them give us the opportunity to always learn more about the variety of fruits and vegetables we cook. Through our constant exchanges and conversations, we adapt our orders and our methods to their deliveries. It's an important commitment for us, at the very foundation of our profession as cooks.

ONIONS

POTATOES

Mr. Bertrand and his partner Lucille grow several dozen varieties of onions in his garden. Among them are Vidalias, a fragile variety that requires particularly temperate climes to thrive, which is why they are rarely produced in Quebec. Vidalia onions are delicate and sweet, and we use them both raw and cooked. Mr. Bertrand also produces a very old variety of grey shallot sometimes known as Griselle. It's a very fine, very small, and very savoury shallot. But they're getting harder and harder to find, not to mention the fact that restaurant owners are often discouraged by the time required to peel them. This is why seeds have been developed which give a shallot that is both larger and easier to peel. We've rediscovered Griselle thanks to Mr. Bertrand.

In Quebec, potatoes were long considered the "vegetable of the poor." In recent years there has been renewed interest in this plant from South America. Yves Decelles, a.k.a. Mr. Passionate Potato, grows his potatoes on his few acres of land near Saint-Aimé, along the Yamaska River. A passionate soul, he has documented the histories of the varieties he grows. The Ozette variety, for example, was imported by the Spanish into Washington State before being cultivated by the Haida, a native American tribe who have kept the strain alive ever since. Mr. Decelles' work has been central to the revitalization of potatoes among restaurant owners. For the past few years, chefs have begun adding specific varieties of potatoes to their menus.

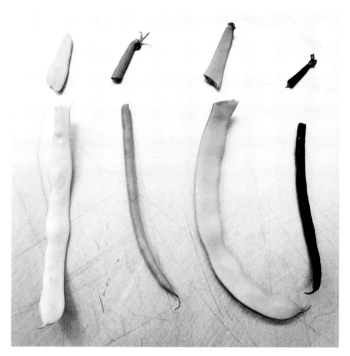

FRENCH BEANS

Mr. Bertrand is a passionate man when it comes to beans; one day he hopes to write an entire book on the subject! Over the past fifteen years, he has gathered more than two hundred varieties of beans to determine which are best suited to his land and his palate. Beans are climbing plants that need sun to develop their chlorophyll. Mr. Bertrand grows them on contraptions made from fishing nets that hang three meters off the ground. This system helps the beans develop bolder, more complete flavours, but requires much more space. Each year, he brings us a selection of his tastiest fare: fine, fillet and Morgan beans. The cranberry beans we receive are picked ripe, which gives the seeds their creamy flavor.

RASPBERRIES

Among the berries we use in the kitchen, Normand particularly likes raspberries, be they red or black. As a child, he remembers having eaten himself sick with them! Wild raspberries, called *Catherinettes* in Quebec, have a slightly more floral taste than your regular red raspberries. The main difference between varieties is felt in the acidity level, largely influenced by when the fruit is picked. Some people don't enjoy wild raspberries, due to their larger seeds, but their taste is much more pronounced, with undertones of Dijon mustard. At the restaurant we usually serve them fresh in season, and transform them into purées, vinegar and raspberry water in order to serve them throughout winter.

TOMATOES

The tomatoes we use at *Toqué!* mainly come from Pierre-André Daigneault and Jean-Pierre Bertrand's gardens. Pierre-André is the first person to have supplied us with heirloom tomatoes. These old varieties like the Beefsteak or the full-fleshed Striped German disappeared from local markets in the 1960s since they are often irregular or covered in spots. Because of this—despite being much more savoury—they didn't sell as well as the flawless genetically modified versions.

Both the use and cultivation of tomatoes depend on the variety.

For our preserves, we use the San Marzano, a tasty Italian variety that the Birri brothers supply us out of their Jean-Talon Market headquarters. One year, Charles-Antoine brought the crew to their stand to teach younger cooks about artisan vegetable production. By encouraging them to plant tomatoes in their own flowerpots at home, these up-and-coming cooks had the chance to experience the evolution of the plant, from seed to succulent fruit. It was important that our cooks learn not to reject a fruit or vegetable because of a small, superficial defect.

STRAWBERRIES

In Quebec, the season for field berries is fairly short. For the past few years, quality greenhouse production has been expanding. This lets us cook with field berries for an extended period, while always using local products. It took Mr. Legault more than three years of experimentation to set up a profitable operation. At first, it was pretty experimental: we tested a dozen varieties that were different in flavour and palette. Among them was an English variety called Eros. Today, Mr. Legault mainly sends us Darselect, a French variety. His strawberries are systematically picked the same day, then cooked over the following days. In this way, we are supplied with field berries up to the beginning of autumn. Mr. Legault developed an ingenious system to maximize his workspace and get the best return on very high heating and lighting costs: his strawberry pots are hung from the roof of his greenhouses, allowing him to grow beans and cucumbers at ground level.

SUMMER IS A PARTICULARLY BUSY TIME FOR THE TEAM, WITH LARGE BASKETS OF FRUITS AND VEGETABLES COMING IN EVERY DAY. FOR AMIN, ONE OF OUR SOUS-CHEFS, IT'S A PARTICULARLY STIMULATING TIME, THOUGH STRESSFUL: "AT *TOQUÉ!*, ROUTINE SIMPLY DOESN'T EXIST. WHEN THE TIME IS RIGHT AND THE PRODUCTS COME IN, THE EXCITEMENT AND STRESS RISE AND FALL THROUGHOUT THE DAY. WE HAVE SO MANY PRODUCTS IN OUR REFRIGERATOR THAT WE BARELY HAVE TIME TO PREPARE OUR MISE EN PLACE." OUR PHILOSOPHY IS BASED ON WORKING WITH FRESH PRODUCTS, AND THE ENTIRE ORGANIZATION OF THE KITCHEN REVOLVES AROUND THIS SIMPLE IDEA. MARC-ANTOINE, TASKED WITH THE MANAGEMENT OF THE KITCHEN AND THE INCOMING ORDERS, EXPLAINS: "EVERYTHING IS UNIQUE AT *TOQUÉ!*: THE PHILOSOPHY, THE KNOW-HOW, THE THOUGHT PROCESSES, THE ORGANIZATION... NOTHING IS DONE LIKE ANYWHERE ELSE!"

IN ORDER TO REMAIN AS CREATIVE AS POSSIBLE, WE'RE ALWAYS WILLING TO ADAPT TO OUR PRODUCTS. IN THIS WAY, AND THANKS TO OUR OBSESSIVE SECOND-USE MENTALITY, WE MANAGE TO WORK WITH A CHANGING MENU WHILE WASTING NOTHING.

COCKTAILS

Instead of throwing out our strawberry hulls, we decided to try and find a way to use them. By letting them steep overnight in sugar, we obtained a sweet strawberry water that is now used as the base for quite a few of our recipes.

APPLE AND VANILLA GRASS COCKTAIL

SERVES 4
PREPARATION: 10 MIN
REST: 30 MIN

· 240 ml (8 oz) Cortland apple juice, extracted with a juice extractor
· 2 branches of vanilla grass
· 120 ml (4 oz) vodka

1 In a small saucepan over low heat, bring the apple juice to a simmer, and add the vanilla grass. Turn the heat off and cover. Allow to steep for 30 minutes. Remove the vanilla grass.

2 In a shaker, mix all the ingredients together with ice. Filter with an ice strainer and pour into martini glasses.

STRAWBERRY HULL MARTINIS

SERVES 4
PREPARATION: 5 MIN

· 3 tbsp lemon juice
· 240 ml (8 oz) vodka
· 480 ml (16 oz) strawberry water [P. 260]

1 In a shaker, mix all the ingredients together with ice. Filter with an ice strainer and pour into martini glasses.

TIP
+ Keeping in mind the concept of creating infusions out of trimmings, we also make pineapple and black-currant water. We use it as a base for cocktails or to prepare sorbet.

BLACKCURRANT COCKTAIL

SERVES 4
PREPARATION: 5 MIN

· 60 ml (2 oz) blackcurrant water [P. 263]
· 4 tbsp lemon juice
· 120 ml (4 oz) Ungava gin

1 In a shaker, mix all the ingredients together with ice. Filter with an ice strainer and pour into martini glasses.

SNACKS

REPLANTED CARROTS AND RADISHES

SERVES 4
PREPARATION: 5 MIN

· A few small carrots of different colours with stalks
· A few French radishes
· 60 g (¼ cup) salt
· 240 g (1 cup) sugar
· 2 tbsp powdered curry

1 Wash the carrots and radishes well under cold water and keep them slightly moist. In a bowl, combine the salt, sugar and curry, and divide this mixture among 4 cups. Plant the roots in the cups and serve with drinks.

PANCETTA ALMONDS

SERVES 4
PREPARATION: 5 MIN

· A few fresh almonds, shelled
· 60 g (2 oz) pancetta, thinly sliced

1 Wrap the almonds with pancetta. Serve at room temperature or warm up under the grill for about 5 seconds, until the pancetta begins to glisten. Serve with drinks.

FRIED GARLIC OR SALSIFY SHOOTS

SERVES 4
PREPARATION: 15 MIN

· Canola oil (for frying)
· 4 garlic shoots, split in half lengthwise, or a few whole salsify shoots
· Salt

1 In a fryer, heat the oil to 190°C (375°F) and fry the garlic shoots for 30 seconds. Strain on a paper towel. Salt to taste and serve.

RUTABAGA

MAKES 750 ML (3 CUPS)
PREPARATION: 30 MIN
COOKING: 1 HR

Rutabaga Mousse
· 1 rutabaga, peeled and sliced
· 250 ml (1 cup) milk
· 125 ml (½ cup) 35 % cream

Cocoa Butter
· 60 g (¼ cup) butter
· 1 tbsp cocoa powder

Finishing Touches
· Unsweetened chocolate, grated
· Maldon salt

Rutabaga Mousse

1 In a saucepan over low heat, cook the rutabaga in milk for approximately 1 hour. Drain and set the cooking milk aside. In a food processor, purée the rutabaga, then add milk until you get a creamy texture. Mix 300 ml (1¼ cups) of the purée with the cream, and pour the preparation into a whipped cream dispenser. Load 2 N_2O chargers, shaking after each addition. [P. 451]

Cocoa Butter

2 In a saucepan over low heat, fry the butter until hazelnut in colour. Add the cocoa, remove from heat, and mix well with a whisk.

Finishing Touches

3 Bring water to boil in a pot, remove from heat, and place the whipped cream dispenser in the pot. Wait 10 minutes for the container to heat up (Important: do not let the dispenser boil).

4 Place the rutabaga mousse in bowls or cups. Add a little hot cocoa butter, and garnish with a sprinkling of unsweetened chocolate and Maldon salt.

SWEET CORN

We like to offer dishes that bring back memories in a few bites. With our corn on the cob recipe, we wanted to pay tribute to a well-known Quebec tradition. In summer, families and friends get together for huge, outdoor corn roasts—an *épluchette de blé d'Inde*: everyone eats corn and drinks beer. The cobs are salty, sweet, buttery and delicious!

SWEET CORN WITH BUTTER AND SALT

· 12 ears of sweet corn, shucked
· 120 g (½ cup) butter
· Salt

1 In a large pan filled with salted boiling water, cook the corn for about 10 minutes and strain. Roll the cobs in butter and salt to taste.

SWEET CORN WITH BUTTER AND SALT AND NOTHING BETWEEN THE TEETH

SERVES 8
PREPARATION: 1:30 HRS

· 12 ears of sweet corn, shucked
· 1 litre (4 cups) milk
· 160 ml (⅔ cup) 35 % cream
· 120 g (½ cup) butter
· Fine salt

1 With a knife, remove the corn from the ear. Place the shelled corn in a saucepan and cover with the milk. Cook over medium heat until the corn bursts. Purée with a food processor. Pass through a conical strainer and allow to rest in the refrigerator.

2 Mix the cooled corn purée with cream. In a 450 ml whipped cream dispenser, pour 400 ml (1⅔ cups) of corn purée and add two N_2O chargers. Shake well and allow to rest in the refrigerator [P. 451].

3 Melt the butter in a pan. Place portions of corn foam in a few bowls or cups. Drizzle with melted butter and add a pinch of salt.

TIP
+ What's best about the dish, unlike the traditional recipe, is that you'll have nothing stuck between your teeth!

SWEET CORN

Corn has been used in Quebec cuisine for the longest time. Normand remembers making juice with the corn he received in August, since these late summer specimens were filled with water. The secret of this sauce is that it thickens due to the starch in the corn. It's a sauce that now accompanies many of our dishes. After some pretty thorough testing using the gravy as a base, corn ice cream was born. Its texture is so smooth that you'd think it was made from cream or milk.

SWEET CORN ICE CREAM ON CORN SUGAR

MAKES 500 ML (2 CUPS) OF ICE CREAM
PREPARATION: 1H30

Corn Ice Cream
· 24 ears of corn, shucked
· Salt
· **Corn Sugar**
· 2 tbsp powdered albumen
· 240 g (1 cup) sugar
· 6 tbsp water

Corn Ice Cream

1 Remove the corn from the ear and run it through a juicer. Strain the juice and keep the pulp to make sweet corn sugar.

2 In a double boiler over low heat, cook the corn juice while scraping the bottom of the double boiler with a rubber or plastic spatula. As soon as the juice becomes hot, stir until the corn's starch thickens the preparation. Remove from heat. (The preparation is ready once it coats the back of a wooden spoon.) Pass through a sieve and set aside to cool.

3 Salt to taste. Pass through an ice-cream maker and place in the freezer.

Corn Sugar

4 In a bowl, combine the albumen and 160 g (½ cup) of the reserved corn pulp. In a saucepan, bring the sugar and water to a boil until the temperature reaches 135°C (275°F). Add the corn pulp and cook for 1 minute while stirring constantly with a spatula. Remove from heat and continue to stir until the sugar has crystallized. Pour on a baking sheet lined with parchment paper.

Finishing Touches

5 On each plate, spread 1 tbsp corn sugar. Place a scoop of ice cream on top of the sugar and serve immediately.

TIP
+ Serve this ice cream as an appetizer.

RAW AND COOKED VEGETABLES

The concept behind this recipe was to play with both raw and cooked vegetables to obtain new textures. Chef Michel Bras was the first to create a dish to showcase vegetables: Gargouillou.

VEGETABLE SALAD

SERVES 4
PREPARATION: 1 HR

· 4 green asparagus, peeled
· 4 white asparagus, peeled
· 8 baby carrots, sliced in half
· 1 small fennel, in sticks
· A few seasonal string beans
· 1 Chiogga beet, thinly sliced
· A few french radishes, sliced in half
· 1 small Kohlrabi, thinly sliced
· 1 small spring onion, thinly sliced
· A few cherry tomatoes, sliced in half
· A few seasonal berries

Vinaigrette
· 1 tbsp honey
· 2 tbsp rice vinegar
· 60 ml (¼ cup) olive oil
· Salt and freshly ground black pepper
· 60 ml (¼ cup) Herbalicious [P. 445]

1 In a saucepan filled with salted boiling water, blanch the asparagus, carrots, fennel and string beans for a few seconds. Remove and cool. [TIP]

2 Meanwhile, in a bowl of ice water, soak the beets, kohlrabi, onions and radishes for a few minutes.

Vinaigrette
3 Whisk all the ingredients together in a bowl.

Finishing Touches
4 Once the vegetables are ready, strain them and combine with the tomatoes and berries. Stir in the vinaigrette. Serve immediately.

TIP
+ Blanched green vegetables quickly lose their colour. If they're not served immediately, it's important to cool them off in ice to fix the chlorophyll. Just reheat them before serving. Don't blanch your vegetables too long if you want them to remain crunchy.

POTATOES

ROASTED POTATO PEELS

PREPARATION: 1 HR

· 1 kg (2 lbs) potato peels, washed

1 Preheat the oven to 180°C (350°F), on a baking sheet lined with parchment paper, spread a single layer of potato peels. Bake for about 1 hour, until they're well roasted. (Cooking times may vary, so monitor the cooking and rotate the baking sheet from time to time.)

TIP

+ If you prefer, fry the potato peels in vegetable oil heated to 180°C (350°F).

POTATO MOUSSE

MAKES 2 LITRES (8 CUPS)
PREPARATION: 1 HR
COOKING: 1 HR

· 1 kg (2 lbs) roasted potato peels
  [PREVIOUS RECIPE]
· 4 litres (16 cups) water
· 5 tbsp low-salt organic soy sauce
· Salt
· 150 g (⅔ cup) butter

1 Place the roasted potato peels in a saucepan. Add the water and let simmer until the volume has reduced by half. Pass through a conical strainer. Reserve the liquid and throw the peels way.

2 Mix the reserved cooking water with the soy sauce, and salt to taste. Whisk the butter into this liquid, and pour it into a tall saucepan (the liquid should not reach higher than the halfway mark). Foam the mixture for a few seconds with a hand mixer. With a large spoon, carefully remove the foam on top of the liquid. Serve as a garnish with meat or fish.

TIP

+ The leftover stock is perfect for making mushroom soup.

THE LIFE
OF TOMATOES

Every year when autumn comes around, we prepare preserves for *Toqué!* and *Brasserie T!* We make sure to use every part of the tomato, and avoid wasting anything: seeds and scum are transformed into vinaigrette, tomato paste, chips and more...

Tomato preserves

Wash and quarter the tomatoes. Pass through a tomato grinder. If you don't have a tomato grinder, just toss them whole in a food processor, and filter through a conical strainer. Use the juice for preserves, and set the skins and seeds aside for a later use.

In a saucepan, over medium heat, let the juice cook until reduced by half while skimming the surface from time to time. Set the scum (the layer of froth skimmed from the surface) aside. Pour the reduced juice into sterilized jars. Place the lids, but make sure you don't tighten them too much.

Preheat the oven to 180°C (350°F). Place the jars on a baking sheet in the oven for about 20 minutes, or until the contents begin to boil lightly. Carefully remove the jars from the oven and allow to rest at room temperature for 24 hours without moving them. If the canning process is successful, the seals of the jars will *pop* as they cool. This means they're properly sealed.

Using skin and seeds

In a saucepan, mix a portion of the skin and seeds (previously set aside) with three parts water. Reduce the liquid by half over medium heat. Pass through a conical strainer and keep the juice. Throw out the contents of the strainer. Bring the juice back to a boil, add a little honey, and again reduce by half until syrupy. Add cider vinegar to taste, and enough olive oil to make a vinaigrette. Continue reducing, and you'll end up with tomato caramel.

Using scum

Keep the scum as you boil your tomatoes and strain in a muslin cloth for 24 hours. Separate the water and paste.

The strained water can be used to make cocktails by adding vodka, for example. You can also make jelly with it; just bloom gelatin sheets in cold water, warm the tomato water and add salt and pepper to taste before adding the strained gelatin. Pour this mixture into moulds, allow to cool in the refrigerator, and slice into cubes to serve as a garnish.

With the pulp that remains in the muslin cloth, you can make chips, powder, paste, etc.

To make chips, combine the pulp with egg whites. Spread thinly on parchment paper and dry in the oven at 110°C (225°F) for about 45 minutes, or until the preparation is dry to the touch. The chips are ready to be eaten straight away. However, if you wish, you can pulverize them in a coffee grinder to make tomato powder.

You can also cook the pulp in olive oil in a frying pan while mixing well. The result is a tomato paste that works well as a spread.

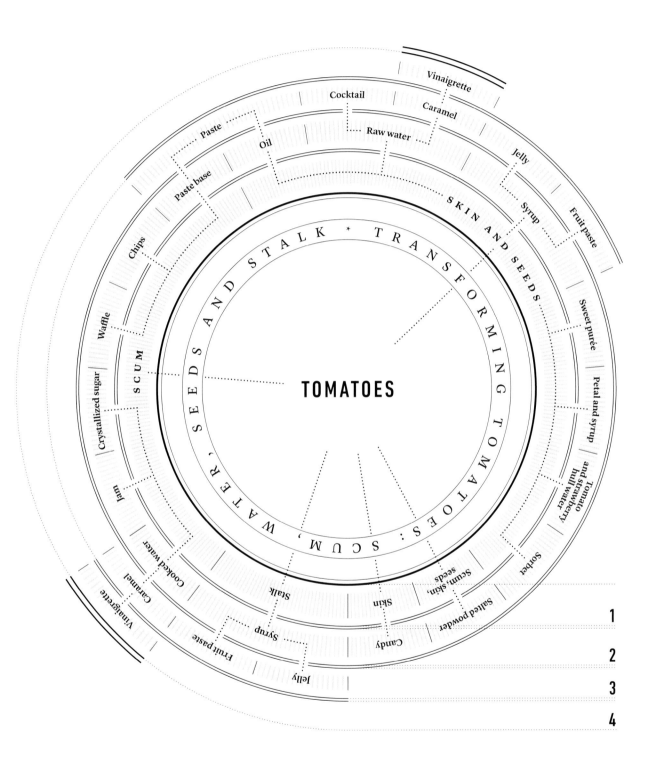

TOMATOES

TRANSFORMING TOMATOES : SCUM, WATER, SEEDS AND STALK * SKIN AND SEEDS

SKIN AND SEEDS

Vinaigrette
Cocktail
Caramel
Paste
Oil
Raw water
Jelly
Paste base
Syrup
Chips
Fruit paste
Waffle
Sweet purée
Crystallized sugar
Petal and syrup
SCUM
Tomato and strawberry hull water
Jam
Sorbet
Scum, skin, seeds
Cooked water
Salted powder
Caramel
Skin
Vinaigrette
Candy
Fruit paste
Jelly
Syrup
Stalk

1
2
3
4

TOMATOES

TOMATOES
AND BURNT BREAD

SERVES 4
PREPARATION: 15 MIN

- 4 slices of fleshy tomato (of the Beefsteak variety) about 2 cm (¾ in) thick
- 4 tbsp olive oil
- Salt and freshly ground black pepper
- 4 tbsp mayonnaise [P. 448]
- 200 g (7 oz) burnt bread [P. 446]
- Basil leaves
- Borage flowers or leaves
- 60 ml (¼ cup) green onion oil [P. 445]

1 Preheat the oven on broil. Place the tomato slices on a baking sheet, sprinkle with olive oil and add salt and pepper to taste. Warm in the oven for 2 to 3 minutes.

2 Spread 1 tbsp mayonnaise on each plate. Place a tomato slice on the mayonnaise. Garnish with burnt bread and the remaining ingredients.

COLD TOMATO SOUP

SERVES 4
PREPARATION: 30 MIN
REFRIGERATION: 4 HRS

- 1 kg (4 cups) of fleshy tomatoes (of the Beefsteak variety), cut into large pieces
- 60 ml (¼ cup) red wine vinegar
- 2 tbsp spicy oil
- 125 ml (½ cup) olive oil
- 5 g (1 tsp) fine salt
- 2 tbsp sugar

1 In a large bowl, combine the tomatoes, vinegar, oils, salt and sugar. Refrigerate for 4 hours.

2 In a blender, purée the preparation and pass through a conical strainer. Serve cold.

TIP

+ If using yellow tomatoes, replace the red wine vinegar with white wine or rice vinegar. As the ingredients are raw, it's possible that the soup will separate before being served. If this is the case, simply mix again with a hand mixer.

TOMATOES

This recipe is inspired by the Nintendo game *Burger Time*, in which the main character adds layer upon layer of ingredients to make sandwiches. We took this playful idea to heart and applied it to the classic North American BLT, but decided to have a bit of fun, and inverted the bread and tomato.

BACKWARDS BLT

SERVES 4
PREPARATION: 1 HR

· 12 thin slices of pancetta (not rolled)
· 4 medium tomatoes
· 4 tbsp chardonnay vinegar
· 4 tbsp olive oil
· Maldon salt and pepper
· 4 tbsp shallots, minced
· 250 ml (1 cup) mayonnaise [P. 448]
· 12 basil leaves
· 12 lettuce leaves
· Chives
· 4 tbsp parmesan cheese, grated
· 4 tbsp fried bread [P. 446]

1 Preheat the oven to 160°C (325°F). Place the pancetta slices between two sheets of parchment paper on a baking sheet. Cook for 10 to 20 minutes until golden and crunchy. Set aside.

2 With a small knife, score an X on the underside of the tomatoes and blanch them in boiling water for 15 seconds. Before peeling, cool the tomatoes in a bowl of ice water. Set aside on paper towels. Remove the heart of each tomato with an apple corer, then slice each fruit horizontally into three equal slices. Keep the slices of each tomato together, so they can be easily restacked later.

Finishing Touches

3 Place the tomato slices on a baking tray, in such a way that each tomato can be easily reconstructed later. Drizzle a little vinegar and olive oil on each slice (except the topmost), and add Maldon salt, pepper, shallots, mayonnaise, a basil leaf, a lettuce leaf, chives, Parmesan cheese and fried bread.

4 Finally, place a slice of pancetta on each tomato slice. Stack the slices one on top of each other to re-form a full tomato. Add a bit of mayonnaise in the hole made by the apple-corer. Sprinkle with olive oil and add Maldon salt.

TIP

+ You can use different types of tomatoes and vary the colours. Avoid tomatoes that are too ripe. Try adding garden herbs and small flowers also.

TOMATOES

Tomato jam is an old Quebecois tradition. Throughout the fall, big unripe tomatoes were picked so they wouldn't freeze. As they weren't ripe, we made jam out of them. From the very first days of the *Toqué!,* we've been adding this jam to many of our desserts.

TOMATO JAM AND WILD GINGER ICE MILK

SERVES 4
PREPARATION: 1:30 HRS
REST: 36 HRS

Tomato Jam
· 1 kg (2 lbs) green zebra tomatoes
· 320 g (1⅓ cups) sugar
· 1 cinnamon stick
· Zest of ½ lemon
· 20 g (¾ oz) whole almonds

Wild Ginger Ice Milk
· 750 ml (3 cups) 3.25 % milk
· 200 g (¾ cup) sugar
· 2 tbsp wild ginger

Basil Pulp
· 2 bunches basil, with leaves plucked
· 3 tbsp water

Basil Sugar
· 2½ tbsp powdered albumen
· 300 g (1¼ cups) sugar
· 125 ml (½ cup) water

Finishing Touches
· 60 ml (¼ cup) sour cream
· 20 ml (4 tsp) molasses
· Olive oil

Tomato Jam

1 Wash the tomatoes thoroughly. Using a sharp knife, remove the stem and score a small X on the bottom of the tomato. Blanch in boiling water for a few seconds, and immediately immerse in iced water. Remove the skins with a small knife.

2 Quarter the tomatoes and remove the seeds. In a bowl, mix the tomato flesh with sugar and marinate overnight. Strain, save the syrup and set the tomatoes aside.

3 In a pot, over low heat, reduce the syrup by half. Lower the heat, add the tomatoes and cook for 1 minute without bringing to a boil. Refrigerate for 12 hours.

4 The next day, repeat the same steps: strain the tomatoes, save the syrup and set the tomatoes aside. In a pot, over low heat, reduce the syrup by half. Lower the heat, add the tomatoes, and cook for 1 minute without bringing to a boil. Refrigerate for 12 hours.

5 On the third day, strain the tomatoes, save the syrup, and set the tomatoes aside. In a pot, over low heat, bring the syrup to a temperature of 110°C (230°F). Add the cinnamon, lemon zest, and tomatoes, and cook for 2 minutes without bringing to a boil. Add the almonds, remove from heat, and refrigerate.

Wild Ginger Ice Milk

6 In a pot, heat the milk and sugar. Remove from heat and add the wild ginger. Cover and let steep for 15 minutes. Strain and cool. Pass through an ice-cream maker and place in the freezer.

Basil Pulp

7 In a pot filled with boiling water, blanch the basil leaves for 15 seconds. Cool down immediately by soaking them in a bowl of ice water. Strain and mix in a food processor to obtain a paste. Adding a few tablespoons of water will make the paste form more easily. Set aside.

Basil Sugar

8 Mix the reserved basil pulp with the albumen. In a pot over high heat, cook the sugar and water to a temperature of 135°C (275°F). Add the basil pulp and cook for 2 minutes over medium heat, stirring from time to time with a spatula. Turn the heat off, and whisk vigorously for 45 seconds until crystallized. Then, scrape the sides of the pot to remove the granular powder. Spread this preparation on parchment paper and crush the largest pieces. Set aside in a cool, dry place.

Finishing Touches

9 On each plate, draw a few lines of sour cream and molasses. Add a scoop of wild ginger ice milk and a few spoonfuls of tomato jam. Sprinkle the basil sugar over the whole plate and add a dash of olive oil.

TIP

+ You can replace the wild ginger with 2 tbsp of thyme.

PEAS

SERVES 4
PREPARATION: 2 HRS

Beet Caramel
· 10 large red beets, peeled
· 1 tbsp honey

Pureed Peas
· 500 g (2 cups) peas
· About 175 ml (¾ cup)
  vegetable stock [P. 450]
· Salt
· 1 tbsp room temperature butter

Vegetables
· 250 g (1 cup) peas
· 250 g (1 cup) snow peas
· 8 garlic florets
· 500 ml (2 cups) canola oil (for frying)

Pigeon Supremes
· 2 tbsp olive oil
· 2 tbsp butter
· 4 pigeon supremes
· Salt and freshly ground black pepper
· Tub o' Duck Fat [P. 449]

Field Berries with Smoked Fat
· 125 ml (½ cup) smoked duck fat [P. 448]
· In season wild berries (red or black
  raspberries, blackcurrants, etc.)

Finishing Touches
· A few daylily flowers

Beet Caramel
1 Extract the beet juice in a juice
  extractor. Heat the juice and skim
  the surface. Add the honey and
  reduce over medium heat until
  the mixture has the consistency of
  molasses.

Pureed Peas
2 In a pot filled with salted boiling
  water, blanch the peas until tender.
  Cool in a bowl of ice water and
  strain. In a blender, purée immediately with a bit of vegetable stock
  to obtain a smooth but firm purée.
  Salt and add the butter. Cool on ice
  and pass through a sieve.

Vegetables
3 In a pot of salted boiling water,
  cook the peas and snow peas
  for about 2 minutes, so they remain
  slightly crunchy. Cool in ice water
  and strain.

4 Cut the garlic florets in half lengthwise. In a fryer, heat the canola
  oil to 200°C (400°F). Fry the florets
  for a few seconds, until they become crunchy. Pat dry with paper
  towels. Salt to taste and set aside.

Pigeon Supremes
5 In a pan over medium heat, lightly
  colour the butter and oil. Season
  the pigeon supremes and place
  them skin down in the pan. Place
  a weight on top to ensure even
  cooking and prevent curling.
  Sear over high heat until the skin
  is golden.

6 Immerse the pigeon in the Tub o'
  Duck Fat for 3 minutes. Cover with
  aluminium foil and allow to rest
  at room temperature for 6 minutes
  before serving.

Field Berries with Smoked Fat
7 Heat the smoked fat, add the berries and keep this mixture warm off
  the heat.

Finishing Touches
8 Place the cooked peas and snow
  peas in a sieve and immerse
  them quickly in boiling water to
  warm. Reheat the pea purée first,
  followed by the peas.

9 Place the pigeon, sliced in two,
  at the centre of each plate. Lightly
  coat with smoked duck fat and
  beet caramel. Alongside the
  meat, place a spoonful of pea purée
  and a medley of warm peas, berries, daylily flowers, and fried garlic
  florets.

THE LIFE OF
BERRIES

STRAWBERRY STEM WATER

REFRIGERATE: 48 HRS

· 500 g (1 lb) strawberry hulls
· 160 g (⅔ cup) sugar

In a large container, mix the strawberry hulls and sugar and cover with water. Refrigerate for 48 hours. Pour through a conical strainer without pressing on the strawberry hulls. Save the water.

BERRY SORBET

REFRIGERATE: 36 HRS

· 500 g (1 lb) berries,
  cut into pieces
· 240 g (1 cup) sugar
· Juice of 1 lemon

In a bowl, soak the berries in sugar and lemon and refrigerate for 24 hours. Purée in a food processor and filter through a conical strainer. Set the pulp aside for a later use, and use the purée for the sorbet. Pass the purée through an ice-cream maker and store in the freezer.

BERRY VINEGAR

INFUSION: 2 WEEKS
REST: 1 MONTH

· 625 ml (2½ cups) red wine vinegar
  or rice vinegar

Pour 250 g (1 cup) of the fruit pulp [PREVIOUS RECIPE] into a glass bowl. In a pot, warm the vinegar over low heat, then pour it over the fruit pulp. Leave to steep in the refrigerator for 2 weeks.

Filter the vinegar in a conical strainer and pour into a decanter. Refrigerate for 1 month.

Pour the vinegar through a coffee filter and save the pulp. Bottle the liquid. This vinegar will keep in the fridge for several months.

FRUIT SUGAR

· 2 tbsp powdered egg whites
· 300 g (1¼ cups) sugar
· 125 ml (½ cup) water

Mix 160 g (⅔ cup) of fruit purée [SORBET RECIPE] with the egg whites. In a pot over high heat, cook the sugar and water until the mixture reaches 135°C (275°F). Add the purée and cook for 1 minute over medium heat, stirring well with a spatula. Turn off the heat and whisk vigorously for 45 seconds until the mixture crystallizes. Scrape the sides of the bowl well until you get a granular powder. Sprinkle it on parchment paper, crushing the larger pieces. Keep in a cool, dry place

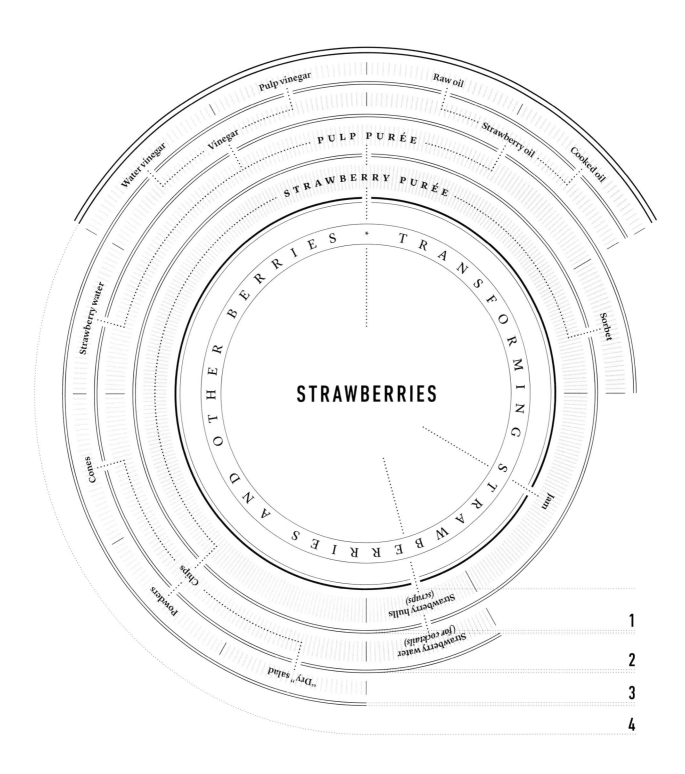

Pulp vinegar   Raw oil

Water vinegar   Vinegar   PULP PURÉE   Strawberry oil   Cooked oil

STRAWBERRY PURÉE

OTHER BERRIES ∗ TRANSFORMING STRAWBERRIES AND

STRAWBERRIES

Strawberry water

Sorbet

Cones

Jam

Powders   Chips

Strawberry hulls (scraps)

Strawberry water (for cocktails)

"Dry" salad

1

2

3

4

In order to have a wide variety of ingredients to work with during the long winter months, we have turned to our traditions to develop a number of simple techniques to utilize berries to the fullest. By separating the juice from the pulp, we obtain purée, sauce, jelly, chips, caramel, syrup, fruit paste, etc. The process can be applied to most berries (blueberries, raspberries, etc.). Some of these recipes can also be used with other fruits like pineapple or citrus fruits.

VINEGARED PULP

· 250 g (1 cup) vinegared pulp [BERRY VINEGAR RECIPE]

Use as a purée with venison, meat, foie gras or white fish.

FRUIT WATER

MAKES 1 L (4 CUPS)

· 200 g (¾ cup) berry pulp
· 800 ml (3¼ cups) water

In a pot, bring the berry pulp [BERRY SORBET RECIPE] and water to a boil. Turn off the heat and steep for 10 to 15 minutes. Pour through a conical strainer lined with a coffee filter. Refrigerate the water. No need to add sugar since the pulp is naturally sweetened.

FRUIT OILS

You can make two types of fruit oil: raw and cooked.

Raw Fruit Oil
· 500 ml (2 cups) grape seed oil

Cooked Fruit Oil
· 500 g (2 cups) grape seed oil

Raw Fruit Oil
In a food processor, mix the oil with 500 g (2 cups) of berry pulp [BERRY SORBET RECIPE] for 3 minutes.

Cooked Fruit Oil
In a pot over low heat, heat the oil with 500 g (2 cups) of berry pulp [BERRY SORBET RECIPE] for 5 minutes. Use as a seasoning for lettuce or as a garnish, but not as a cooking oil.

STRAWBERRIES

WASABI STRAWBERRIES

MAKES 12 BITES
PREPARATION: 45 MIN

· 90 g (2 cups) tarragon or basil leaves
· 250 ml (1 cup) warm water
· 2½ gelatin sheets
· 6 large strawberries
· 2 g (½ tsp) wasabi paste

1 In a pot of boiling water, blanch the herbs for 10 seconds. Cool in ice water and strain well. In a blender, purée the herbs, gradually adding the warm water. Pass through a coffee filter.

2 Bloom the gelatin in cold water. Reheat a little of the tarragon liquid and use it to dissolve the strained gelatin. Add the rest of the herb liquid and let rest at room temperature.

3 Slice the strawberries in half. Make sure they are stable on the plates when adding the jelly.

4 Place a dab of wasabi in the centre of the strawberry halves. Cover with jelly (if it has set, gently reheat in a double boiler).

5 Refrigerate until the jelly sets.

HAM AND STRAWBERRIES WITH MOLASSES AND LIME ZEST

SERVES 4
PREPARATION: 10 MIN

· 1 basket of strawberries, hulled and sliced in half
· 2 tbsp molasses
· Zest of 1 lime
· 200 g (7 oz) thin slices of dried ham
· 1 pinch freshly ground black pepper
· 2 tbsp olive oil

1 Place the strawberries in an irregular fashion on a large plate. Slowly pour the molasses over the strawberries. Add the lime zest, ham, pepper and olive oil.

TIP
+ You could serve this appetizer on a large sheet of parchment paper placed in the middle of the table.

ANOTHER ROUND
FOR SAMUEL...

ANDRÉ BEAUFORT
Pinot Noir, Chardonnay, Pinot Meunier
CHAMPAGNE

In this recipe, molasses and lime enhance the strawberries' flavour. The mix of these three ingredients may seem improbable, but it works wonderfully. We often pair strawberries with champagne, and here we've chosen a dry but mellow champagne—for a delicious touch of hedonism. Henriot makes plush, generous, rather full wines that go well with strawberries and molasses.

CHAMPAGNE

André Beaufort

BRUT
MILLESIME 2002

Lot no 02 degorgé en 01/2012   ALC. 12% BY VOL 750 ML

De vignes cultivées sans engrais chimique, sans désherbant, sans in-
secticide ni fongicide de synthèse, Elles reçoivent du compost végétal
et sont soignées par aromathérapie et homéopathie.

STRAWBERRIES

Our terrine is representative of the way we cook and the methods we employ to use trimmings instead of wasting them. It's a dessert that allows us to use fruits that are delicious in flavour but perhaps imperfect in appearance.

STRAWBERRY TERRINE

SERVES 8 TO 10
PREPARATION: 1:30 HRS
REST: 12 HRS

Strawberry Water
· 1.5 kg (3 lbs) strawberries, quartered
· 750 ml (3 cups) water
· 125 ml (½ cup) honey
· Juice of 3 lemons
· 14 gelatin sheets

Terrine
· 3 strawberry baskets, hulled and sliced in half

Strawberry Crunch
· 740 ml (3 cups) strawberry purée
· 60 g (¼ cup) egg whites

Strawberry Caramel
· 120 g (½ cup) sugar

Finishing Touches
· Strawberry sorbet [P. 260]
· Field berry sugar [P. 260]
· Fresh strawberries, to taste

Strawberry Water
1 In a large bowl, combine the strawberries, water, honey and lemon juice. Cover the bowl with plastic film and place in a double boiler. Simmer for 30 minutes until the strawberries lose their colour. Without pressing on the strawberries, gently pass through a conical strainer to obtain a clear juice.

2 Heat 1 litre (4 cups) of the strawberry water and set the rest aside to make strawberry caramel. Bloom the gelatin in very cold water. Strain and mix well with the warm liquid. Set aside at room temperature.

Terrine
3 Take a tall and narrow terrine or 1.5 litre (6 cup) loaf pan. Line with plastic film, leaving enough around the edges to fold over the top of the mould.

4 Gently fill the mould three-quarters of the way with strawberries; avoid pressing too hard on the fruit. Close the plastic film over the strawberries and place a (not too heavy) weight on top (ideal here would be a weight made of dried peas wrapped in aluminium foil). Refrigerate overnight.

Strawberry Crunch
5 Preheat the oven to 100°C (210°F). In a bowl, carefully mix the strawberry purée with the egg whites. With an offset spatula, spread a uniform 2 mm thick layer of purée onto a silicone baking mat. Bake for 20 to 30 minutes, or until the preparation is dry to the touch (your finger shouldn't leave a mark).

Strawberry Caramel
6 In a pot, combine the reserved strawberry water and sugar. Reduce over medium heat until the mixture is syrupy in consistency.

Finishing Touches
7 Turn out the strawberry terrine. Place a 2 cm (¾ in) thick slice of terrine on each plate. Garnish with a scoop of sorbet placed on a dusting of field berry sugar. Drizzle with caramel and sprinkle with strawberry crunch and fresh strawberries.

TIP
+ If there is any terrine leftover, you can serve it chopped with oysters or salads.

CRANBERRIES

GIRLY CRANBERRIES

SERVES 4 TO 6
PREPARATION: 1:30 HRS
COOKING: 1:30 HRS

Cranberry Purée
· 1 kg (2 lbs) cranberries
· 375 ml (1½ cups) water
· 120 g (½ cup) sugar

Cranberry Sorbet
· 250 ml (1 cup) simple syrup [P. 448]
· Cranberry pulp

Cranberry Syrup
· 60 g (¼ cup) sugar

Cranberry Chips
· 6 egg whites
· 240 g (1 cup) sugar

Finishing Touches
· 60 ml (¼ cup) thyme oil [P. 449]
· 125 ml (½ cup) whipped cream
· Fresh thyme
· Maldon salt
· 2 tbsp dried olives, chopped [P. 288]

Cranberry Purée

1 In a pot over medium heat, cook the cranberries with the water and sugar between 10 and 15 minutes until all the berries have burst. Pass through a sieve without pressing on the fruit too hard. Keep the water to make the syrup. Mix the pulp in a blender and set aside to use for the chip and sorbet recipes.

Cranberry Sorbet

2 Mix 900 g (3 cups) of the cranberry purée with the simple syrup. Pass through an ice-cream maker. Store in the freezer.

Cranberry Syrup

3 In a pot over medium heat, simmer the reserved cranberry water and the sugar until the mixture has a syrupy consistency.

Cranberry Chips

4 Preheat the oven to 110°C (225°F). Using a stand mixer, whisk the egg whites, gradually adding the sugar in 3 batches. Using a spatula, delicately fold a quarter of this meringue mixture into 100 g (½ cups) of the reserved cranberry purée. Gently fold in the rest of the meringue. With an offset spatula, spread a 5 mm (¼ in) thick layer of the preparation onto a silicone baking mat. Carefully divide into four sections by scoring a cross with the end of a wooden spoon. Separate the four pieces so they do not touch each other to ensure even cooking.

5 Bake for 25 minutes. Rotate the baking mat 180 degrees, and cook for another 25 minutes. Carefully flip the meringue squares onto a baking sheet lined with parchment paper and cook for a further 25 minutes or until dry to the touch (your finger shouldn't leave a mark). Adjust the cooking time accordingly. Slice into 5 cm × 8 cm (2 in × 3 in) rectangles with a serrated knife.

Finishing Touches

6 Drizzle thyme oil and cranberry syrup over each plate. Add a scoop of sorbet. Spread cream on each chip, adding thyme, Maldon salt and dried olives. Stack together.

BLUEBERRIES

BLUEBERRY TARTLETS

SERVES 4
PREPARATION: 1:30 HRS
REST: 12 HRS

Vanilla Mascarpone Cream
· 180 g (¾ cup) mascarpone
· 2 tbsp honey
· ½ vanilla bean
· 2 tbsp 35 % cream

Breton Dough
· 4 egg yolks
· 240 g (1 cup) sugar
· ½ vanilla bean
· 240 g (1 cup) butter
· 245 g (1¾ cups) flour
· 1 pinch salt

Blueberry Sorbet
· 500 g (1 lb) blueberries
· 120 g (½ cup) sugar
· 60 ml (¼ cup) lemon juice

Finishing Touches
· 2 tbsp honey
· Wild fruit sugar [P. 260]
· 450 g (3 cups) wild blueberries

Vanilla Mascarpone Cream
1 The day before: in a round-bottomed mixing bowl, gently whisk the mascarpone, honey and vanilla. Slowly add the cream and let steep in the refrigerator.

Breton Dough
2 The day before: in a bowl, cream the yolks and sugar. In another bowl, mix the vanilla with the butter, and then incorporate the egg mixture. Add the flour and salt and knead into a dough. Refrigerate overnight.

3 The next day: preheat the oven to 180°C (350°F). Roll out the dough to a thickness of 5 mm (¼ in). On a lightly floured surface, cut out circles of pastry using a cooking cutter. Place in small buttered aluminum tartlet moulds and fill each one with a few dried peas. Bake for 25 minutes in a conventional oven or 12 minutes in a convection oven.

Blueberry Sorbet
4 In a pot over medium heat, cook all the ingredients until the blueberries are well cooked. Purée in a blender and pass through a sieve. Process the most runny portion of the blueberry mixture in an ice cream maker and freeze until ready to use.

Finishing Touches
5 Place a spoonful of the vanilla mascarpone cream into each pastry. In a pan over medium-high heat, heat the honey and add the blueberries. Warm up quickly and pass through a sieve, making sure the berries are not too wet. Place the warm blueberries on top of the cream in the tartlets. Serve with a scoop of sorbet placed on a dusting of fruit sugar.

DRY SALAD

It all began when a giant pot hole appeared on Saint Lawrence Boulevard at the corner of Ontario. Charles-Antoine wanted to make a salad that would look like that pile of rubble. We first made chips with almond skins, pea pods, squash pulp and beet trimmings. Little by little, we added other ingredients, but those first four mark the beginning of the 2 × 2.

2 × 2

SERVES 4
PREPARATION: 1:30 HRS
REST: 24 HRS

Wild Berry Sorbet
· 500 g (1 lb) wild berries, cleaned and hulled (blackberries, strawberries, raspberries, blueberries, or sea buckthorn berries)
· 120 g (½ cup) sugar
· 5 ml (1 tsp) lemon juice

White Chocolate Mousse
· 100 g (3½ oz) Valrhona Ivory chocolate
· 200 ml (¾ cup + 4 tsp) 35 % cream
· 160 g (⅔ cup) 10 % Mediterranean yogurt

Dry Salad
· 220 g (1 cup) berry purée (blackberries, strawberries, raspberries, blueberries, or sea buckthorn berries)
· 1 egg white

Finishing Touches
· 500 g (1 lb) mixed seasonal field and wild berries (black and red raspberries, blackcurrants, red currant, ground cherries, strawberries)
· 60 ml (¼ cup) simple syrup [P. 448]

Wild Berry Sorbet
1 In a large bowl, combine the fruit with the sugar and lemon juice. Refrigerate for 24 hours. Purée in a blender and filter through a sieve. (Keep the pulp left in the sieve for another use [P. 260]). Process in an ice-cream maker and place in the freezer.

White Chocolate Mousse
2 Place the chocolate in a bowl. In a pot, over medium heat, bring the cream to a boil while stirring constantly. Pour over the chocolate. When the chocolate has fully melted, place the bowl in another bowl filled with ice water and mix well to cool the mixture and ensure it doesn't separate. Add the yogurt and mix well. Pour into a whipped cream dispenser and add two N₂O chargers while stirring after every addition. Keep the dispenser in the refrigerator at least one hour before use. [P. 451]

Dry Salad
3 Preheat the oven to 100°C (210°F). Using an electric hand mixer, mix the fruit purée and egg white in a large bowl. With an offset spatula, spread a 2 mm layer of this mixture onto a silicone baking mat. Place on 2 baking sheets and bake for 20 to 30 minutes until the mixture becomes dry to the touch (your finger shouldn't leave a mark). Adjust the cooking time if necessary.

Finishing Touches
4 In a bowl, mix the simple syrup with the fruit.

5 Serve in soup plates or cups. Cover with white chocolate mousse and large pieces of dry salad. Top with a scoop of sorbet.

FRUIT PASTE

FRUIT PASTE À LA MONTREAL
CONVENTION CENTRE

REST: 1 HR
PREPARATION: 1 HR
MAKES 1 FRUIT PASTE SQUARE OF
20 CM X 20 CM X 1 CM (8 IN × 8 IN × 1/2 IN).

*In order to obtain a perfect fruit paste,
the quantities are only given using
the metric system*

· 400 g fruit purée (blueberries, sea
  buckthorn berries, strawberries,
  raspberries, peaches, apples, pears
  or cranberries)
· 100 ml water
· 300 g sugar
· 70 g glucose
· 100 g simple syrup
  (only for cranberry fruit paste; [P. 448])
· 70 g sugar
· 15 g yellow pectin
· 10 ml (2 tsp) lemon juice
· 2 g citric acid
· 60 g organic sugar

1 In a pot over medium heat, bring
the fruit purée, water, sugar and
glucose to a boil. (If you're making
cranberry fruit paste, also add
the simple syrup here.) Quickly
mix together the sugar and pectin
and gradually add to the boiling
purée, stirring well. Lower the heat
and stir gently with a spatula for
around 15 minutes. Turn the off
the heat. Mix together the lemon
juice and citric acid and add to
the purée. Pour the preparation into
a 20 cm × 20cm (8 in × 8 in) mould
lined with plastic film. Leave to rest
at room temperature for 1 hour.

2 Cut the fruit paste into pieces of the
desired size and roll in the organic
sugar before serving as a petit-four.

TIP
+ Unsweetened fruit paste makes
a delightful accompaniment
to cheese.

SOUFFLÉS

FRUIT SOUFFLÉS

SERVES 6
PREPARATION: 1 HR

Fruit Base for Soufflés

· 250 g (1 cup) strawberry, raspberry, blueberry, apple or ground cherry purée
· 3 tbsp sugar (doubled for ground cherries)
· ½ tbsp corn starch (doubled for ground cherries)
· 2 tbsp water

Soufflés

· 8 egg whites
· 120 g (½ cup) sugar
· 4 tbsp icing sugar

Fruit Base for Soufflés

1 In a pot, bring the fruit purée and sugar to a boil. In a bowl, mix the cornstarch and water. Pour over the purée, bring to a boil, and whisk vigorously for 1 minute. Pour into a bowl, cover with plastic film and refrigerate.

Soufflés

2 Use 6 soufflé moulds with a width of 10 cm (4 in) and a depth of 7 cm (2¾ in). Brush the moulds twice with butter using a vertical stroke and place in the refrigerator.

3 With a stand mixer, whisk the egg whites until they begin to swell. Continue whisking while slowly adding a third of the sugar. When the egg whites have doubled in volume, add another third of the sugar. Finally, when the mixture begins to stiffen, add the remaining sugar and whisk until firm peaks form.

4 With a spatula, gently fold in part of the meringue into the fruit base. Carfully incorporate the rest, making sure the mixture is homogenous but airy.

Cooking

5 Spoon the preparation into a pastry bag. Pipe the mixture into the moulds and smooth over with a spatula. Place your thumb about 1 cm (½ in) deep against the side of the dish and drag it along the edge, creating a small indentation that will ensure the preparation doesn't stick as it cooks.

6 Preheat the oven to 195°C (380°F). Cook the soufflés and monitor cooking progress—without opening the oven door. Depending on the fruit, the soufflés should cook for about 20 minutes, or until they have doubled in height. Remove from the oven and sprinkle with icing sugar. Serve immediately.

TIP
+ In a convection oven, cooking time for the soufflés can be reduced to 8 minutes at 195°C (380°F).

APPLES

POM POM POM

SERVES 4
PREPARATION: 1 HR
COOKING: 2HRS
REST: 6 HRS

Apple Compote

· 2 kg (4½ lbs) Cortland or McIntosh apples, whole and unpeeled

Apple Sorbet

· 120 g (½ cup) sugar

Apple Chips

· 2 apples (e.g., Empire, Granny Smith, Honeycrisp)
· 60 ml (¼ cup) simple syrup [P. 448]

Apple Mousse

· 375 ml (1½ cups) apple juice
· 2 branches of vanilla grass
· 2 gelatin sheets

Oatmeal Crumble

· 75 g (¾ cup) oatmeal
· 75 g (½ cup) brown sugar
· 80 g (⅓ cup) butter
· 75 g (½ cup) flour
· 75 g (½ cup) almond powder

Apple Compote

1 Preheat the oven to 180°C (350°F). Place the apples on a metal grill and cook for 1 hour, or until the heart has begun to soften. Pass through a sieve and reserve the purée for the sorbet.

Apple Sorbet

2 In a pot over medium heat, heat the reserved apple compote with the sugar until it begins to simmer. Remove from heat and allow to cool. Process in an ice-cream maker.

Apple Chips

3 Preheat the oven to 105°C (220°F). Core the apples and slice them into 1 mm thick slices using a mandoline. Dip the slices in the simple syrup, and shake off any excess liquid. Lay out on a silicone baking mat and cook for 10 minutes. Flip the slices, rotate the baking sheet, and cook for another 10 minutes. If the chips aren't crunchy, cook them for a further 5 minutes until they have the desired texture.

Apple Mousse

4 In a pot over low heat, bring the apple juice and vanilla grass to a boil. Remove from heat, cover and steep for 20 minutes. Remove the vanilla grass. Bloom the gelatin in a bowl of cold water, strain and mix in with the juice. Refrigerate to cool.

5 Pass the cooled juice through a conical strainer, and pour into a small whipped cream dispenser. Add two N_2O chargers. Place the dispenser in the refrigerator for 6 hours [P. 451].

Oatmeal Crumble

6 Preheat the oven to 160°C (325°F). Using a stand mixer, mix together all the ingredients until homogenous. Spread on a baking tray lined with parchment paper. Bake for 20 minutes, stirring halfway through or as soon as the sides of crumble start to colour. The crumble is ready when golden.

Finishing Touches

7 On each plate, create alternate layers of apple chips and mousse. Serve with the oatmeal crumble and a scoop of ice cream.

APPLES

CARAMEL BUBBLES

SERVES 4

Apple Purée
· 1 kg (2 lbs) apples
· 910 ml (3⅔ cups) water
· 360 g (1½ cups) sugar

Apple Mousse
· 2 g vanilla grass, roughly chopped (approximately 18 stems)
· 4 gelatin sheets

Isomalt Bubbles
· 360 g (2 cups) Isomalt
Isomalt is a sweetener derived from sucrose. Once heated, it remains translucent.

Cracked Pepper Ice Milk
· 750 ml (3 cups) 3.25 % milk
· 200 g (¾ cup) sugar
· 1 tsp cracked pepper

Finishing Touches
· 20 g (4 tsp) blueberry sugar [P. 260]
· 20 g (4 tsp) raspberry sugar [P. 260]

Apple Purée

1 Quarter the apples. Bring all the ingredients to a boil in a pot. Simmer for approximately 30 minutes until the fruit turns to compote. Remove from heat and immediately run through a sieve. Reduce the preparation to a smooth purée in a blender and set aside.

Apple Mousse

2 In a pot, heat 870 g (3 cups) of the apple purée until it begins to simmer. Turn off the heat and add the vanilla grass. Cover and steep for 15 minutes.

3 Bloom the gelatin in a bowl of ice water. Pour the apple purée into a conical strainer and heat. Strain the gelatin and stir it into the purée away from the heat source until it dissolves. Allow to cool to room temperature, then pour into a whipped cream dispenser. Load two N₂O chargers, stirring well after each addition. Refrigerate for 6 hours before serving [P. 451].

Isomalt Bubbles

4 In a pot over medium heat, melt the Isomalt until it becomes liquid. Remove from heat and place the pot in cold water to prevent further cooking.

5 Plunge the base of a round metal pastry cutter in the melted Isomalt. Lift it up, and let it drip a little, until there's only a thin filament left (the Isomalt should stick to the side of the cylinder). Blow softly from the other end of the cutter to make the sugar swell into a bubble. When the bubble is big enough, separate it from the cutter with scissors, and then cut the sugar filament at the other end. Continue making bubbles in this manner. The bubbles will keep for a day in a sealed, dry container.

Cracked Pepper Ice Milk

6 Heat the milk and sugar in a pot. Remove the pot from the heat and add the pepper. Cover and allow to steep for 15 minutes. Pour through a conical strainer and process the cooled liquid in an ice cream maker. Store the ice milk in the freezer.

Finishing Touches

7 In each Isomalt bubble, right at the bottom, add a little blueberry and raspberry sugar. Fill with apple mousse by carefully inserting the tip of the dispenser. Set a bubble on each plate with a scoop of cracked pepper ice milk. Serve immediately as the bubbles will melt quickly.

PEARS

POACHED PEARS
WITH BEET JUICE

SERVES 4
PREPARATION: 2 HRS
(POACH THE PEARS THE DAY BEFORE)
REST: 12 HRS

Poached Pears

· 8 medium-sized beets, peeled
· 2 unpeeled red apples
· 4 pears

Goat Cheese Ice Cream

· 500 g (1 lb) fresh goat cheese
  at room temperature
· 430 ml (1¾ cups) water
· 250 ml (1 cup) simple syrup [P. 448]
· Salt
· 7 gelatin sheets

Beet Sugar

· 2 tbsp powdered albumen
· 300 g (1¼ cups) sugar
· 125 ml (½ cup) water

Thyme Honey

· 60 ml (¼ cup) honey
· 4 sprigs thyme (leaves only)
· 5 ml (1 tsp) water

Poached Pears

1 The day before, extract the beet juice with a juice extractor and keep the pulp to make beet sugar. Then extract the juice from the apples.

2 In a pot over low heat, heat both juices together while skimming the surface until the liquid becomes clear. (The liquid is ready when no more scum forms.)

3 Peel the pears and core them using a melon baller. Bring the juice to a simmer, and poach the pears for 10 to 12 minutes until they become soft without loosing their shape. Refrigerate the pears in the juice overnight.

Goat Cheese Ice Cream

4 Bloom the gelatin in a bowl of cold water. Crumble the goat cheese in a heat-resistant bowl. In a pot, over low heat, heat the water, simple syrup and salt. Incorporate the gelatin into the hot mixture. Pour onto the cheese and stir well. Allow to cool, then process in an ice-cream maker. Reserve in the freezer.

Beet Sugar

5 Mix 2 tbsp of the reserved beet pulp and 1 tbsp of the pear cooking juice with the albumen.

6 Heat the sugar and water in a pot over high heat until the temperature reaches 135°C (275°F). Add the beet pulp and cook 1 minute over medium heat, stirring well with a spatula. Remove from heat and whisk vigorously for 45 seconds or until crystallized. Scrape the sides of the pot to remove the granular powder. Spread the preparation on parchment paper and crush the largest pieces. Set aside in a cool, dry place.

Thyme Honey

7 In a pot, bring the honey to a boil. Remove from heat and add the thyme and water. Stir and allow to rest.

Finishing Touches

8 Drizzle thyme honey on each plate. Sprinkle a dusting of beet sugar in the middle. Stuff the pears with goat cheese ice cream and place on the beet sugar.

TIP

+ Heat the rest of the pear's cooking juice with 120 g (½ cup) of sugar and reduce until syrupy in consistency. Incorporate a little of this mixture in a vinaigrette, or serve as a sauce for fish.

PEACHES

This dessert brings together all the elements of a savoury dish. Inspired by a rustic Catalan recipe made of figs and black olives, we elaborated a similar dessert using peaches and Kalamata olives. Charles-Antoine realized that an element was missing that might bind the different parts of the dish together. Being such a fan of olive oil desserts, he came up with a whipped cream cut with olive oil. As the dish evolved, Samuel, our sommelier, proposed that we add an oxidative wine. The resulting combination of yellow wine, olive and peach is fantastic.

PEACHES WITH YELLOW WINE AND DRIED OLIVES

SERVES 4
PREPARATION: 2 HRS
COOKING: 2:45 HRS

Peaches
· 1 litre (4 cups) simple syrup
· 4 ripe peaches, sliced in half and pitted

Peach Sorbet
· 8 medium peaches
· 240 g (1 cup) sugar

Dry Meringue
· 3 egg whites
· 1 vanilla pod, sliced in half
· 240 g (1 cup) sugar

Yellow Wine Cream
· 125 ml (½ cup) 35 % cream
· 2 tbsp yellow wine
· 1 tbsp icing sugar

Dried Olives
· 60 g (2 oz) Kalamata olives, pitted
· 120 g (½ cup) sugar
· 250 ml (1 cup) water

Finishing Touches
· 4 tbsp honey
· 2 tbsp olive oil

Peaches
1 In a large pot, bring the simple syrup to a simmer, and then add the peaches without stacking them. Cook for about 5 minutes until quite tender. Allow to cool in the syrup, then refrigerate.

Peach Sorbet
2 In a large pot of boiling water, blanch the peaches for 2 to 5 minutes. Then skin, pit and chop the peaches. In a food processor, reduce the peaches to a fine purée with the sugar. Pass through a sieve, then cool in the refrigerator. Process in an ice cream maker and store in the freezer.

Dry Meringue
3 Preheat the oven to 105°C (220°F). With a stand mixer, whisk the egg whites with the vanilla and gradually add the sugar until firm peaks form.

4 You will need several 30 × 40 cm (12 × 16 in) baking trays and double the amount of parchment paper cut to the size of the trays. Roughly spread the mixture onto a sheet of parchment paper and cover with another sheet. With a rolling pin, spread the preparation around by rolling gently. Remove any excess mixture that might have escaped from between the sheets of parchment paper. Remove the topmost sheet of parchment paper and place the one coated with the mixture onto the baking sheet. Bake for about 25 minutes until the preparation is dry to the touch (your finger shouldn't leave a mark).

Yellow Wine Cream
5 In a bowl, whip the cream until soft peaks form. Incorporate the yellow wine and icing sugar, and store in the refrigerator.

Dried Olives

6 Soak the olives in cold water for 30 minutes, then slice them into quarters. In a pot over low heat, cook the olives and sugar for about 20 minutes. Pass through a sieve and reserve the liquid to make caramel.

7 Preheat the oven to 105°C (220°F). Spread a single layer of olives on a baking sheet and cook for about 2 hours (cooking time will vary depending on the oven and the olives). Remove one olive from the oven. If it becomes crunchy as it cools, it's perfectly cooked. If not, cook for a further 15 minutes and test again until the desired texture is achieved. Let cool. Roughly chop the olives and store in a cool, dry place.

Olive Caramel

8 In a pot, bring the olive's cooking liquid to a boil and reduce until it has the consistency of molasses.

Finishing Touches

9 In a pan, heat the honey until it begins to boil. Lower the heat and softly cook the peaches, stirring constantly. Drizzle a spoonful of yellow wine cream and half a tablespoon of olive oil onto each plate. Garnish with dried olives, and draw a line of olive caramel. Add the warm peaches and garnish with meringue. Add a scoop of peach sorbet and serve immediately.

TIP

+ You can replace peaches by pears in this recipe, but the cooking time will be longer. Both the dried olives and the caramel can be prepared in advance.

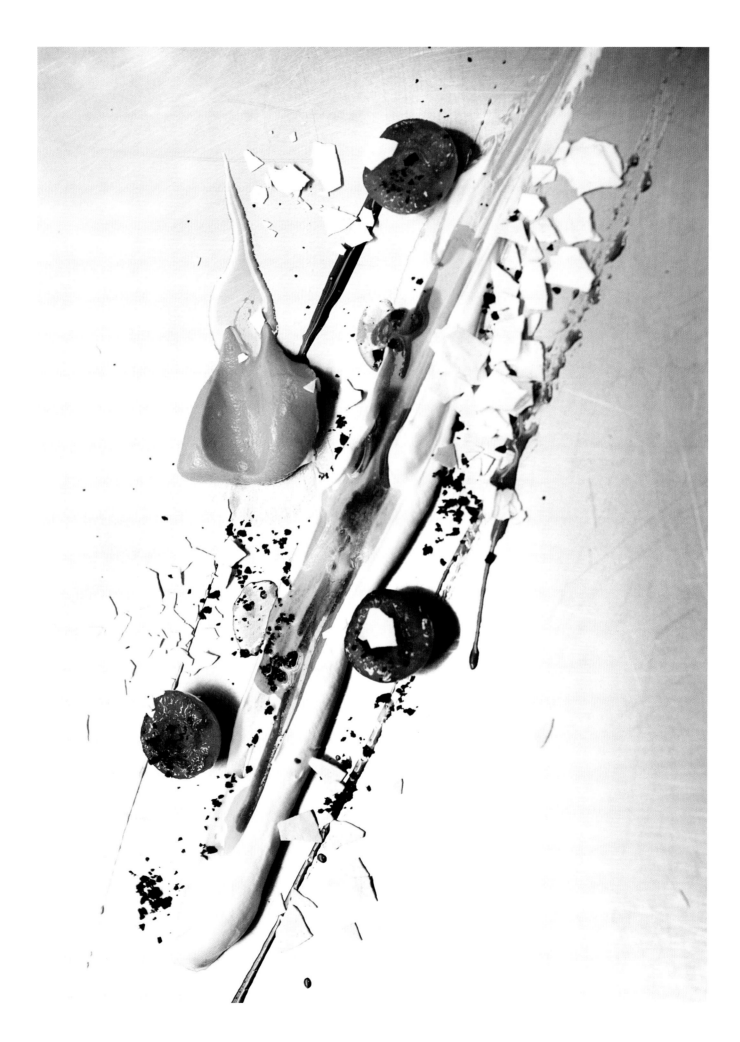

ANOTHER ROUND
FOR SAMUEL...

CHRISTIAN BARTHOMEUF
Ice Cider
EASTERN TOWNSHIPS, QUEBEC

Everything in Peaches with Yellow Wine and Dried Olives echoes ice cider! Ice cider was invented by Christian Barthomeuf, organic viticulture and viniculture pioneer and owner of the Clos Saragnat vineyard His ice cider is by far the most complex in existence, with notes of caramel and salted butter.

Clos Saragnat

MELON

MR. BERTRAND'S MELON VILLAGE WITH SMOKED FAT

SERVES 4
PREPARATION: 15 MIN

· 1 medium very ripe cantaloupe,
  sliced in half and seeded
· 2 tbsp smoked duck fat, warm [P. 448]
· Maldon salt

1 Slice the melon. Cover in smoked
  fat and sprinkle with Maldon salt.

"MY FATHER'S GLORY" MELON DESSERT

SERVES 8
REST: 12 HRS
PREPARATION: 45 MINUTES

Pastis Watermelon
· 1 small watermelon
· Pastis

Lavender Ice Cream
· 8 egg yolks
· 120 g (½ cup) sugar
· 500 ml (2 cups) 3.25 % milk
· 4 g (1 tsp) lavender flowers

Finishing Touches
· 1 small honeydew melon, peeled
  and seeded
· 1 small cantaloupe, peeled
  and seeded
· Dried olives and olive caramel [P. 288]
· Olive oil
· A few rosemary flowers

Pastis Watermelon
1 With a melon baller, remove 320 g
  (2 cups) of watermelon balls of
  2 cm (¾ in) in diameter. Cover with
  pastis and refrigerate overnight.

Lavender Ice Cream
2 Whisk the egg yolks and sugar in
  pot. In a separate pan over low
  heat, bring the milk and lavender
  to a simmer. Remove from heat
  and allow to steep, uncovered, for
  10 minutes, then filter.

3 Gradually add the warm milk to
  the eggs, stirring well to make sure
  the eggs do not cook. Place the mixture back on the burner and cook,
  stirring constantly until the preparation coats the back of a spoon.
  Allow to cool in the refrigerator.
  Process in an ice cream maker and
  store in the freezer for no longer
  than 2 hours to ensure that the ice
  cream isn't too hard when serving.

Finishing Touches
4 Cool the service plates in the
  freezer.

5 With a mandoline, cut the honeydew melon and the cantaloupe
  into thin slices. Serve with lavender ice cream (if the ice cream is
  too hard, stirring it vigorously will
  soften it up, the desired consistency is akin to an iced purée).
  Garnish with dried olives, pastis
  watermelon and melon. Add a dash
  of olive oil, rosemary flowers and
  olive caramel.

TIP
+ Once the watermelon has soaked
  all night in the refrigerator, keep
  the pastis to make a few melon-
  flavoured drinks. If there are
  watermelon balls left, freeze them
  and use them as ice cubes.

NOTHING

SERVES 4
PREPARATION: 1 HR

Nothing Ice Cream
· 8 egg yolks
· 80 g (⅓ cup) sugar
· 250 ml (1 cup) milk
· 250 ml (1 cup) 35 % cream

Fruit Powder
· 125 ml (½ cup) orange
  (or any citrus) juice
· 1 tbsp albumen powder
· 60 ml (¼ cup) water
· 240 g (1 cup) sugar

Nothing Ice Cream

1 In a bowl, whisk the egg yolks and sugar. In a pot over low heat, heat the milk and cream without bringing to a boil. Pour a little warm liquid over the eggs without mixing. Then gradually add the rest of the liquid, stirring constantly so the eggs don't cook. Pour everything back into the pot and cook, stirring constantly until the mixture coats the back of a spoon. Pass through a conical strainer and set to cool in the refrigerator. Process in an ice cream-maker and store in the freezer.

Fruit Powder

2 In a pot, reduce the juice by half. In a bowl, thoroughly mix the juice with the albumen powder. In a separate pot, bring the water and sugar to a boil. Cook over high heat until the temperature reaches 135°C (275°F). Immediately add the orange juice preparation. Cook over medium heat for 2 minutes until crystallized. Remove from heat and place the pot on a damp cloth while continuing to stir vigorously until a powder is obtained. Crush the powder to make it finer.

Finishing Touches

3 Serve with a scoop of fruit powder ice cream. Since the ice cream has no flavour, it can be flavoured with different fruit powders, herb and spice sugars, or even fruit syrups.

BANANA

BANANA SORBET
AND MOUSSE WITH DRY
SAFFRON MERINGUE

SERVES 8
COOKING: 50 MIN
PREPARATION: 1 HR
REST: 6 HRS

Banana Infusion
· 400 g (14 oz) bananas, chopped
· 625 ml (2½ cups) 3.25 % milk
· 180 ml (¾ cup) 35 % cream
· 120 g (½ cup) sugar
· ½ vanilla pod

Banana Ice Cream
· 6 egg yolks

Banana Mousse
· 500 ml (2 cups) 35 % cream
· 2 egg yolks
· 1 tbsp cornstarch

Banana Powder
· 4 tbsp albumen
· 4 tbsp simple syrup [P. 448]

Finishing Touches
· Molasses
· Dry Saffron Meringue [P. 288]; replace
the vanilla with 2 tbsp of saffron

Banana Infusion
1 In a pot, over medium heat, bring all the ingredients to a boil. Lower the heat and let simmer for 5 minutes. Remove from heat, cover and let steep for 15 minutes. Strain. Set the infusion aside and keep the leftover pulp in the sieve to make banana powder.

Banana Ice Cream
2 Mix 750 ml (3 cups) banana infusion with the egg yolks. Cook this mixture over low heat, stirring constantly until it coats the back of a spoon. Cool quickly and process in an ice cream maker before storing in the freezer.

Banana Mousse
3 In a pot, heat 250 ml (1 cup) of banana infusion and the cream. In a bowl, mix the egg yolks and cornstarch. Pour a little of the warm banana infusion over the eggs. Stir and pour back in the pot. Bring back to a boil, whisking constantly. When the preparation has thickened, pour on a baking tray, place plastic film directly on top of the mixture and cool in the refrigerator.

4 Process the preparation in a blender and pour into a large whipped cream dispenser. Add two N2O chargers, shaking between charges. Refrigerate the dispenser for at least six hours [P. 451].

Banana Powder
5 Preheat the oven to 105°C (220°F). In a blender, mix the reserved banana pulp, albumen and simple syrup. Spread on a silicone baking mat. Bake for 25 minutes. Rotate the baking sheet and cook for another 25 minutes until the preparation is dry to the touch (your finger shouldn't leave a trace). Cool at room temperature. Pulverize in a coffee grinder.

Finishing Touches
6 Draw a few lines of molasses on a plate. Place a scoop of banana ice cream in a large bowl. Coat with banana mousse using the whipped cream dispenser. Roll in the meringue and serve in the plate. Garnish with banana powder.

CHOCOLATE

CHOCOLATE PURSE

SERVES 8
PREPARATION: 1:30 HRS
REST: 24 HRS

Orange Biscuit

· 120 g (1 cup) icing sugar
· 35 g (¼ cup) flour
· 2 tbsp cocoa powder
· Ground Guinea pepper
· 60 ml (¼ cup) orange juice
· 1 tbsp butter, melted

Tiramisu Ice Cream

· 8 egg yolks
· 80 g (⅓ cup) sugar
· 500 ml (2 cups) 3.25 % milk
· 60 ml (¼ cup) liquid espresso
· 65 g (¼ cup) mascarpone

Raspberry Sugar

· 60 g (¼ cup) raspberry purée
· 1 tbsp albumen
· 240 g (1 cup) sugar
· 60 ml (¼ cup) water

Praline Filling

· 225 g (8 oz) Valrhona Caraïbe chocolate
· 60 g (¼ cup) butter
· 30 g (1 oz) almond hazelnut praline
· 200 ml (¾ cup + 4 tsp) 35 % cream
· 2 tbsp glucose

Finishing Touches

· A few strawberries, diced
· Pink peppercorns, lightly crushed
· Icing sugar

Orange Biscuit

1 The day before, combine the icing sugar, flour, cocoa and Guinea pepper. Add the orange juice and butter and mix well until a ball forms. Wrap with plastic film and refrigerate for 24 hours.

2 The next day, preheat the oven to 180°C (350°F). With an offset spatula, thinly spread the preparation onto a silicone baking mat, making rectangles of 15 cm × 10 cm (6 in × 4 in). Bake for 6 to 10 minutes, rotating the baking sheet midway through cooking. It is normal for bubbles to form during baking. The preparation is ready when the biscuits turn light brown. Set aside to cool.

Tiramisu Ice Cream

3 In a bowl, whisk the egg yolks and sugar. In a pot over low heat, bring the milk to a simmer. Remove from the heat and leave uncovered for 10 minutes. Pour a little warm milk on the eggs and mix well. Gradually add the rest of the milk, stirring constantly and taking care not to cook the eggs. Pour everything back in the pot and return to the heat, stirring constantly until the preparation coats the back of the spoon. Allow to temper, then incorporate the espresso and mascarpone. Process in an ice cream maker and place in the freezer for no more than 2 hours so that the ice cream is still fairly soft when serving.

Raspberry Sugar

4 In a bowl, mix the raspberry purée with the albumen. In a pot, bring the sugar and water to a boil. Cook over high heat to a temperature of 135°C (275°F). Turn off the heat and add the purée. Cook over medium heat for two minutes until crystallized. Remove from heat and place the pot on a damp cloth while vigorously stirring with a wooden spoon until a powder is obtained. Crush to make a finer powder.

Praline Filling

5 In a bowl, mix the chocolate, butter and praline. In a pot, over medium heat, bring the cream and glucose to a boil. Pour the warm mixture over the chocolate and emulsify with a whisk. Set aside.

Finishing Touches

6 Before serving, preheat the oven to 180°C (350°F). Reheat the orange biscuits on a silicone baking mat for 30 seconds to soften them a little.

7 Garnish the biscuits immediately with a little praline filling in the centre of each one. Add the strawberries and a dusting of raspberry sugar and pink pepper. While the biscuits are still warm, close them like little purses by pressing the four points together. Serve with a scoop of tiramisu ice cream. Sprinkle with icing sugar and serve immediately.

OUR LAND

Denis Ferrer

BOILEAU, OUTAOUAIS

It was a chance encounter that led me to my career path. My parents were vintners near Collioure and Banyuls in the south of France. Initially, when I came to Quebec, I had a bakery that doubled as a cheese shop. Mr. Harpur, who owns Harpur Farms, was one of my customers. He wanted to start a deer farming business similar to those in New Zealand, and needed someone to bring his product to market. I joined his operation, and we've been partners ever since.

Denis is a well-known figure in the restaurant business, and a truly curious individual. At the annual Toqué! dinner we hold for our producers, he's always peppering the other producers with questions about their progress and hardships, regardless of the business they're in.

NORMAND LAPRISE

THE STORY OF HARPUR FARMS

Founded in 1992, Harpur Farms is one of the biggest farming operations in North America: we have some 2,500 head of deer in our parks. Contrary to standard industry practice, we let our deer roam freely within our 1,000-acre grounds to promote the development of their muscles. The farm is divided into several parks. The biggest, which surrounds a hill, is about 300 acres. It never contains more than 250 animals.

We make sure that our deer have constant access to food, while remaining eco-friendly. The animals' semi-wild life greatly reduces their stress levels. We know that in addition to causing many diseases, stress affects the deer's ability to gain weight as well as the quality of the meat. By providing the herd with a total ration, i.e., allowing the animals to eat at will, we lessen the stress associated with finding sustenance. Our goal is to maintain the balance between nature and herd, and so we rarely get involved with the deer's daily existence. For instance, we isolate them during their breeding period (deer mate only once a year), but we are not involved in the birthing process. Our work focuses on making sure everything goes well, in recording births and following the fawns' progress. Interfering is always more harmful than simply letting nature take its course. In the end, nature knows best.

CONTROLLED PRODUCTION

We exert control over every step of the production process, from feeding to slaughter at the abattoir. We used to do business with a non-affiliated slaughterhouse. However, we had no control over their methods nor access to the premises. Our own process differs from that of major producers: we hang and age our carcasses. For that reason, we thought it best to build our own facilities. We also use a high-quality cutting process in order to meet each of our clients' specific needs.

I favour sensible farming—which requires you trusting your producer—over organic farming. You have to work with care, respecting nature while keeping a close eye on the different stages of rearing and production. All these elements are critical to the quality of the *Cerf de Boileau*. With our label, you get what you pay for. We used to try supplying restaurants year round. Since then, we've narrowed our production to a five- to six-month period to increase profitability.

MEETING NORMAND LAPRISE

Normand was one of our first customers. We've been working together since 1996. The people at *Toqué!* have played an important role in our growth, offering us visibility in the restaurant industry and adapting their orders and menus to our production. They've helped us develop our product as well. In association with McGill University, we conducted a study on deer's eating habits by trying different types of feed in our parks. We then had a blind taste test with the *Toqué!* crew and, of course, they all preferred the meat produced by the most expensive diet!

Normand is probably the most honest chef I know. He has always felt duty bound to identify each food by its maker or place of origin. We owe the name *Cerf de Boileau* to him, because that's how he described it on his menu.

From Breeding to Slaughter

The conversations we have with our producers determine our approach to cooking; that's why we're in constant contact with them. Different factors affect the taste of meat: the animal's quality of life, its nutrition, how it was slaughtered, etc. In his efforts to enhance the quality of his production, Denis Ferrer has always been open to feedback from the restaurateurs he supplies. Producers are better able to identify our needs because of the types of relationships we entertain. Hence, when Gaspor Farms approached us with the idea of developing milk-fed piglets, we advised them, as did chefs Alexandre Loiseau and Martin Picard, to opt for a slightly more mature product than a suckling pig, which is generally quite small and therefore harder to cook and less profitable. As a result, they modified their original methods and now feed pigs milk and corn until they weigh 8 kilos.

At *Toqué!,* we like to cook with meats that are rarely found in Quebec. Squab pigeon is one of our favourite meats. In Quebec, a few brave farmers made a foray in this unusual direction, giving us access to very high-quality poultry. It's the case with Turlo Farm's Nicolas and Rhéa, who spare no effort in their squab raising endeavour. By regularly offering dishes prepared from squab pigeon on our menus, we support small businesses by offering them greater stability.

Thanks to our constant, almost daily contact with each of our farmers, we know the origin of our meats. It can be hard for butchers to properly identify their products' origin, given the number of middlemen with whom they must deal. We butcher our meat on site at *Toqué!,* which enables us to order entire animals straight from the producer. We then prepare the cuts that suit our needs or age the meat if we wish. This approach has led us to develop close ties with Bio Rousseau farm, a lamb producer from Saint-Gabriel-de-Rimouski. It's an approach that also makes us that much more creative, since we get to use an assortment of cooking techniques to utilize all of the animal's parts: sausage, loin roll, leg of lamb kebab, confit shoulder, etc. Our diverse menus help us avoid losses, and we divide our lamb between *Toqué!* and *Brasserie T!*

BLACK CURRANT BRANCHES

Dianne is always on the lookout for something new. Charles-Antoine jokingly calls her the "whatchamacallit grower." When spring has just barely begun and things are still a bit slow, Dianne takes the time to comb through her garden to bring us her offbeat discoveries. One day, she bundled black currant branches on which buds had started to grow. We used them for steeping, smoking foods and making syrups. We even created a snow-white sorbet that tasted even more like black currant than the actual violet sorbet made from the fruit. Black currant branches eventually took another form in our Jar of Pigeon recipe.

DOG ROSE

Dog rose, or *rosa canina*, is a wild, thorny bush that grows on river banks close to Kamouraska, among other places. Its fruit, the rose hip, is like a small red apple, which has to be picked after the first autumn frosts—that's when you can tell whether or not it is ripe. It can be used in sauces, jams or juices.

SOIL

The link between quality soil and quality products is unde-niable. Rich earth yields good vegetables every time. Moreover, different types of production call for different varieties of earth. That's why the soil on which Denis Ferrer raises his *Cerfs de Boileau* must be fertile in order to give the animal appropriate conditions for healthy growth. When cooking, we sometimes use soil as an ingre-dient. By boiling and steeping acidic soil, we've managed to make caramel with a woody taste, not unlike maple syrup. Soil can also be used for cooking. During a nocturnal visit to Dianne's garden, the gang decided to place eggs in the campfire's embers so that they would be ready to eat the next morning. Back in the kitchen, we replicated this process by cooking eggs in a mixture of soil and branches and dried coriander.

CHICKEN

At Ferme le Crépuscule, Jean-Pierre Clavet raises organic chickens. He's a staunch ally—our association goes all the way back to the restaurant's beginnings. He loves to tell the story of our first meeting, when all our cooks started inspecting his chickens from every possible angle. At the time, we were already quite selective, especially for a product as common as chicken. His poultry has a unique taste, because he feeds his chicken soy for protein and corn for energy. In the last two years, he has added cranber-ries to their diet, having found that the fruit improves the quality of the meat, making it juicier and more flavourful. At the restaurant, we like to cook his chicken in a casserole with fir, herbs and citrus fruits.

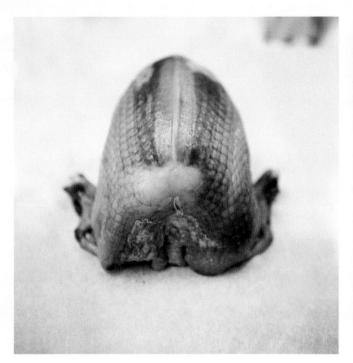

SQUAB PIGEON

MILK-FED PIGLET

While the Turlo and Miboulay farms with which we do business do not produce organic foods, they do farm sensibly. Their production is natural and does not in any way resemble poultry fattening. Because our climate is colder than Europe's, Quebec squabs are raised inside a large building rather than outdoors. This requires a good ventilation system as well as everything else growing pigeons need to fully develop, make their nests and feed: minerals, lime, oyster shells, corn, soy, etc. There is a hierarchy in the pigeon loft. A pigeon couple's power and influence over the other couples increases with the height of its nest. The male and female will keep the same nest throughout their lives. At birth, squabs need their parents' warmth, so the couple shares the incubation period. Squab meat is particularly tender due the fact that their muscles aren't called on much.

In Portugal, Spain and Latin America, milk-fed piglet is a fairly popular ancestral culinary tradition. Gaspor's production was inspired by the approach used for veal. It took the producer a year to work out a milking system similar to a sow's, but with a machine that could support the piglet. Restaurateurs were attentive throughout the research process. The piglet Gaspor supplies us is not genetically modified; instead, it comes from an understanding of the animal's morphology. The meat is very tasty, and in no way comparable to other types of pork you'll find on the market. Unlike pork meat, you can't see the fibre; the grain of the meat is dense, compact and juicy, and the fat we use to make our sausage stays as soft as butter. The milk-fed piglet's skin is fairly thin, making it crispy when cooked.

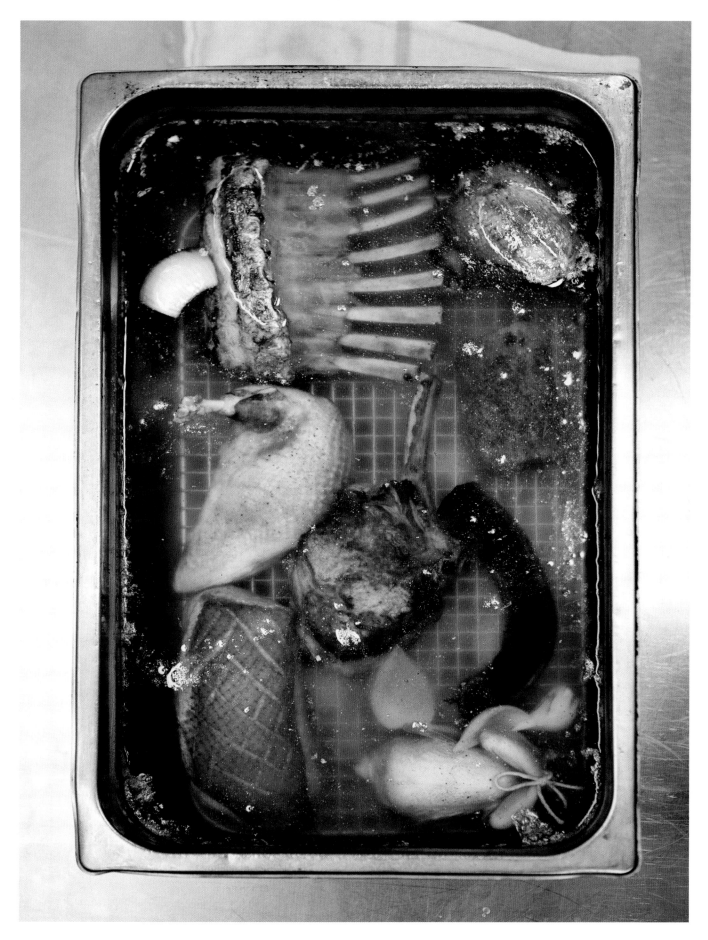

FOIE GRAS

Gavage was already being used by the ancient Egyptians, who, having noticed that geese livers grew larger before migration, force-fed them crushed grains. However, foie gras as we now know it comes from the south of France. Véronique Fleury, who was born in the Landes, is following the footsteps of her mother, who tube-fed ducks herself. When she arrived in Quebec in 1987, Véronique and her sisters-in-law founded Le Duc d'Albret, the first traditional gavage company in North America. In 1999, she went out on her own with La Canardière. The animal is respected throughout the tube-feeding process. The corn is precooked in scalding water and lightly oiled, with the dose gradually increasing to give the bird time to digest. The duck is then taken to the abattoir and delivered to *Toqué!* the very next day in order to keep the product as fresh as possible. As with our former supplier Mr. Delaunay, one of Quebec's foie gras pioneers, as well as products from Palmex farms with whom we collaborated for quite some time, this foie gras is sharp yellow and extremely savoury. It's a foie gras that doesn't lose that much volume when pan-fried. While it doesn't keep for very long, its taste is incomparable. Pan-fried foie gras is our reigning classic. We have always served it with seasonal fare.

CHEESES

Pierre-Yves Chaput made it possible for Normand to offer a broad selection of cheeses in the 1990s. He trained as a master cheesemaker in France before importing artisan French cheeses to Quebec. Consequently, we were able to serve authentic cheeses at *Citrus* from the outset. Pierre-Yves has a cellar where he ages his product. Not only did he help Quebeckers discover a host of cheeses, but he encouraged makers to develop local artisanal expertise. One such maker is Maurice Dufour. Over the past few years, he has succeeded in developing an extensive variety of first-rate cheeses in the Charlevoix County town of Baie Saint-Paul.

Despite the fact that Quebec artisans are continuing to hone their know-how, their products are rarely sold beyond our borders. Expanding into foreign markets requires large investments that, in most cases, only large businesses can afford. We believe it would be beneficial if the name of every cheese produced in Quebec was followed by the name of the region in which it was produced, as with the *Cheddar de l'Ile-aux-Grues* and the *Tomme de Brebis de Charlevoix*. Identifying cheeses in this manner increases traceability and, with it, food safety, as well as giving a measure of recognition to our producers.

SOME OF OUR CUSTOMERS HAVE BEEN WITH US SINCE OUR VERY FIRST DAY. EVER SINCE THEY MET NORMAND AT *CITRUS*, PIERRE AND CLAUDE HAVE BEEN LOYAL CUSTOMERS, COMING TO THE RESTAURANT EVERY THURSDAY NIGHT. WE NICKNAMED THEM MR. AND MRS. FOIE GRAS BECAUSE FOR THE LONGEST TIME, THEY'D ORDER THE DISH LIKE CLOCKWORK.

PIERRE : WE LOVE FOIE GRAS. WE USED TO EAT IT EVERY WEEK! CLAUDE : WE HAD IT AS AN APPETIZER AND A DESSERT. PIERRE : WHEN OUR MAIN COURSE WAS DONE, WE'D ASK OURSELVES, "WHAT WAS THE BEST PART?" AND IT WAS ALWAYS THE FOIE GRAS. CLAUDE : SO WE'D HAVE IT AGAIN TO FINISH OUR MEAL! PIERRE : IT WAS FOIE GRAS AND MORE FOIE GRAS! NOW, WE EAT IT LESS OFTEN, FOR HEALTH REASONS... CLAUDE : THOUGH WE STILL ORDER IT ONCE IN A WHILE, ESPECIALLY AT *TOQUÉ!*, WHERE THEY CONSTANTLY REINVENT IT. I REMEMBER PAN-FRIED FOIE GRAS SERVED WITH FIGS. WE ONCE CALCULATED THE AMOUNT OF FOIE GRAS WE HAD EATEN AT TOQUÉ!, AND IT CAME OUT TO MORE THAN 700 MEALS. PIERRE : THAT'S LIKE 1,000 DIFFERENT DISHES!

COCKTAILS

MEAD SLUSH COCKTAIL

SERVES 4
PREPARATION: 15 MIN
REST: 12 HRS

· 240 ml (8 oz) Blizz mead [TIP]
· 240 ml (8 oz) Marie-Clos rosé mead
· 8 saffron pistils

1 Pour the Blizz mead into a container and freeze overnight.

2 The next day, use a fork to rake the frozen mead into slush. Freeze the slush until you're ready to use it.

3 In freezer-chilled martini glasses, add 2 tbsp of slush, 2 saffron pistils and 60 ml (2 oz) of rosé mead.

TIP

+ Marie-Clos is raspberry mead, and the Blizz is semi-dry mead. Despite its alcohol content, mead (honey wine) can be frozen since it contains a lot of water. You can also make slush with sake (rice wine) or serve it on small, red fruit.

BEETS

BEET CRISPY CREAM WITH SMOKED SALMON EGGS

SERVES 4
PREPARATION: 15 MIN
COOKING: 45 MIN

- 2 crapaudine beets (an oblong, rough-skinned variety) or other type of red beet
- 120 g (½ cup) butter, melted
- Salt and freshly ground black pepper

Finishing Touches
- 125 ml (½ cup) 35 % fresh cream
- 30 ml (2 tbsp) green onion oil [P. 445]
- 2 tbsp beet caramel [P. 258]
- 90 g (3 oz) smoked salmon roe
- Some amaranth leaves
- A bit of bronze fennel

1 Cut the beets into thin slices (1 to 2 mm) with a mandoline.

2 Preheat the oven to 135°C (275°F). On a baking sheet lined with parchment paper, spread out the beets, brush on the butter, and season both sides. Cover with another sheet of parchment and bake for 45 minutes, flipping the slices every 15 minutes. Remove them from the oven when crispy.

Finishing Touches
3 Whip the cream until soft peaks form, and add salt and pepper to taste. Add the green onion oil and beet caramel and mix lightly to keep the marble effect.

4 On each plate, draw a line of cream, adding salmon roe, beet chips and herbs.

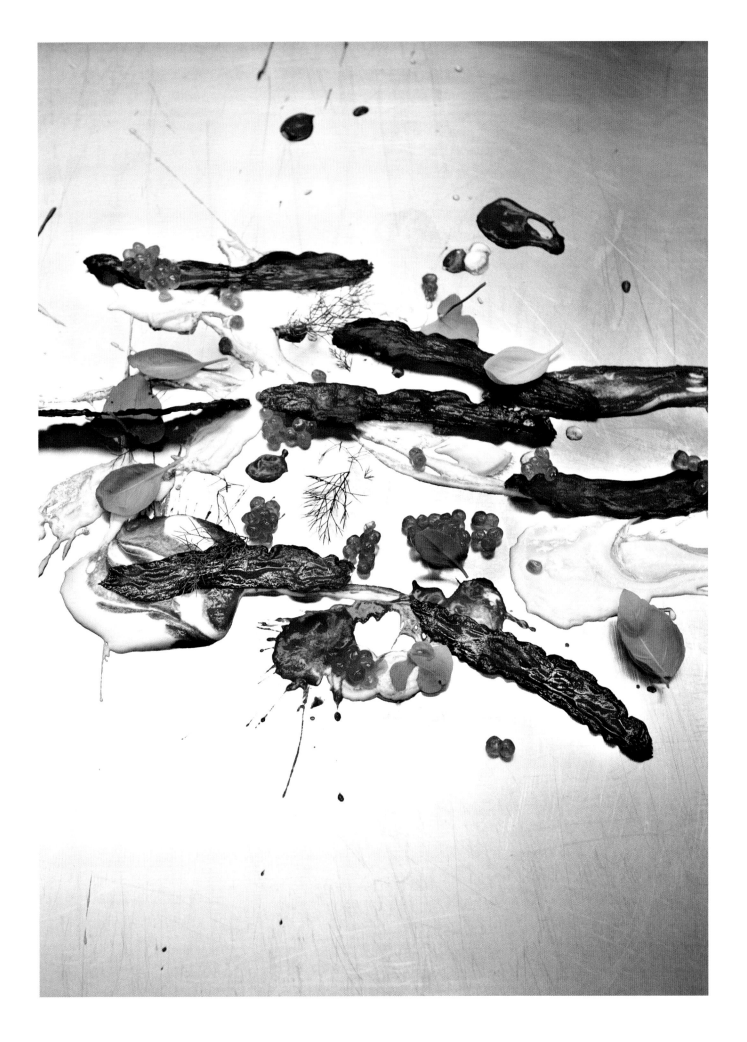

ANOTHER ROUND
FOR SAMUEL...

JULIEN GUILLOT
Gamay, Pinot noir
BOURGOGNE

CYRIL DUBREY
Merlot Noir, Cabernet Franc, Cabernet Sauvignon
BORDEAUX

The wines we pair with summer beets are different from those we pair with the autumn kind. The former are so sweet and pure-tasting that we treat them as fruit. With fall beets, however, we play more with the earthy, autumnal aspect of the root. It is essential that the evolution of the beet's taste be noted when matching it with a wine. The closer we are to fall, the more attention we pay to the wine's age.

DEPUIS 910

2010 PRODUIT DE FRANCE

Clos des vignes du Maynes

MÂCON CRUZILLE

APPELLATION MÂCON CRUZILLE CONTROLÉE

MANGANITE

MIS EN BOUTEILLE PAR JULIEN GUILLOT À SAGY 71260 CRUZILLE

PROPRIÉTAIRE RÉCOLTANT

VIN ISSU DE RAISINS DE L'AGRICULTURE BIOLOGIQUE
CERTIFIÉ PAR QUALITÉ FRANCE SA LE GUILLAUMET 92046 PARIS LA DÉFENSE

GRAND VIN DE GRAVES

1999   1999

CHÂTEAU MIREBEAU

PESSAC-LEOGNAN

APPELLATION PESSAC-LÉOGNAN CONTRÔLÉE

MIS EN BOUTEILLE AU CHÂTEAU   S.C.A. CH. D'ARDENNES EXPLOITANT
CYRIL DUBREY VIGNERON
À MARTILLAC (GIRONDE)
FRANCE

PRODUCT OF FRANCE · BORDEAUX

DELI MEATS

This *Brasserie T!* classic was inspired by a recipe for Toulouse sausage. We've added our own twist and renamed it "Montreal Sausage" as a way of clearly stating that the skills, know-how and products are from here. Although Quebec's cultural melting pot is part of our identity, protecting our heritage is of utmost importance.

MONTREAL SAUSAGE
À LA BRASSERIE T!

MAKES 10 SAUSAGES
PREPARATION: 45 MIN
DRYING: 24-48 HRS (OPTIONAL)
REST: 12 HRS

· 750 g (1½ lbs) pork shoulder and neck
· 300 g (10 oz) pork fat
· 6 tbsp white wine
· 100 g (3½ oz) duck gizzard confit, roughly diced
· 5 g (1 tsp) nitrite salt or 1 tbsp coarse salt
· 2 g (1 tsp) ground black pepper
· 1 hog casing

1 On the first day, roughly chop the meat and pork fat. Place the pieces in a large bowl, add the white wine, and marinate in the fridge overnight.

2 The following day, pass the meat and pork fat together though a meat grinder. Add the gizzard confit and the nitrite salt. Blend using a table mixer with a hook while adding the pepper.

3 Insert the sausage filler on the table mixer. Position the hog casing correctly, then make a knot at one end to keep the stuffing from sliding out. Pour in the stuffing, twisting the casing every 12 cm (5 in). Make another knot at the end of the last sausage.

4 Optional step: hang the sausages in the fridge and dry for 1 or 2 days.

Cooking

5 Fill a pot with cold water and, over medium heat, poach the sausages until the water starts to bubble. Remove from heat, leaving the sausages in the water for 5 minutes. Drain and refrigerate. Poaching lets you serve the sausages cold or pan-fried.

DELI MEATS

CHICKEN SKIN TERRINE

MAKES 1 TERRINE
PREPARATION: 1 HR
COOKING: 1:30 HRS

- 625 g (1¼ lbs) chicken skin
- 625 g (1¼ lbs) pork fat
- 200 g (½ cup) onions, finely chopped
- 2 tbsp olive oil
- 1 pale ale
- 5 g (1 tsp) nitrite salt
  or 1 tbsp coarse salt
- 2 g (1 tsp) ground black pepper
- 120 g (4 oz) pork caul fat

1 Mince the chicken skin in the meat grinder before cooking it in a pot over medium-low heat for approximately 15 minutes. Pass through a sieve, and keep the skin. Refrigerate the melted chicken fat for later use [TIP].

2 Put the pork fat through the meat grinder and mix it with the chicken skin.

3 In a frying pan over high heat, sweat the onions in olive oil for a few minutes. Pour in the beer. Once the mixture has reduced halfway, remove it from heat and allow to sit at room temperature.

4 Preheat the oven to 150°C (300°F), and place a double boiler inside.

5 Combine all the ingredients in a large bowl. Line the bottom of a terrine mould with the caul fat, letting it spill over on each side. Put the preparation into the mould, close the caul fat, and cut off the excess. Cook the terrine in the double boiler in the oven for approximately 1½ hours.

TIP
+ The melted chicken fat can be used to stir-fry vegetables.

DELI MEATS

HEAD CHEESE

MAKES 1 TERRINE
COOKING: 4 HRS
REST: 24 HRS

· 1 piglet head (preferably cut in two)

Cooking Stock

· 2 carrots
· 2 onions
· 1 bunch parsley
· 2 litres (8 cups) pork stock
· 5 litres (20 cups) water

Head Cheese

· 1 red pepper, diced
· 1 shallot, minced
· ½ bunch chives, minced
· Zest of 1 lemon
· Salt and freshly ground black pepper

Cooking Stock

1 Dice the vegetables into medium-sized cubes and place them in a pot before adding the remaining ingredients. Bring to a boil. Put the piglet head in the broth, and simmer over medium heat for 4 hours. Drain and let sit at room temperature.

2 Bone the head and refrigerate the meat, fat and rind before cutting everything into 1 cm (½ in) cubes. Set aside.

3 Filter the broth through a conical strainer, and reduce over medium heat until there is only 500 ml (2 cups) of liquid left. Let the liquid sit in the pot.

Head Cheese

4 Pour the hot broth into a bowl. Add the meat, fat and rind cubes, the red pepper, shallot, chives and lemon zest. Add salt and pepper to taste.

5 Cover the bottom of a terrine mould with plastic film and pour in the preparation. Refrigerate for 24 hours before serving.

CHICKEN

CHICKEN CASSEROLE

SERVES 4
PREPARATION: 30 MIN
COOKING: 1:30 HRS
REST: 2 HRS

Luting Paste
· 3 egg whites
· 80 ml (⅓ cup) water
· 450 g (3 cups) flour

Chicken Casserole
· 1 chicken, approximately 2 kg (4 lbs)
· 300 g (1 cup) coarse salt
· A few sprigs of thyme
· A few sprigs of fir
· 1 orange, quartered
· 1 lemon, quartered
· 375 g (3 cups) vegetable *mirepoix* (medium-diced carrots, leeks, onion and garlic), lightly browned
· 1 head garlic, cut into 4

Luting Paste
1 Install a hook on your table mixer. Mix all the ingredients together at medium speed. Roll the dough into a ball, wrap in plastic and refrigerate for 2 hours.

Chicken Casserole
2 Place the chicken in a large dish and cover with the coarse salt. Refrigerate for 2 hours. Rinse with cold water and pat dry.

3 Preheat the oven to 200°C (400°F). Stuff the chicken with the thyme and fir tree branches, citrus fruits, mirepoix and garlic. Tie the chicken well with string, and place it in a casserole dish. Use luting paste to form an airtight seal between the casserole and its lid, hence locking in the air and steam while the dish is cooking.

4 Bake for approximately 40 to 45 minutes per kilogram (1 kg = 2 lbs). Let the casserole sit at room temperature for 15 minutes before serving. Use a hammer and screwdriver to break the seal.

TIPS
+ You can substitute the casserole dish and lid with two same-sized, round-bottomed mixing bowls.

+ Reduce the cooking juices to make sauce.

QUAIL

SMOKED QUAIL

SERVES 4
PREPARATION: 1:30 HRS

· 4 whole quails

Seaweed Broth
· 15 g (½ oz) kombu seaweed
· 2 litres (8 cups) water
· 400 g (1⅔ cups) sugar
· 750 ml (3 cups) sake

Smoking
· A few branches of fir tree
· 1 cup smoking wood

Cooking
· Tub o' Duck Fat [P. 449]

Seaweed Broth

1 Preheat the oven to 170°C (340°F). In a pot over low heat, steep the seaweed in the sugar and water for approximately 15 minutes. Filter in a conical strainer. Mix the water infusion with the sake, and simmer over low heat.

2 Soak the quails in the broth for 10 seconds and then place them on a baking sheet. Bake for 5 minutes. Repeat this step two more times.

Smoking

3 Place the branches of fir tree and smoking wood in the smoker before lighting it. Smoke the hot quails for 15 to 20 minutes.

Cooking

4 Cook the quails in the Tub o' Duck Fat for 8 to 10 minutes. Let them sit at room temperature for 5 minutes before removing the supremes and legs from the torso (as with chicken). You can also serve the quails whole.

TIP
+ In *The Art of Living According to Joe Beef,* David McMillan and Frédéric Morin give excellent instructions on how to make a smoker.

QUAIL

QUAIL RUMP SALAD

MAKES 4 PORTIONS
PREPARATION: 45 MIN

· 12 quail rumps (rear cut of the quail that includes the legs)

Sauce
· 375 ml (1½ cups) honey
· 125 ml (½ cup) soy sauce
· 1½ tbsp lemon juice
· ½ tbsp sriracha sauce (Thai hot pepper sauce)
· 60 ml (¼ cup) olive oil
· 1 clove garlic, peeled
· 1 or 2 sprigs thyme, leaves only

Finishing Touches
· Seasonal salad

Sauce
1 In a bowl, stir all the ingredients together until homogenous in texture.

2 Preheat the oven to 190°C (375°F). Place the quail rumps on a grill set on a baking sheet. Brush on a third of the sauce. Bake for 10 minutes. Remove from the oven and again brush on a third of the sauce. Cook for 10 minutes and apply the remaining sauce. Cook for 10 more minutes.

Finishing Touches
3 Place the quail rumps on the salad just before serving.

QUAIL

QUAIL CONFIT

SERVES 4
PREPARATION: 30 MIN
COOKING: 15 MIN
REST: 1 HR

· 4 quails
· 1½ litres (6 cups) cold brine [P. 446]
· Tub o' Duck Fat [P. 449]
· 1 lemon, quartered
· 1 head garlic, crushed
· 2 sprigs thyme, cut in two

1 Soak the quails in the brine for 1 hour in the fridge.

2 In a pot, heat the duck fat to 80°C (175°F). Once drained, stuff the quails with the lemon, garlic and thyme. With their legs well tied, plunge the quails in the duck fat. Leave them in for approximately 15 minutes and then let them sit for a few minutes.

3 Serve whole or boned. If the quails are not quite cooked through, drizzle with 2 tbsp of duck fat and cook for a few more minutes in the oven (preheated to 180°C (350°F)).

TIP
+ This quail recipe is delicious with grapefruit syrup confit [P. 356].

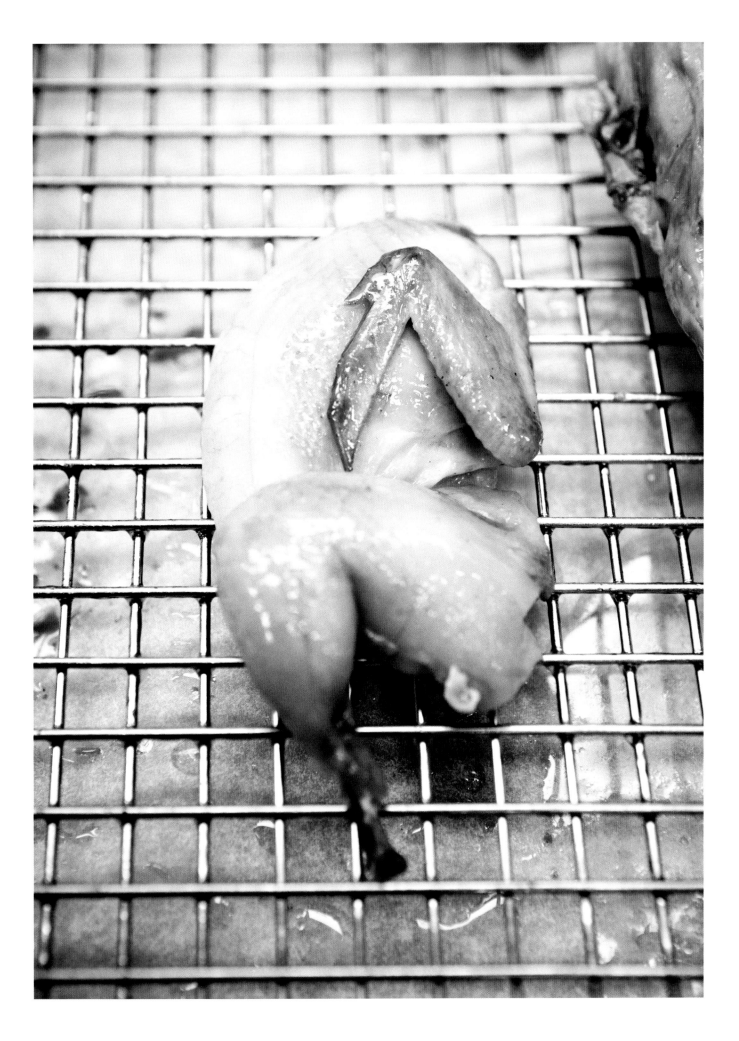

PIGEON

While filming *Well Done*, we stopped at a gas station in a small town on the Gaspé peninsula. The station had one of those machines that lets you buy toys and stuffed animals. We got Jigglypuff, a Pokemon character, who has since lived in our kitchen. One day, Charles-Antoine saw him in a spice jar, giving him the idea to cook pigeon using the concept of a lute-sealed pot. This became our Jar of Pigeon. We use spice jars when cooking casseroles; for bigger items, we use a pair of round-bottomed bowls, or *culs-de-poule*, which we seal with lute paste.

JAR OF PIGEON

SERVES 2
PREPARATION: 1 HR
REST: 2 HRS

· 2 × 1 litre (4 cup) jars with wide openings (e.g. Fido)

Luting Paste
· 3 egg whites
· 80 ml (⅓ cup) water
· 450 g (3 cups) flour

Pigeon
· 5 tbsp olive oil
· Peel of 1 orange
· Peel of 1 lemon
· A few branches (fir, thyme or black currant)
· 2 cloves garlic, crushed
· 60 ml (¼ cup) maple syrup
· Salt and freshly ground black pepper
· 2 pigeon torsos (without the legs), of approximately 250 g (9 oz) each

Luting Paste
1 Install a hook on your table mixer. Mix all the ingredients thoroughly at medium speed. Roll the dough into a ball, wrap in plastic and refrigerate for 2 hours.

Pigeon
2 In a hot frying pan over high heat, heat 2 tbsp of olive oil. Brown the orange and lemon peels, branches and cloves garlic. Divide into each jar and pour in equal amounts of maple syrup.

3 Season the pigeons. Place them in a hot frying pan and quickly brown over medium-high heat in the remaining olive oil. Put them in jars, and close the lids.

4 Preheat the oven to 200°C (400°F). Seal where the jar and lid meet with the luting paste. Place the jars on a baking sheet covered with a damp cloth and bake.

Cooking time
200-205 g = 10 minutes
205-215 g = 11 minutes
215-225 g = 13 minutes
225-240 g = 14 minutes
240-255 g = 15 minutes

5 Remove the jars from the oven, and let them sit unopened for 10 minutes before finally taking the pigeons out. Let the flavouring liquid drip off and keep the cooking juices. Plate the pigeon supremes. Cover them with the saved liquid. Serve immediately.

FOIE GRAS

PRESSED FOIE GRAS

MAKES 1 TERRINE
PREPARATION: 30 MIN
REST: 24 HRS

· 1 whole lobe of foie gras,
  approximately 625 g (1¼ lbs)
· 1 tsp salt
· 1 tsp sugar
· Ground black pepper

1 Line a terrine mould with plastic wrap, with excess on every side. Cut a piece of cardboard the shape of the mould, to be placed on the foie gras later.

2 Cut the lobe of foie gras lengthwise into slices approximately 2 cm (¾ in) thick, and carefully devein.

3 Preheat the oven to 95°C (200°F). Place the foie gras slices on a grill set on a baking sheet. Add the salt and sugar mixture and pepper to taste. Bake for approximately 10 minutes, until the foie gras starts to render its fat.

4 Lay the pieces of foie gras in the mould, making sure making sure no air pockets remain. Seal the plastic wrap, cover the mould with the piece of cardboard, and lay a weight (not too heavy) over it. Refrigerate overnight.

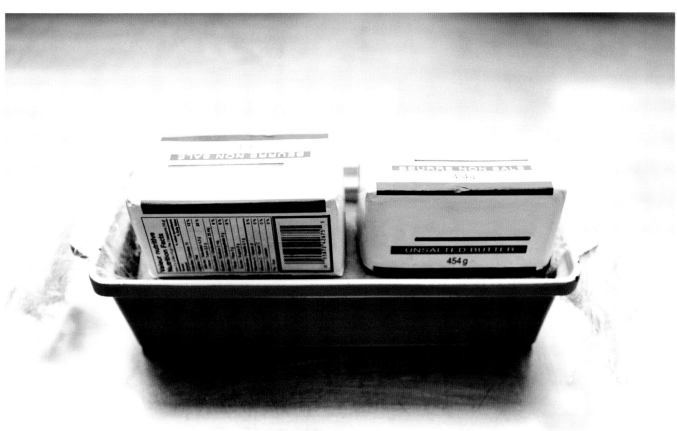

FOIE GRAS

*Our thanks to Anne-Sophie Pic
for this grapefruit recipe.*

SERVES 4
PREPARATION: 45 MIN
GRAPEFRUIT CONFIT: 5 DAYS
DRESSING REST TIME: 12 HRS

Grapefruit Confit

· 4 grapefruits, thoroughly washed
· 2 litres (8 cups) water
· 2 kg (4 lbs) sugar
· 5 × 480 g (2 cups) sugar

Grapefruit Caramel

· 10 unpeeled grapefruits
· 4 tbsp honey

Brandy and Black Truffle Dressing

· 125 ml (½ cup) brandy
· 60 ml (¼ cup) honey
· 4 tbsp black truffle, cut into pieces
· 250 ml (1 cup) grape seed oil
· Salt

Sautéed Endives with Peanuts

· 4 tbsp unsalted peanuts
· 2 red endives
· 2 white endives
· 1 tbsp olive oil
· 1 tbsp brandy
· 1 tbsp maple syrup
· Salt and freshly ground black pepper

Finishing Touches

· 200 g (7 oz) Pressed Foie Gras [P. 354]
· 1 grapefruit, peeled and cut into wedges
· Pieces of day-old sweet roll
· 1 shallot, finely minced
· 1 tbsp fir powder [P. 443]

Grapefruit Confit

1 Poke each grapefruit 50 times with a toothpick. Pour the water into a pot, add the grapefruits and boil. Cook for 2 minutes. Allow them to cool in the cooking water.

2 In another pot over medium heat, melt 2 kg (4 lbs) of sugar in the grapefruits' cooking water until a syrup forms. Cut the grapefruits in half and add them to the syrup. Simmer for 30 minutes. Refrigerate for 24 hours.

3 The following day, remove the grapefruits from the syrup, add 480 g (2 cups) of sugar and bring to a boil. Pour the scalding hot syrup on the grapefruits. Let everything cool to room temperature and refrigerate for 24 hours. In all, you must carry out this step once a day for 5 consecutive days.

Grapefruit Caramel

4 Press the juice from the 10 grape-fruits and pour it through a conical strainer. In a pot over low heat, reduce the juice with honey until syrupy. Set aside.

Brandy and Black Truffle Dressing

5 Stir together the brandy, honey and truffle pieces. Mix with a hand blender, adding grape seed oil to thicken the dressing. Salt to taste and refrigerate for at least 12 hours to let the taste of truffle soak in.

Sautéed Endives with Peanuts

6 In a frying pan over medium heat, roast the peanuts, then set them aside. Sear the endives in olive oil and deglaze with brandy. Flambé and add maple syrup. Add salt and pepper to taste. Place in a bowl and mix in the peanuts.

Finishing Touches

7 Cut the grapefruit confit into wedges and the Pressed Foie Gras into thin slivers. Cut the sweet rolls into chunks, and burn with a torch.

8 Put endives on each plate, add the grapefruit confit and fresh grapefruit wedges, shallots, foie gras slivers and burnt sweet roll. Drizzle with grapefruit caramel and truffle dressing and sprinkle with fir powder.

FOIE GRAS

SEARED FOIE GRAS, H₂O, RHUBARB AND STRAWBERRIES

SERVES 4
PREPARATION: 2 HRS

Rhubarb Water
· 6 rhubarb sticks, roughly chopped
· 1 tbsp honey

Strawberry and Red Pepper Water
· 4 red peppers
· 250 g (8 oz) strawberries, in quarters
· 2 tbsp honey

Strawberry and Red Pepper Jelly
· 2½ gelatin sheets

Daikon Confit
· 1 medium-sized daikon radish, peeled
· 120 g (½ cup) sugar
· 500 ml (2 cups) water

Acidic Mix
· 5 g (1 tsp) citric acid powder
· 2 g (1 tsp) long pepper
· 1 tbsp organic sugar

Foie Gras
· 4 foie gras slices, 75 g (2½ oz) each
· Salt

Finishing Touches
· A few strawberries, cut into pieces
· A few flowers (borage and pansies)
· 2 tbsp tarragon oil [P. 449]

Rhubarb Water
1 Juice the rhubarb in a juicer. Bring to a boil with the honey in a pot over medium-high heat. Strain through a coffee filter and set aside.

Strawberry and Red Pepper Water
2 Juice the red pepper in a juicer. Bring to a boil in a pot over medium-high heat. Pour through a coffee filter.

3 In a pot, pour the still-hot pepper juice on the strawberries and honey. Cover and simmer over medium heat for 5 minutes. Turn off the heat, and let sit for 5 minutes. Run through a sieve without pressing the fruit: we want clear water without pulp. Refrigerate 250 ml (1 cup) of the flavoured water and keep the rest for later use.

Strawberry and Red Pepper Jelly
4 Bloom the gelatin in ice water. In a pot, boil the strawberry and red pepper water previously set aside.

5 Drain, and mix well with the hot strawberry and red pepper water. Refrigerate.

Daikon Confit
6 Cut the daikon into slices 1 cm (½ in) thick. Sprinkle the sugar in the bottom of a saucepan. Place the daikon over the sugar making sure the slices do not touch each other. Pour in water and cook over low heat for 30 minutes, until the daikon is tender. Let them cool to room temperature.

Acidic Mix
7 In a coffee grinder, crush all the ingredients into a powder and set aside.

Foie Gras
8 Preheat the oven to 190°C (375°F). Salt the foie gras slices. In a hot, non-stick frying pan over very high heat (without fat), sear the slices on both sides. Place the foie gras (without fat) on a baking sheet and cook for 1 to 2 minutes, until tender.

Finishing Touches
9 Pour the rhubarb water into soup plates, centre the daikon confit in each, and circle the confit with strawberries, flowers, and cubes of strawberry and red pepper jelly. Add a splash of tarragon oil. Top the daikon with foie gras. Add a little acidic mix to one side of the dish so you can add a pinch on each bite of foie gras as you eat.

FOIE GRAS

SERVES 4
PREPARATION: 1 HR

Foie Gras
· 2 g (1 tsp) cumin seeds
· 100 g (3½ oz) Pressed Foie Gras
[P. 354]

Caramel
· 3 tbsp water
· 120 g (½ cup) sugar
· 60 ml (¼ cup) glucose
· 10 g (2 tsp) butter, room temperature

Foie Gras

1 In a frying pan over medium-high heat, roast the cumin seeds for a few seconds until they're lightly browned. Reduce to a powder with a pestle and mortar.

2 Cut the foie gras into 4 cm × 6 cm (1½ in × 2⅓ in) cubes and set aside.

Caramel

3 In a pot over medium heat, add water, sugar and glucose in turn. Melt the sugar, lower the heat, and cook to a temperature of 145°C (203°F). Turn off the heat and add the butter. Stir quickly, and then immediately pour the mixture onto a silicone baking mat. Let the mixture set before breaking it up and reducing it to a fine powder in a food processor.

4 Preheat the oven to 180°C (350°F). Place a silicone baking mat on a baking sheet and spread with caramel powder in strips 4 cm (1½ in) wide. Melt them in the oven for 1 to 2 minutes. Slide the mat off the baking sheet, and cover with parchment paper. Flatten the caramel with a rolling pin.

5 Once the caramel has cooled completely, bake it again at 180°C (350°F) for 30 seconds. Use a very sharp knife to cut 5 cm × 7 cm (2 in x 2¾ in) squares. Keep the caramel squares at room temperature in an airtight container, separated by parchment paper.

6 When serving, put a slice of chilled foie gras on a metal sheet. Add a pinch of cumin and a caramel square. Quickly melt the caramel with a torch so it coats the foie gras nicely.

TIP
+ Before serving appetizers, prepare bite-sized Pressed Foie Gras cubes, which you can sprinkle with grated smoked herring to add a smoky flavour. You can also serve Caramel Foie Gras as a dessert with red berry salad.

FOIE GRAS

Foie Gras Tissot is one of the dishes that came out of a good bottle of wine. During an event we were attending with our friend and Jura winemaker Stéphane Tissot, he brought us a Savagnin wine with a light smoky personality. It's an assemblage of several different grape varieties that was just asking for this pairing. Wines like this one give us the opportunity to riff on several eccentric notes such as burnt, acidic and smoky.

FOIE GRAS TISSOT

SERVES 4
PREPARATION: 45 MIN

Liquid Apple Jelly

· 5 or 6 Cortland apples, quartered without removing peel or seeds
· 1 litre (4 cups) water
· Yellow pectin powder
· Sugar
· Lemon juice

Acidic Cumin

· 2 g (1 tsp) cumin seeds
· 5 g (1 tsp) citric acid powder
· 5 g (1 tsp) salt
· 1 tbsp sugar

Finishing Touches

· 250 g (8 oz) Pressed Foie Gras [P. 354]
· A variety of fruit chips [DRY SALAD, P. 276]
· A few strawberries, halved
· 2 tbsp argan oil

Liquid Apple Jelly

1 In a pot over low heat, cook the apples in water for 20 minutes. Pour into a coffee filter, and keep the juice.

2 Measure the amount of juice you get before you pour it into a pot. Use a ratio of 20 g (⅔ oz) of pectin and 300 g (1¼ cups) sugar for every 1 litre (4 cups) of juice. Boil the juice with the required amount of pectin. Mixing well, gradually add the sugar and cook until it has completely dissolved. Reduce by a third, then refrigerate until ready to serve. Tweak the jelly's consistency with lemon juice to get a smooth, velvety purée.

Acidic Cumin

3 In a pan over medium-high heat, roast the cumin seeds for a few seconds until they're lightly browned, then use a coffee grinder to reduce all the ingredients to a powder.

Finishing Touches

4 Place your knife under running warm water to heat the blade. Cut the foie gras into 1 cm (½ in) thick slices. On each slice, put 1 tbsp liquid apple jelly, a mix of fruit chips and strawberries. Sprinkle lightly with the cumin mix and add a few drops of argan oil.

TIP

+ When preparing the liquid apple jelly, you can take what's left in the sieve and press it in a conical strainer. Add sugar and reduce to a purée. Throwing in a few sticks of butter while the purée is still hot gives you apple butter.

ANOTHER ROUND
FOR SAMUEL...

GIULIO ARMANI
*Malvasia di Candia aromatica, Marsanne, Ortugo,
unidentified indigenous grape varieties*
EMILIA-ROMAGNA

While the tendency is to serve foie gras with sweet, mellow wines, at *Toqué!* we pair it with dry whites instead. Foie gras is very versatile and therefore goes well with a pretty wide range of wines: smooth, tannic reds or powerful whites. We nearly always favour big, generous white wines with pleasing depth and a rich, powerful taste. On occasion, we'll select wines with oxidative characteristics, such as *vins jaunes* (yellow wines). For some time now, we have also been opting for macerated whites, a process that enables winemakers to release the tannins, polyphenols and many aromas contained in the grape's skin. Such wines are found most commonly in Italy and Slovenia. They're so powerful you can barely drink them on their own; you have to couple them with a hearty dish. With foie gras, such tannic wines gain in power and aroma. Examples include Denavolo wines (Emilia Romagna, Italy), Frank Cornelissen Munjebel Bianco (Sicily, Italy) or Radikon (Julian March, Italy).

DINAVOLINO

VINO BIANCO

PRODOTTO ALL'ORIGINE DA AZAGR · DENAVOLO · RIVERGARO · ITALIA
CONTAINS SULFITES · CONTIENE SOLFITI · CONTIENT SULFITES · ENTHALT SULFITE
℮ 75 cl PRODOTTO IN ITALIA L 10 11,5% vol

BEEF

BEEF ROSSINI WITH FLOWERS AND BERRIES

SERVES 4
PREPARATION: 30 MIN
COOKING: 15 MIN
REST: 12 HRS

Fir Beef

· 4 pieces beef tenderloin, approximately 150 g (5 oz) each
· 50 g (½ cup) balsam fir powder [P. 443]
· 3 tbsp fir-flavoured Maldon salt [P. 443]; coarse grind
· 2 tbsp extra virgin olive oil
· 2 tbsp butter
· Tub o' Duck Fat [P. 449]

Finishing Touches

· 80 ml (⅓ cup) raspberry oil [P. 263]
· 4 tbsp bordelaise sauce [P. 450], heated
· 100 g (3½ oz) pressed foie gras, in slivers [P. 354]
· 80 ml (⅓ cup) smoked fat and berries (raspberries, black currants, red currants)
· A few flowers (chervil, marigold, calendula, daylily, beebalm)

Fir Beef

1 Cover the beef tenderloins with the fir powder preparation. Wrap them separately in plastic, making a sausage. Refrigerate for 12 hours. Remove the wrap to cook, add fir-flavoured Maldon salt, and let the preparation sit at room temperature for 15 to 20 minutes.

2 In a large frying pan, heat the olive oil with butter until it is hot and frothy. Sear the meat on both sides, then submerge it in the Tub o' Duck Fat for 8 to 12 minutes until cooked to preference. Let it sit for a few minutes.

Finishing Touches

3 Trace a line of raspberry oil on the plates, and place a very hot portion of meat, sliced in half, on top. Dress with bordelaise sauce, and garnish with pressed foie gras slivers.

4 Scatter a few flowers and some of the berries prepared in smoked fat [P. 448] over the dish. Serve immediately.

TIP
+ You can replace beef with venison.

ANOTHER ROUND
FOR SAMUEL...

LUCA ROAGNA
Nebbiolo
PIEDMONT

Fir, liquorice and anise are all in the same aromatic range. We like to match these aromas with wines of the Piedmont Nebbiolo variety, such as Barbaresco and Barolo. The remarkably powerful tannins of a Nebbiolo wine are polished by the taste of blood found in meats such as beef, duck or pigeon, which are served quite rare. By cutting the tannins, we bring these wines' fat, round qualities to the fore. What's more, Nebbiolo wines have a slight liquorice flavour, which we play with by adding herbs such as bronze fennel or anise to the sauces we serve with our meats.

VENISON

SERVES 4
PREPARATION: 1 HR
COOKING: 3 HRS

Cabbage Chips

· 1 tbsp coarse salt
· The 15 best outer cabbage leaves
· 250 ml (1 cup) olive oil
· Salt

Dog Rose Purée

· 1 kg (4 cups) dog rose berries
· 500 ml (2 cups) water
· 120 g (¼ cup) honey
· 125 ml (½ cup) chardonnay vinegar

Venison

· 4 venison ribs, 200 g (7 oz) each, with bones, or 4 loins, 150 g (5 oz) each
· Salt and freshly ground black pepper
· Tub o' Duck Fat [P. 449]
· 2 tbsp butter

Finishing Touches

· 125 ml (½ cup) bordelaise sauce
[P. 443]

Cabbage Chips

1 Preheat the oven to 120°C (250°F).

2 In a large pot, boil water and add the coarse salt. Cut the cabbage leaves on either side of their ribs, keeping only the thin leafy part. Blanch the leaves in boiling water for 4 minutes or until quite tender. Drip-dry the leaves on absorbent paper. Brush olive oil on both sides, and then lay them out on baking sheets lined with parchment paper.

3 Bake the cabbage leaves for 2 hours, flipping them every 30 minutes. The chips must be translucent and dry on both sides. They should be crispy once cooled. Store in a dry place.

Dog Rose Purée

4 Fill the sink with cold water and wash the dog rose berries twice before removing their stems. In a large, thick-bottomed pot, simmer the berries in water for approximately 30 minutes, stirring often until the fruits burst. Remove from the heat and let sit at room temperature. Drain with a sieve, pressing the berries with a ladle to fully extract the pulp and juice.

5 In a pot over low heat, froth the honey without colouring it. Add the vinegar and dog rose berry pulp. Stir the mixture well and reduce by half over low heat (the preparation will thicken while reducing. The more you reduce, the more you lose the bright red colour of the berries). Put a little purée on a cold plate to check its texture. If it coats well, it's ready. Taste, and add honey as needed, keeping in mind that it will further thicken the purée. When you're happy with the taste and consistency, purée the mixture in a blender until smooth.

Venison

6 In a very hot pan, sear the meat in frothy butter. Let it sit, covered, for 5 minutes.

7 Let the meat sit at room temperature for 20 minutes. Add salt and pepper to taste. Cook in the Tub o' Duck Fat for 8 minutes.

Finishing Touches

8 Preheat the oven on broil. On a baking sheet, sear the meat for approximately 1 minute, throwing on a few spoonfuls of duck fat. Serve each portion with 2 tbsp of dog rose purée, a little bordelaise sauce and some cabbage chips.

VENISON

VENISON TONGUE SASHIMI

SERVES 4
PREPARATION: 1 HR
COOKING: 1:30 HRS
REST: 12 HRS

Sashimi

· 2 venison tongues
· 1 L (4 cups) brine [P. 446]
· 500 g (4 cups) vegetable *mirepoix* (medium-diced carrots, leeks, onion and garlic)
· 250 g (8 oz) bacon, 2 mm thick slices
· Grape seed oil

Salad

· ½ celeriac, julienned
· A few green onions, cut diagonally
· 2 tbsp olive oil
· 2 tbsp rice vinegar
· 1 tbsp honey
· Salt and freshly ground black pepper

Finishing Touches

· 1 tbsp organic sugar
· 60 ml (¼ cup) vegetable glaze [P. 450]
· 25 ml (5 tsp) green onion oil [P. 445]
· 30 g (¼ cup) popcorn powder [P. 448]
· 1 small, sautéed leek

Sashimi

1 Put the venison tongues in the brine and refrigerate for 12 hours.

2 The next day, preheat the oven to 200°C (400°F). Drain the tongues and put them in a pot with the mirepoix. Cover with water (to twice their height) and bring to a simmer.

3 Place the pot in the oven and cook for approximately 1½ hours (the skin comes off when the tongues are ready). Peel the hot tongues and refrigerate in the cooking stock.

4 Cut the tongues into thin slices (approximately 2 mm thick), length-wise. Alternate between tongue and bacon slices (3 or 4 of each), and lay them in a rectangular shape on parchment paper slightly moistened with grape seed oil. Refrigerate.

Salad

5 In a large bowl, mix the celeriac and green onions. In a small bowl, mix the olive oil, rice vinegar and honey. Drizzle the dressing on the salad. Add salt and pepper to taste.

Finishing Touches

6 Turn out the tongue and bacon onto a plate. Sprinkle with sugar and caramelize with a torch.

7 Garnish the sashimi with vegetable glaze and green onion oil and dust with popcorn powder. Serve with the salad and sautéed leek.

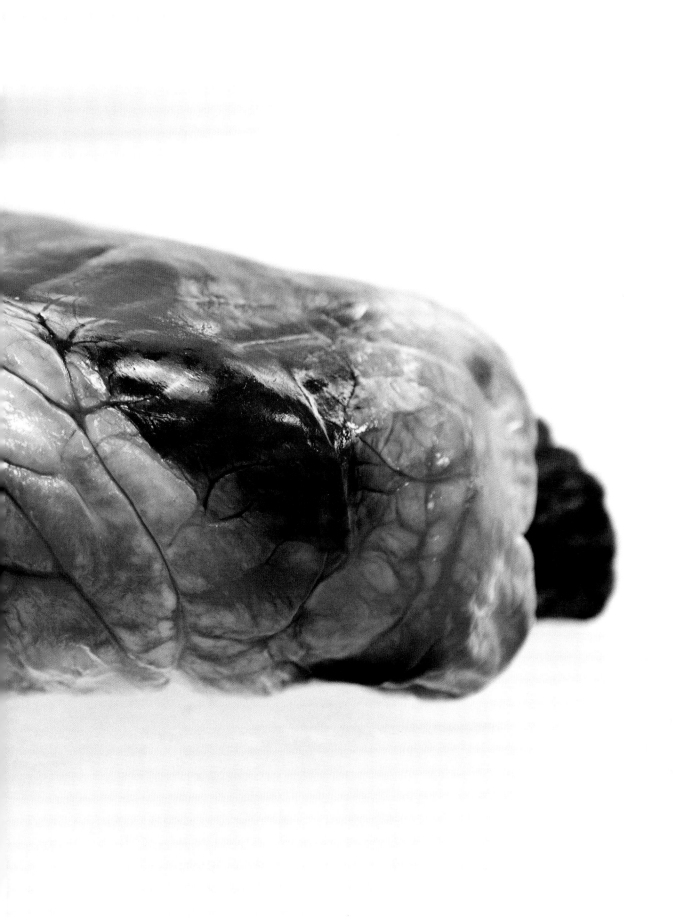

VENISON

VENISON HEART

SERVES 4
PREPARATION: 30 MIN

· 1 venison heart
· 120 g (½ cup) salt
· 250 g (1 cup) duck fat
· 1 fir tree branch
· 1 head garlic, crushed

1 Clean the venison heart by removing the excess fat and large veins. Put the heart in a dish and cover evenly with salt. Refrigerate for 30 minutes and then rinse with cold water.

2 In a pot over medium heat, heat the duck fat with the fir tree branch until it's nice and hot.

3 Put the venison heart in a baking dish and cover evenly with very hot duck fat. Let it sit at room temperature for 30 minutes. Take the heart out of the fat and cut into thin slices. Serve lukewarm on a salad.

TIP

+ We feel it tastes best when cooked medium-rare. If you use beef heart, double the quantities and cooking times.

VENISON

DAYLILY SALAD WITH VENISON HEART, CALAMARI

SERVES 4
PREPARATION: 30 MIN

Seaweed Mix

· 9 g (3 tsp) seaweed powder
· 9 g (3 tsp) roasted sesame seeds
· 9 g (3 tsp) Maldon salt

Daylily Salad

· 15 leafless daylily shoots
· 5 g (125 ml) plain popcorn
· 30 g (¼ cup) wild leek bulbs, sliced thinly
· 30 g (¼ cup) green onions, cut diagonally
· 60 ml (¼ cup) olive oil
· 60 ml (¼ cup) chardonnay vinegar

Venison Heart and Calamari

· 120 g (4 oz) venison heart confit in duck fat [P. 448]
· 120 g (4 oz) calamari heads, sliced very thinly
· Salt and freshly ground black pepper
· 3 tbsp olive oil

Finishing Touches

· 60 ml (¼ cup) red pepper purée [P. 66]
· 60 ml (¼ cup) Herbalicious [P. 445]
· 2 tbsp seaweed mixture

Seaweed Mix

1 Pulse the ingredients together in a coffee grinder. Repeat 2 more times. (If the grinder is too small, pulse portions of the spices together. The end result mustn't be too fine; the sesame seeds must remain almost whole.)

Daylily Salad

2 In a bowl, mix the daylily shoots, popcorn, wild leek and green onions. Add olive oil, vinegar and 9 g (3 tsp) of seaweed mixture. Blend well and set aside.

Venison Heart and Calamari

3 Remove the venison heart confit from the duck fat. Slice it thinly and keep at room temperature.

4 Season the calamari. Pan-fry in a little olive oil over high heat for 30 seconds.

Finishing Touches

5 Add the calamari to the daylily salad and toss. Add the venison heart and mix well. On each plate, portion out the Herbalicious mixture, salad, pepper purée and remaining seaweed mixture.

PIGLET

ROAST PIGLET BELLY
WITH HOT SHRIMP
AND ENDIVE SALAD

SERVES 4
PREPARATION: 1:15 HRS
COOKING: 4 HRS
REST: 2 HRS

Piglet Belly

· One 500 g (1 lb) piglet belly
· 250 g (1 cup) salt
· 2 tbsp olive oil

Maple Sauce

· 4 tbsp yellow or hot dog mustard
· 125 ml (½ cup) maple syrup
· 2 tbsp chardonnay vinegar
· 2 tbsp olive oil
· Salt and freshly ground black pepper

Honey Dressing

· 3 tbsp rice vinegar
· 1 tbsp honey

Finishing Touches

· 2 tbsp olive oil
· 2 endives, leaves only
· 120 g (½ cup) Matane shrimp
· Wild daisy shoots or arugula
· A few green onions, cut diagonally

Piglet Belly

1 In a dish, cover the piglet belly evenly with salt and refrigerate for 2 hours. Rinse with cold water and pat dry.

2 Preheat the oven to 160°C (325°F). Set a grill in a dripping pan, and add enough water to cover the bottom. Place the belly on the grill but make sure it doesn't touch the water. Cover with aluminum foil, and cook for 3 hours. Let it cool to room temperature between 2 sheets of parchment paper. Place a weight on top.

3 Preheat the oven to 200°C (400°F). Place the belly (skin facing down) in a non-stick, ovenproof frying pan coated with olive oil. Place a weight on top (e.g. another frying pan) to ensure the meat gets nice and crispy. Bake for 45 minutes and set aside.

Maple Sauce

4 In a bowl, combine all the ingredients and set aside.

Honey Dressing

5 Combine the ingredients and set aside.

Finishing Touches

6 In a frying pan over high heat, heat the olive oil and quickly sauté the endives so they're hot but not browned. Place them in a bowl and top with honey dressing. Add the shrimp, daisy shoots and green onions, and mix well before you put some on each plate. Add slices of pork and drizzle with maple sauce.

TIP

+ Cut the pork with a bread knife with the skin side on the cutting board.

SOIL

Basically, earth caramel is all about infusion. We start by clarifying the earth before drying it and infusing it.

SMOKED SWEET

SERVES 4 TO 6
REFRIGERATE 1:30 HRS
PREPARATION: 4 DAYS (EARTH CARAMEL)

Earth Caramel
· 1 bag of earth [TIP]
· 1 litre (4 cups) water
· 80 g (¼ cup) glucose
· 900 g (3¾ cups) sugar
· 250 ml (1 cup) water

Smoked Sorbet
· 3 gelatin sheets
· 375 ml (3 cups) water
· 200 ml (¾ cup + 4 tsp) simple syrup [P. 448]
· 100 ml (⅓ cup + 4 tsp) smoked water (to make smoked water, save the melted ice water in the smoked cream recipe; [MOCK SMOKED SALMON, P. 138].)

Cocoa Nougatine
· 7 tbsp water
· 300 g (1¼ cup) sugar
· 70 g (¾ cup) cocoa powder
· 100 g (3½ oz) roasted hazelnuts, roughly chopped
· 100 g (3½ oz) roasted pistachios, roughly chopped
· 100 g (3½ oz) roasted almonds, roughly chopped

Chocolate Sauce
· 75 g (2½ oz) Valrhona Caraibe chocolate
· 75 g (2½ oz) Valrhona Manjari chocolate
· 7 tbsp milk
· 200 ml (¾ cup + 4 tsp) 35 % cream

Earth Caramel
1 Preheat the oven to 180°C (350°F). In a pot, boil the earth and water for approximately 10 minutes, until pulp stops forming. Skim the surface with a skimmer, and spread this pulp on a baking sheet. Leave it in the oven until the earth dries out.

2 Place a coffee filter in a bowl and let the mixture drip through overnight. Repeat the same steps every day for 4 consecutive days.

3 Refrigerate the earth and water in separate containers. Sift the preparation to dry the earth. Keep the larger pieces to make 3 packets with 3 layers each of muslin (like tea bags).

4 In a pot over medium heat, let the packets of earth simmer along with the other ingredients and 250 ml (1 cup) of chilled earth water, reducing the mixture by two thirds.

5 Pull the packets from the pot. Reduce the preparation by half, until it reaches 135°C (275°F) and has a caramel-like texture. Keep at room temperature.

Smoked Sorbet

6 Bloom the gelatin in a bowl of cold water and drain. Boil the water in a pot before dissolving the gelatin in it. Pour this mixture in a bowl an add the simple syrup and smoked water. Once lukewarm, process it in an ice cream maker and freeze.

Cocoa Nougatine

7 In a pot, heat water and sugar to 145°C (293°F) until it has a clear caramel colour. Turn off the heat, add cocoa powder and mix well, before stirring in the roughly cut hazelnuts, pistachios and almonds with a spatula. Pour immediately onto a baking sheet and cool to room temperature. Once set, break it into small pieces and reduce to a granular powder in the food processor. Set aside in a dry place.

Chocolate Sauce

8 Put the two chocolates in a bowl. Bring the milk and cream to a boil and pour immediately onto the chocolate. Whisk.

Finishing Touches

9 Serve a scoop of smoked sorbet on a splash of nougatine to help it hold. Top with lukewarm chocolate sauce, which will harden on the sorbet, forming a shell. Garnish with earth caramel to taste.

TIPS

+ It's extremely important to use top quality soil. The best is acidic soil found near coniferous trees. Make sure it was not in contact with inedible elements.

+ You can use cocoa nougatine to garnish ice cream, cakes and profiteroles.

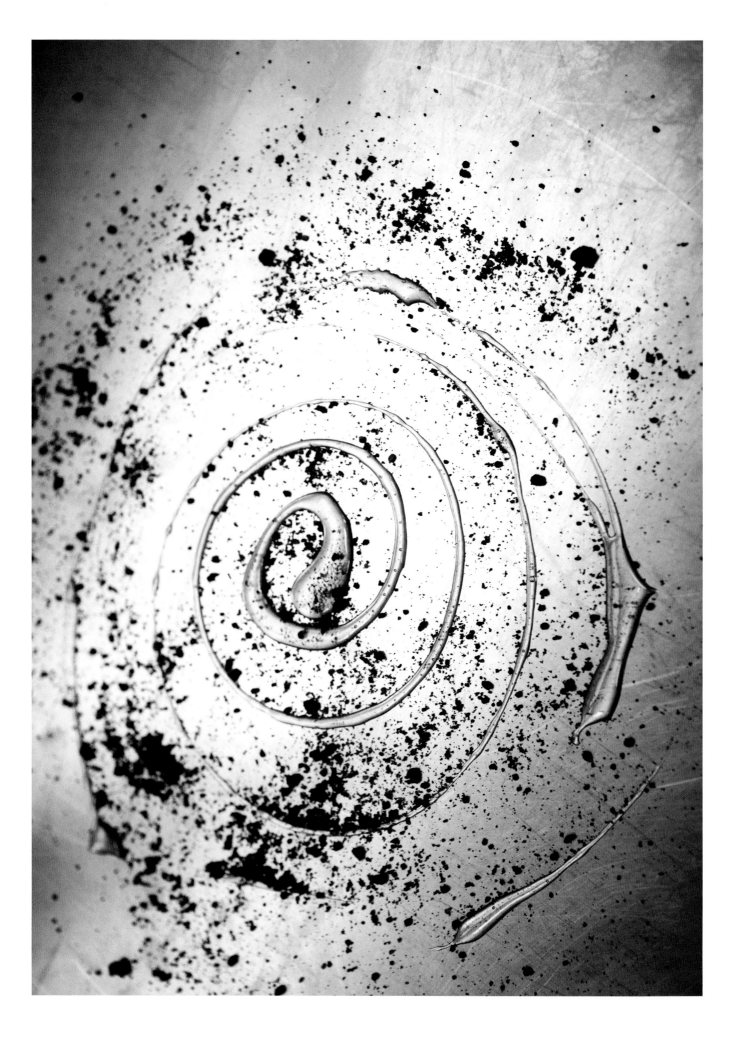

TRUFFLES

Truffles are among the few foods we import. Quality truffles are firm and dark-skinned and have a powerful aroma. Anne-Sophie Pic, owner and chef at the Maison Pic in Valence, introduced us to Mr. Ayme's truffles. We've been ordering his truffles since. We generally use truffles raw, cutting them into thin slices with an eye to keeping them as flavourful as possible. These slices must be crisp when you bite into them. We use the trimmings or less attractive truffles in various preparations. The earthy taste unique to this mushroom goes well with eggs, white fish, scallops, beets and cavatelli pasta.

BONE MARROW SALAD WITH TRUFFLES

SERVES 4
PREPARATION: 1:30 HRS

Bone Marrow
· 4 marrow bones, cut in two lengthwise (ask the butcher)

Salad
· 2 tbsp olive oil
· ½ Lebanese cucumber, roughly cut
· 1 shallot, fine-cut
· 4 tbsp olive oil bread [P. 446]
· 1 tbsp Dijon mustard
· 1 tbsp aged balsamic vinegar
· A few thin truffle slices

Finishing Touches
· 125 ml (½ cup) bordelaise sauce [P. 443]
· 100 g (3½ oz) parmesan cheese, freshly grated

Bone Marrow
1 Place the marrow bones in a bowl of cold water to soak overnight in the fridge.

2 The following day, preheat the oven to 180°C (350°F). Drain and cook the bones on a baking sheet. Lay the bones on an aluminium rack with the marrow facing upwards for approximately 10 minutes. Cook until the marrow comes off the bone easily, then refrigerate. Wash the bones well and set aside.

Salad
3 In 4 bowls, make 4 same-sized salads using all the ingredients and some of the truffle slices (separating the salad into different bowls makes the plating easier).

Finishing Touches
4 Preheat the oven to 150°C (300°F). Cut the cooled marrow into cubes, set them on a baking sheet, and heat them in the oven for approximately 2 minutes.

5 Divide the marrow among the bowls and mix. Place a chilled bone on every plate. Fill the bones with salad, and top with bordelaise sauce. Dust on some parmesan and garnish with the remaining truffle slices.

TIP
+ You can substitute the olive oil bread with croutons topped with mushroom gum [P. 70]. The salad must be kept light.

TRUFFLES

TRUFFLE CAVATELLI

SERVES 6
PREPARATION: 1:30 HRS
REST: 2 HRS

Cavatelli
· 200 g (7 oz) ricotta
· 1 egg yolk
· 125 g (½ cup) fine semolina flour

Sauce
· 2 cloves garlic, minced
· 2 tbsp olive oil
· 330 ml (1⅓ cups) 35 % cream
· Salt and freshly ground black pepper

Finishing Touches
· A little truffle, minced
· 125 g (½ cup) parmesan cheese, grated
· Some chives, minced

Cavatelli
1 In a round-bottomed mixing bowl, mix the ricotta and egg yolk by hand until even in texture. Add the flour and mix until a firm dough forms. Do not overwork the dough. Knead into a ball and wrap in plastic. Refrigerate for 2 hours.

2 Divide the dough in two, and roll each half into a cylinder 2 cm (¾ in) in diameter. Cut each cylinder into 2 cm (¾ in) thick slices. Roll the cavatelli on the back of a fork or gnocchi board to hollow them out and to make grooves on the outside.

Sauce
3 In a frying pan, brown the garlic in olive oil. Add the cream, season to taste, and reduce by half over medium heat. Set aside.

Finishing Touches
4 Cook the pasta in a large pot filled with boiling, salted water: the pasta is done 15 seconds after its floats to the surface. Drain immediately.

5 Heat the sauce. Add the truffle pieces, pasta and parmesan cheese. Reheat and garnish with chives.

TRUFFLES

Once upon a time at *Citrus,* Normand made a striped bass dish with a leek and potato based hash, topped with thin strips of truffle. This dish stayed on the menu for a long time. On occasion it was overcooked, causing the garnish to nearly turn into a purée. One day, this happy accident inspired Normand to create a gratin dish with layers of leek, potato, spinach and fresh goat cheese. Long featured on the *Toqué!* menu, the Goat Cheese Gratin [P. 402] is now available at *Brasserie T!*.

[P. 402]

STRIPED BASS WITH TRUFFLES

SERVES 4
PREPARATION: 45 MIN

Leek & Potato Mix
· 200 g (2 cups) leeks, diced
· 2 tbsp butter
· 320 g (2 cups) potatoes, peeled and diced
· Salt and freshly ground black pepper
· 750 ml (3 cups) white poultry stock [P. 450]

Striped Bass
· 4 × 150 g (5 oz) filets of wild striped bass with the skin
· 8 slices of black truffle, 1 mm thick
· 2 tbsp olive oil
· 1 tbsp butter

Finishing Touches
· 1 tbsp butter
· 2 tbsp black truffle, minced
· Chervil, chopped

Leek & Potato Mix
1 In a pot over medium heat, sweat the leeks in butter. Add the potatoes and salt and pepper to taste. Moisten with the poultry stock and simmer gently until the potatoes get soft.

Striped Bass
2 Make 2 incisions halfway through the fish on the skin-side of the filets. Insert the truffle slices in these incisions.

3 Preheat the oven to 180°C (350°F). Season the filets. In a very hot frying pan, heat the olive oil and butter. Cook the fish skin-side down. When they're nice and coloured, lay the filets on a baking sheet skin-side up. Cook for 5 to 6 minutes, ensuring the centre of the fish remains tender.

Finishing Touches
4 While the fish is in the oven, heat up the leek and potato mix and adjust the seasoning. Add the butter and minced truffle. Serve a heaped spoonful on every plate. Set the fish on the vegetables and garnish with chervil.

TIP
+ To get the most of the truffle, make a straight cut with a knife and do the actual slicing with a mandoline. Mince the remaining truffle to flavour the leek and potato mix.

TRUFFLES

The term "truffled" applies to anything stuffed or infused with truffles. To maximize our flavours, we keep ours in a mason jar with eggs to take advantage of the eggs' porosity. You can then prepare sundry dishes (scrambled eggs, omelettes, English cream, ice cream, dacquoise, etc.) without having to add truffle.

ALL THINGS TRUFFLE

SERVES 4
PREPARATION: 1 HR
REST: 6 HRS

Truffle Ice Cream
· 250 ml (1 cup) 35 % cream
· 250 ml (1 cup) 3.25 % milk
· 8 egg yolks, truffle-flavoured [ABOVE]
· 90 g (⅓ cup + 2 tsp) sugar

Truffle Mousse
· 1 gelatin sheet
· 375 ml (1½ cups) milk
· 6 egg yolks, truffle-flavoured [ABOVE]
· 70 g (¼ cup + 2 tsp) sugar

Dried Truffle Meringue
· 3 truffle-perfumed egg whites
· 240 g (1 cup) sugar
· 5 g (1 tsp) truffle, fine-cut

Finishing Touches
· A few thin truffle slices (optional)

Truffle Ice Cream
1 In a pot over medium heat, warm the cream and milk. In a bowl, whisk the egg yolks with sugar until creamed. Pour a little warm milk on the eggs, stir, then pour into a pot. Warm over medium heat, stirring continuously until the preparation coats the back of a spoon. Pour into a conical strainer. Let the preparation cool, run it through an ice cream maker, and freeze.

Truffle Mousse
2 Bloom the gelatin in a bowl of cold water. In a pot over medium heat, heat the milk. In a bowl, whisk the egg yolks with sugar until creamed. Pour a little hot milk on the eggs, stir, then pour into a pot. Warm over medium heat, stirring continuously until the preparation coats the back of a spoon. Add the strained gelatin, mix well, and pour into a conical strainer.

3 Let the preparation cool to room temperature and pour it into a whipped cream dispenser. Load two N₂O gas chargers, stirring after each addition, and keep the dispenser in the refrigerator for 6 hours. [P. 451]

Dried Truffle Meringue
4 Preheat the oven to 105°C (220°F). In a table mixer, whisk the egg whites until fluffy, gradually adding sugar until stiff peaks form. Add the truffle pieces. Spread the mixture on parchment paper, top with another sheet of parchment, and flatten with a spatula into a thin layer of meringue. Remove any excess. Separate the sheets of parchment paper and bake each one on a baking sheet for 20 minutes.

Finishing Touches
5 Serve the truffle mousse in deep bowls or cups. Cover with dried meringue, and top with a scoop of truffle ice cream. Garnish with truffle slices.

TRUFFLES

For this dish, we used ganache and truffle trimmings to make mock truffles. We made irregular-shaped balls that we blackened with dark chocolate to the approximate colour of real truffles. We then made cocoa nougatine, which we chopped to give it a rocky look.

MOCK CHOCOLATE TRUFFLES

MAKES APPROXIMATELY 15 MOCK TRUFFLES
REFRIGERATE 12 HRS

Mock Truffles
· 400 g (14 oz) Valrhona Caraibe chocolate
· 60 g (2 oz) Valrhona Tanariva chocolate
· 60 ml (¼ cup) brandy
· 400 ml (1⅔ cups) 35 % cream
· 60 ml (¼ cup) glucose or corn syrup
· 120 g (½ cup) cold butter, cut into small pieces
· Slices of fresh black truffle (optional)
· Cocoa powder

Nougatine (mock earth)
· 300 g (1¼ cups) sugar
· 7 tbsp water
· 300 g (2 cups) hazelnuts or a mix of pistachios, almonds and hazelnuts
· 60 g (¼ cup) cocoa powder

Mock Truffle
1 Mix the chocolates and brandy in a food processor. In a pot, bring the cream and glucose to a boil and pour on the chocolate. Emulsify in the food processor, gradually adding the butter, blending it completely into the mixture. Add the truffle slices. Let the ganache sit overnight in a covered bowl in a cool, dry place.

2 The following day, roll the ganache into fairly round balls approximately 3 cm (1¼ in) in diameter. Place them on a sheet and refrigerate to cool. Roll the mock truffles in cocoa powder.

Nougatine (mock earth)
3 In a pot, heat the sugar and water to 145°C (293°F) to make caramel. Turn off the heat, add the hazelnuts and cocoa. Spread the preparation on a sheet, and cool to room temperature. Reduce to a granular powder in a food processor.

Finishing Touches
4 Scatter a little nougatine on every plate, and place a mock truffle in the middle.

TIP
+ At the restaurant, rather than roll the mock truffles in cocoa, we use a paint gun to coat them with a mixture of chocolate and food dye to make them look like real truffles.

CHEESE

For the past few years, we've been serving cheese as a dish. In this way, cheese is always a part of our tasting menu, and eases the transition to dessert.

PSEUDO PIZZAS

SERVES 4
PREPARATION: 35 MINUTES

Parmesan Cream
· 60 ml (¼ cup) 35 % cream
· 1 tbsp parmesan cheese, grated
· Fine grain salt

Pseudo Pizzas
· A few cherry tomatoes, cut in half
· Olive oil bread [P. 446]
· 60 ml (¼ cup) parmesan cream
· A few leaves of basil
· 4 thin slices of Comtomme cheese, approximately 30 g (1 oz) each
· 2 tbsp red pepper glaze [P. 66]
· 2 tbsp olive oil
· Maldon salt and freshly ground black pepper

Parmesan Cream
1 In a bowl, whip the cream until soft in texture. Add the parmesan cheese, and salt to taste. Refrigerate.

Pseudo Pizzas
2 Preheat the oven on broil. Place the cherry tomatoes in the 4 ovenproof plates, along with slices of olive oil bread, 1 tbsp of parmesan cream and a few leaves of basil.

3 Top with a slice of Comtomme cheese and melt for 10 seconds without browning, until the cheese drapes over the garnish. Add a few dabs of red pepper glaze and dashes of olive oil. Add Maldon salt and black pepper to taste.

TIP
+ Prepare the Pseudo Pizzas on a large service plate so people can share. You can make this recipe with raclette cheese or another tomme. You can also adapt the toppings to the season: mushrooms, peppers, herbs, basil, etc.

CHEESE

GOAT CHEESE GRATIN
SERVES 6

Leek & Potato Mix
· 1 leek, diced in 1 cm (½ in) cubes
· 2 tbsp butter
· 500 g (1 lb) Yukon Gold potatoes, peeled and diced in 1 cm (½ in) cubes

Beet Juice
· 8 medium-sized beets, peeled, cut into pieces
· 2 Golden Delicious apples, seeded and cut into pieces

Balsamic Dressing
· 3 tbsp balsamic vinegar
· 2 tbsp mustard
· Maldon salt and freshly ground black pepper
· 60 ml (¼ cup) olive oil
· 60 ml (¼ cup) peanut oil
· 1 tbsp hot water (optional)

Spinach
· 90 g (3 oz) spinach
· 1 tbsp olive oil

Finishing Touches
· 250 g (9 oz) unripened goat cheese
· 6 handfuls of mesclun

Leek & Potato Mix
1 In a pot over medium heat, sweat the leek in butter. Add the potatoes, cover with water, add a lid and simmer until soft. Drain off any excess liquid and cool to room temperature on a large plate.

Beet Juice
2 Juice the beets and apples, and pour into a pot. Reduce by half over medium heat, occasionally skimming the surface.

Balsamic Dressing
3 In a bowl, mix the vinegar, mustard, Maldon salt and pepper. Trickle in the oils, emulsifying. Add hot water if the consistency is too thick.

Spinach
4 In a frying pan over high heat, sauté the spinach in olive oil. Add salt and pepper to taste, and set aside on paper towels.

Finishing Touches
5 Preheat the oven on broil. Fill a baking ring halfway up with potatoes. Add a layer of spinach, and top up with goat cheese, smoothed out with a spatula. Do the same with the other 5 potato rings. Bake for a few moments until golden.

6 Turn out the potatoes *au gratin* onto deep plates. Toss the mesclun with dressing and put some in each plate. Add a little beet juice around the potatoes and serve right away.

CHEESE

BLUE CHEESE
AND MERINGUE

SERVES 4
PREPARATION: 30 MIN
COOKING: 1:30 HRS

· 3 egg whites
· 180 g (¾ cup) sugar
· 6 tbsp 35 % cream
· 100 g (3½ oz) Ciel de Charlevoix
  cheese, cut into big pieces

1 In a bowl, with an electric mixer, add a little sugar and beat the egg whites until fluffy. Keep beating the egg whites until they've risen three quarters of the way. Gradually add the remaining sugar in 5 or 6 stages to get stiff peaks.

2 Preheat the oven to 105°C (220°F). On a baking sheet with parchment paper, spread the egg whites to a thickness of 1½ cm (⅔ in). Bake for 1½ hours, rotating the sheet halfway through for even cooking.

3 In a bowl, whip the cream until soft peaks form.

4 Spoon some whipped cream on each plate. Cover with pieces of cheese and add pieces of broken meringue.

TIP
+ You can substitute the Ciel de Charlevoix with Fourme d'Ambert.

ANOTHER ROUND
FOR SAMUEL...

BÉNÉDICTE ET STÉPHANE TISSOT
Poulsard, Savagnin
JURA

Clients often expect to be served red wine with cheese. However, red wine does not hold up to the lactic aspect of cheeses, so we set about finding the right pairing for our cheese dishes. The cheeses we prepare are best complemented by whites because in addition to "slimming" the cheeses down, we can link wines to the dishes. What's more, by returning to a white wine, you cleanse your palate and give your meal a "fresh start." One example of a wine we serve with Pseudo Pizza is the Macvin du Jura, a mix of Marc du Jura with grape must. On an olfactory level, you'll find the strength and the "jute sack" aspect of an eau de vie. From a gustatory standpoint, though, it's soft and supple with a dried fruit finish.

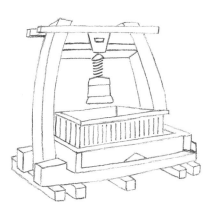

SQUASH

Dianne grows a very juicy, bright orange squash variety known as *Rouge Vif d'Étampes*, nicknamed the Cinderella Pumpkin. While few people eat it since it's relatively unknown, it has a very smooth consistency with which we make a delectable ice cream.

CINDERELLA PUMPKIN ICE CREAM WITH ROASTED SEEDS

SERVES 4
PREPARATION: 1 HR
COOKING: 1:30 HRS

Pumpkin Purée
· 1 Cinderella pumpkin, approximately 3 kg (6 lbs)
· 4 tbsp honey

Cinderella Pumpkin Ice Cream
· 125 ml (½ cup) 35 % cream
· 3 egg yolks
· 60 g (¼ cup) sugar
· 125 ml (½ cup) milk
· 250 g (1 cup) pumpkin purée

Roasted Pumpkin Seeds
· 2 tbsp olive oil

Pumpkin Purée
1 Preheat the oven to 180°C (350°F). Slice the pumpkin in two, remove the seeds, and set them aside. Place the pumpkin, skin up, on a large baking sheet. Bake until the tip of a knife is easily inserted. Remove the flesh with a spoon. Mash the flesh to a smooth purée in a food processor, mixing in the honey.

Cinderella Pumpkin Ice Cream
2 In a bowl, mix the pumpkin purée with 60 ml (¼ cup) of cream, and set aside. In another bowl, whisk the egg yolks with sugar until creamed. In a pot over low heat, heat the milk and remaining cream. Slowly mix a little luke-warm milk into the creamed eggs, and then pour the resultant mixture back into the pot. Cook over medium heat until the prepa-ration coats the back of a spoon. Pour into a conical strainer, then mix with the pumpkin purée. Cool to room temperature, process in an ice cream maker, and freeze.

Roasted Pumpkin Seeds
3 Preheat the oven to 180°C (350°F). After carefully washing the pumpkin seeds, mix them with the olive oil. Spread them onto a baking sheet and roast for 8 to 10 minutes. Let them cool, and shell with a sharp knife.

Finishing Touches
4 Put a scoop of Cinderella pumpkin ice cream in every sherbet glass, and garnish with the roasted seeds.

TIP
+ You can also make this recipe with other types of squash that hold a lot of water.

CITRUS FRUITS

ORANGE, IT'S A PARTY!

SERVES 4
PREPARATION: 1:30 HRS
REFRIGERATE: 4 HRS

Orange Mousse
· 125 ml (½ cup) orange juice
· 2 tbsp lemon juice
· 240 g (1 cup) sugar
· 4 eggs
· 240 g (1 cup) butter, in small pieces

Orange Peels
· 4 oranges

Orange Sugar
· 240 g (1 cup) sugar
· 2 tbsp orange juice
· Zest of 3 oranges

Orange Marmalade
· 3 tbsp orange zest
· 500 g (3 cups) orange pulp
· 250 ml (1 cup) orange juice
· 160 g (⅔ cup) sugar

Meringue Sticks
· 3 egg whites
· 160 g (⅔ cup) sugar
· Red food dye

Finishing Touches
· 2 oranges, supremed

Orange Mousse
1 In a pot over low heat, combine the orange and lemon juice, sugar and eggs. Boil, and remove from the heat as soon as it froths. Turn off the heat, add butter and mix well. Cool in the fridge. Pour into a whipped cream dispenser, and load two N$_2$O chargers. Put dispenser on ice in the refrigerator for a minimum of 4 hours. [P. 451]

Orange Peels
2 Cut off the tops of the oranges. Using a spoon with a sharp edge, scoop out the inside of the orange, without piercing the peel. Set the pulp aside for the marmalade preparation, and place the empty orange peel shells on a sheet in the freezer.

Orange Sugar
3 Mix everything, and set aside.

Orange Marmalade
4 In a saucepan filled with boiling water, blanch the orange zest, then drain. Mix all the ingredients and boil. Lower the heat and simmer the mixture for approximately 1 hour, until the zest is translucent. Remove from the heat and refrigerate.

Meringue Sticks
5 In a bowl, whisk the egg whites until fluffy and slowly add sugar until stiff peaks form. Separate into 3 parts and add 2 drops of food colouring in each one.

6 Preheat the oven to 220°C (425°F). Place the meringue in a pastry bag with a round tip (2 mm in diameter), and draw lines on the parchment paper lining the baking sheet. Bake for 15 minutes.

Finishing Touches
7 Put a spoonful of marmalade and a few orange supremes in each frozen orange peel shell. Top up with orange mousse. Lay a spoonful of orange sugar on every plate as a bed for the shell. Plant a few sticks of coloured meringue in the mousse, and serve immediately.

TIPS
+ You can make different coloured meringue sticks. Always make more than enough, since they tend to break easily.

+ You can garnish this dish with fir sugar.

KILL THE PIG

Félix is one of the cooks who oversees the butchering and preparation for *Brasserie T!*. Born in the Northern Philippines, Félix worked in his native country slaughtering suckling pigs and preparing them in the local traditional manner called *lechón*. He's been part of the kitchen staff for some two years now. We get together on occasion with friends to have a chat over a pig. When Daniel Boulud visited from New York City, we went to Martin Picard's sugar shack. Gaspor brought a piglet, and David McMillan, Frédéric Morin and Daniel Vézina joined us for the show. This ancestral know-how benefits us greatly, providing us with a wellspring of inspiration that lets us further our own techniques.

FÉLIX'S ROAST PIG

Materials
· 1 box of razor blades
· 4 rolls of iron wire or bamboo cord
· 2 × 13 cm (5 in) nails
· 1 sharpened bamboo stick,
  4½ m × 5 cm (15 ft × 2 in)
· 2 Y-shaped tree branches 50 cm
  (1 ½ ft) long
· 8 to 10 bags of wood charcoal
· 1 bamboo branch
· 1 rag
· 1 big bucket of hot water

Ingredients
· 1 pig (*lechón*), 20 kg (44 lbs)
· 3 heads garlic
· 10 bay leaves
· 2 to 3 stems of lemon grass
· 12 tbsp black peppercorns
· 200 g (¾ cup) salt
· 5 shallots

For basting
· 500 ml (2 cups) soy sauce
· 500 ml (2 cups) vegetable oil

1 Slaughter the pig. Wait a few minutes to make sure it's dead. Rinse it with cold water before soaking it in lukewarm water and cleaning it. Caution: if the water is too hot, it will damage the skin.

2 Pour hot water on all the parts that need to be shaved. Use a razor blade to painstakingly remove all the fur, including the finer hairs (nose, toes, etc.). Douse with more hot water, and keep shaving. Following this, soak the legs in hot water to remove the toenails.

3 Cut open the pig with a blade, drain, and rinse thoroughly and repeatedly with cold water.

4 With a knife, cut a hole in the throat and anus. Wash the pig meticulously inside and out, leaving no trace of blood. Insert the bamboo stick in the anus, and make it come out the mouth.

5 Use the iron wire or bamboo cord to tie the front legs together, and do the same with the hind legs. Position the pig in the middle of the bamboo branch, which must be much longer than the animal so you can turn it over the fire. Drive a long nail into the head and another into the back to keep the pig solidly attached to the bamboo while cooking.

6 In a bowl, mix all the aromatics, and put them inside the pig through the hole in its stomach. Stitch it up with a needle and thread or wire. Brush the skin evenly with just enough soy sauce for it to get crispy and fire-engine red.

7 Before you start cooking, measure the pig's length so you'll know how far apart the Y-shaped branches that hold the spit need to be. The pig must be approximately 30 cm (1 ft) from the ground with fire burning on either side.

8 Turn the pig clockwise, slowly and continuously, to cook evenly. With an oil-soaked rag on the end of a bamboo branch, dab lightly over the parts of the skin that turn red in order to keep them from burning. Do this whenever areas of the pig seem to be cooking too quickly. Cooking time is between 3 and 3½ hours, depending on the size of the animal. Add wood charcoal if the fire tapers.

9 You'll know the pig is ready when you stick a knife or fork into one of the meatier parts (e.g., ham or shoulder) and the flesh is tender, offering no resistance. Otherwise, continue cooking.

"I always loved him because of his generosity. He's a man of principles and instinct. He's my favourite chef in the world, the one who inspires me most. One day, I made a dish for him: scampi poached in beer with sauerkraut and a matsutake broth. The sauerkraut and beer remind us of our parties and celebrations, the matsutake of our common Quebecois heritage, and the scampi—well that just reminds me of Normand himself: a guy that's all about delicacy, but with a shell that's hard as a rock!"

Daniel Vézina, Chef at *Laurie Raphaël*

"The *Toqué!* universe is about as wild as *Star Trek*'s universe. I find in it all my favourite heroes: captain James T. Kirk (Normand), lieutenant Hikaru Sulu (Charles) and the beautiful Seven of Nine (Christine)!"

David McMillan, Chef at *Joe Beef*

"If Normand had been given a cupcake for every career he jump started, today, he'd be pretty darn fat!"

Fred Morin, Chef at *Joe Beef*

"Normand is a loyal man. I'm convinced that it's partly thanks to this quality that he's part of the international culinary elite. In my business, you end up working for quite a few chefs in you career, but, naturally, you pick one to whom you'll always remain attached, throughout your life—even if you don't work for him anymore. It's with this loyalty and respect that I view Normand today."

Martin Picard, Chef at *Au pied de cochon*

"Charles-Antoine is incredibly professional and generous. What I admire in him is his loyalty, energy, but more than anything, his "craziness." He still has that child-like spirit. We, French people, love Canadians with their humour that's completely different from ours, and their free spirit. I love North America for that simple reason. I break it down to a New Orleans expression: "Let the good times roll!"

Daniel Boulud, Chef at *Daniel*

"Charles-Antoine is the most generous and intense person I know. He's very creative and sensitive. It can be difficult to work with him since he's so intimidating and loves to work under pressure. Today, more than an unending source of inspiration, Charles is my best friend."

Cheryl Johnson, former sous-chef at *Toqué!*

"Maybe ten years ago, preoccupied by the changes he wanted to make to the menu, Normand woke up in the middle of the night to be alone in the restaurant's kitchen. He was still there by the time the sun came up. When he got back home, he told me about all the new dishes he'd made up. The last one really made an impression. "A cold cod soup, really? " And he told me: "Don't you trust me? " The serving staff was also pretty surprised. Normand got everyone to taste it and the team simply loved it. But never as much as I did. Later, when we talked about that night, he told me he needed a quiet space to cook freely."

Sophie Dormeau, wife of Normand Laprise

"My first meeting with Normand Laprise remains an important moment in my life. During my first visit to Quebec in March 2011, I was graciously hosted by the *Toqué!* team during one of Montreal's festivals, *Montréal en lumière*. Normand and I immediately discovered that we had much in common, starting with the way we represent our values through our cooking. More than that, I think our families are at the heart of our respective processes. We both refuse to be parents that are nothing more than travellers in the lives of our children, since they represent, in a way, what we love about cooking: transmitting, sharing, loving. We are also linked by our common expectations towards the quality of ingredients we use and the care and respect that artisans put into farming and breeding. Normand introduced me to wonderful products, from small aromatic shoots and leaves to maple syrup... I tasted the *Cerf de Boileau*, the famous deer whose meat is incredibly tender and slightly less gamey than its European cousin; a wild scallop caught while ice fishing, a sea buckthorn berry that tasted like passion fruit, a quirky looking carrot with a subtle taste and lettuces with sharp and sophisticated flavours. The professionalism of the cooks in his kitchen also impressed me when it came to choosing the right products. After all, traceability of products is a relatively unknown concept in Canada, and choices are rather limited since producers aren't organized as well as they are in France. However, his staff was able to identify the right ingredient by looking at it from every angle. Cooking under these circumstances creates spontaneity and creativity. All of my discussions with Normand Laprise went to the bottom of things, their source. I even brought funny looking carrot seeds back from my trip, which I then planted in my dearly loved Rhône Valley! There exists, I think, commonalities between the place in which we are born and the emotions that arise from the things we taste: the alluvial plains of our respective homelands, the search for the natural in Montreal and the organic in Valence, the love for our products and those that raise them, a passion for taste and flavours; these are the things that bring us together. Equilibrium, generosity, simplicity and humility are those qualities that make me admire both his character and his cooking. I'm proud to be able to continuously share and communicate with Normand, to flavour and strengthen our young and beautiful friendship."

Anne-Sophie Pic, Chef at *Maison Pic*

APPENDIX

FOUNDATIONS

BALSAM FIR POWDER

Carefully detach the balsam fir needles from the branches, or cut them off with scissors. With a small coffee grinder, pulverise 15 g (¼ cup) of needles at a time.

BALSAM FIR
AND MALDON SALT
· 50 g (½ cup) balsam fir needles.
· 3 tbsp Maldon salt

In a coffee grinder, reduce the balsam fir needles into a powder. Add the Maldon salt and pulse for three seconds.

BALSAM FIR SUGAR
· 5 tbsp fir needles
· 7 tbsp cane sugar

In a coffee grinder, powder the sugar and fir needles together.

BORDELAISE SAUCE

MAKES 250 ML (1 CUP)
PREPARATION: 2 HRS

· 60 ml (¼ cup) olive oil
· 150 g (5 oz) beef trimmings [TIP]
· 2 dried shallots
· 2 cloves garlic, sliced in half
· 5 g (1 tsp) black peppercorns
· 1 tbsp thyme
· 1 tbsp parsley
· 2 tbsp cognac
· 2 tbsp red wine
· 250 ml (1 cup) venison stock, reduced [BROWN STOCK, PAGE 444]
· 500 ml (2 cups) water

In a large pan, over high heat, heat the olive oil and cook the beef trimmings so as to colour them as much as possible. Add the shallots, garlic, peppercorns, thyme and parsley. Colour lightly and deglaze with cognac. Reduce by half and add the red wine. Reduce a little, and then add the stock and water. Simmer 1 hour, or until the water is completely evaporated. Pour through a sieve and set aside.

TIP
+ Gather up a few trimmings when you cut the meat.

BRIOCHE

MAKES 30 BRIOCHES
PREPARATION: 3 HRS
REST: 12 HRS

· 500 g (3½ cups) flour
· 65 g (¼ cup + 1 tsp) sugar
· 10 g (2 tsp) salt
· 18.5 g (⅔ oz) fresh yeast
· 6 eggs
· 250 g (1 cup) cold butter, in pieces
· 1 egg yolk
· 1 pinch salt
· 1 pinch sugar

Using a stand mixer equipped with a hook, at low speed, mix the flour, sugar, salt, yeast and eggs together for about 7 minutes, until smooth. Add the butter, a few pieces at a time, and increase to medium speed. (The dough is ready when it detaches itself from the sides of the bowl.) Put the dough in a bowl and cover with a plastic film. Set aside at room temperature for 2 hours, and then refrigerate overnight.

The next day, punch down the dough. Slice in 30 g (1 oz) pieces and fashion into small balls by moving your hands in a circular motion. Put away on a baking tray while leaving at least 10 cm (4 in) between each ball, and then cover with plastic film. Let rest in a warm area (on the top of an oven or the drier or something similar) for about three hours.

In a small bowl, prepare the glaze by mixing the egg yolk, salt and sugar.

Preheat a convection oven to 180°C (350°F). With the help of a baker's brush, brush each ball with the glaze. With a well-sharpened knife, make a cross on each ball. Bake in the oven for 7 to 10 minutes, until the centre of the brioche is well cooked and the outside has a nice caramelized colour.

BROWN STOCK (MEAT JUS)
PREPARATION: 6 HRS

· 2 kg (4 lbs) bones
· 500 g (1 lb) mirepoix [P.448]
· 1 dash vegetable oil
· 125 g (½ cup) tomato paste
· 1 bouquet garni (mixture of fresh herbs; bay leaves, parsley, thyme, etc.)

Preheat the oven to 200°C (400°F). With a cleaver, break the bones apart. Place on baking sheet and cook until uniformly coloured, stirring regularly.

In a pot, color the mirepoix in oil until coloured. Add the tomato paste, the bouquet garni and the bones. Cover with water. Bring to a boil and simmer 6 hours over medium heat, skimming the surface from time to time. Strain, refrigerate and remove the fat that has formed on the surface. The next day, reduce over medium heat until you reach the consistency of a glaze.

CLARIFIED BUTTER
PREPARATION: 10 MIN

In a small pot, over medium heat, melt the butter completely. Pour through a coffee filter, being careful to filter out the whey (the clear liquid at the bottom of the pan). The purpose of this operation is to remove the impurities that make the butter go rancid and prevent it from supporting high heat. Keep the clarified butter in the refrigerator until ready to use.

COURT-BOUILLON

GIVES 5 LITRES (20 CUPS)
PREPARATION: 1 HR

- 5 litres (20 cups) water
- 1 lemon, chopped
- 1 medium carrot, chopped
- 1 onion, chopped
- 1 tbsp pepper
- 1 bay leaf
- 120 g (½ cup) salt

In a pot, combine all the ingredients and simmer for 1 hour. Remove the vegetables and spices and store in the refrigerator.

FIR SUGAR

- 5 tbsp fir needles
- 7 tbsp cane sugar

Use a coffee grinder to reduce the fir needles and sugar to fine powder, and set aside.

GREEN ONION OIL

MAKES 250 ML (1 CUP)
REST: 12 HRS

- 1½ bunches green onions (only the green part)
- 250 ml (1 cup) olive oil or grape seed oil, at room temperature

Wash the green onions well and thinly chop. In a pot filled with boiling water, blanch them for about 30 seconds. (It's important not to cool the green onions down).

Carefully pat dry and mix with the oil using a hand mixer. Cool on ice. Pour in a container and let rest in the refrigerator for 12 hours. Filter through a conical strainer. Store in a container or glass pipette.

HERBALICIOUS

MAKES 150 G (2 CUPS)
PREPARATION: 15 MIN

- 60 g (1 cup) flat-leaf parsley
- 20 g (1 cup) coriander
- 10 g (1 cup) dill
- 100 g (1 cup) green onion
- 2 tbsp garlic, chopped
- 1 tbsp fresh ginger, chopped
- 250 ml (1 cup) olive oil

Roughly chop the herbs and green onions. In a blender, grind all the ingredients together with the oil. Serve with poultry, grilled fish or in a salad. You can vary the ingredients as well as the quantities depending on what's available.

THE LIFE OF BREAD

We have three ways to recycle the previous day's bread. With fried bread we obtain very fine breadcrumbs with which we coat fish before roasting them. We also like to add it to oil to add a bit of texture to our salads and garnishes. Olive oil bread is sliced, cooked in the oven and used as croutons for salads. Finally, burnt bread is a great way to recycle brioches.

OLIVE OIL BREAD

- 1 loaf of yesterday's bread (without nuts or seeds)
- 160 ml (⅔ cup) olive oil
- Freshly ground black pepper

Preheat the oven to 180°C (350°F). Cut the bread in very thin slices and spread them out on a baking sheet lined with parchment paper. Cover with the olive oil, add pepper to taste and bake for 10 minutes until the bread is crunchy. (Don't let the bread colour too much, it needs to be golden without being burnt.) Let the bread sit on the tray, so that it doesn't lose its oil. If you intend to keep the bread for a later use, cover and store at room temperature.

FRIED BREAD

- 1 loaf of bread (without nuts and seeds)
- Canola oil (for frying)

The day before, slice the bread and let it dry out at room temperature.

The next day, in a food processor, make breadcrumbs with your bread slices. Strain through a metal sieve. Set the breadcrumbs that passed through the sieve aside, and use those left in the sieve for the recipe.

In a fryer, heat the canola oil to 180°C (350°F). Fry the breadcrumbs for 15 seconds, and strain on paper towels. Dry out on a baking tray lined with parchment paper in an oven preheated to 165°C (330°F) for 10 minutes, in order to cook off the surplus oil.

BURNT BREAD

- Yesterday's brioches [P 443]

Tear the previous day's brioches into large pieces and burn them with a blowtorch just before serving. (The sugar in the brioche will help them caramelize slightly.)

LIQUID BRINE

MAKES 1 LITRE (4 CUPS)
PREPARATION: 30 MIN

- 1 litre (4 cups) water
- 5 tbsp fine salt
- 2 tbsp sugar
- 1 bay leaf
- 2 tbsp pepper

In a pot, bring all the ingredients to a boil until the salt has melted. Store in a cool place. Use on poultry or game meat.

MARINATED DAYLILY OR DAISY BUDS

FILLS 2 × 500 ML JARS (2 CUPS)
PREPARATION: 30 MIN
REFRIGERATE 3 WEEKS

· 260 g (1½ cups) daylily or daisy buds
· 400 g (1 cup) coarse salt
· 500 ml (2 cups) rice vinegar
· 120 g (½ cup) granulated white sugar
· 2 g (1 tsp) black peppercorns
· 1 sprig thyme
· 1 bay leaf

Mix the daylily buds and coarse salt. Let them sit for 30 minutes. Rinse off the excess salt with cold water, drain, and seal the buds in a couple of preserve jars.

Meanwhile, in a pot, bring the remaining ingredients to a boil. Pour the mixture immediately onto the daylily buds, and reseal the jars. Keep in the fridge for a minimum of 3 weeks before using. The marinated buds will keep for a few months in the fridge.

The marinated daylily or daisy buds can be used to replace capers.

MARINATED WILD LEEKS

Wild leek, a.k.a. ramp, is a protected species in Quebec. Each person is limited to picking 50 bulbs a year. We marinate wild leeks in order to keep it longer. You can use the plant's leaves without endangering the species.

FILLS 2 × 500 ML JARS (2 CUPS)
PREPARATION: 30 MIN
REST: 3 HRS

· 100 g (3½ oz) wild leek bulbs (about 30), washed
· 100 g (½ cup) coarse salt
· 1 L (4 cups) rice vinegar
· 240 g (1 cup) sugar
· 1 bay leaf
· 2 tbsp pepper

In a bowl, cover the wild leek bulbs with the coarse salt, and let them sit for 3 hours, stirring every 30 minutes. Rinse the salt off completely with cold water and sponge with a cloth. Place the bulbs in a pair of clean 250 ml (1 cup) mason jars.

Mix the vinegar, sugar, bay leaf and black pepper in a pot, and bring to a boil. Pour the mixture immediately onto the bulbs, and seal the jars. Let sit at room temperature for 3 hours. Store the preparation in the fridge for at least 1 month before using. Use the thinly sliced bulbs in salads or heated to accompany roast meats. Marinated wild leek will keep for 1 year in the fridge.

Use the wild leek leaves in herbalicious [P. 445], instead of green onions in the green onion oil [P. 445] or as a fresh herb.

Reuse the infused vinegar—once the jars are empty—to flavour other recipes.

MAYONNAISE

MAKES 300 ML (1 ¼ CUPS)
PREPARATION: 20 MIN

· 1 egg yolk
· ½ tbsp Dijon mustard
· Salt
· 1 tbsp lemon juice
· 180 ml (¾ cup) grape seed oil
· 60 ml (¼ cup) olive oil
· 1 tbsp warm water (optional)

In a bowl, with a hand mixer or a whisk, mix the egg yolk, mustard, salt and lemon juice. Continue whisking the mayonnaise while slowly pouring the grape seed oil and olive oil, so as to let the emulsion form. (If the oil ceases to blend, immediately stop adding more oil and whisk vigorously. When the texture is smooth once again, add the rest of the oil.) At the end of the process, if the texture is too thick, slowly add a touch of warm water while continuously whisking until you reach the desired texture.

AÏOLI

When preparing the mayonnaise add 2 minced garlic cloves with the egg yolk and mustard.

MIREPOIX

A preparation normally made of equal parts celery, onion, leeks, and carrots chopped in pieces of various sizes depending on the cooking time and chosen recipe.

POPCORN POWDER

MAKES ABOUT 80 G (4 CUPS)
PREPARATION: 15 MIN

· 125 g (½ cup) unpopped popcorn
· 2 tbsp neutral oil

In a pot, over medium heat, heat the oil and drop in the unpopped popcorn. Cover and pop while shaking the pot.

Using a coffee grinder, crush the popcorn into a fine powder. You can then either use it as is, or flavour it with grated parmesan or garlic powder.

SIMPLE SYRUP

MAKES 500 ML (2 CUPS)
PREPARATION: 30 MIN

· 250 ml (1 cup) water
· 240 g (1 cup) sugar

In a pot, over medium heat, cook the ingredients while stirring regularly until the sugar has completely dissolved.

SMOKED DUCK FAT

MAKES 500 ML (2 CUPS) SMOKED FAT
INFUSION: 1 HR

· 2 cups (455 g) duck fat
· Smoked duck breast trimmings, minced (surplus fat, etc.)

In an ovenproof pot, melt the duck fat, and then add the duck breast trimmings.

Place the pot in an oven preheated to 95°C (200°F), and let steep for 1 hour. Filter through a conical strainer and set aside.

Depending on the chosen recipe, you can add a few in season berries to the warm smoked fat and serve immediately with poultry or game meat.

TARRAGON, CORIANDER, THYME OR BASIL OIL

· 120 g (3 cups) tarragon, coriander, thyme or basil leaves
· 250 ml (1 cup) grape seed oil or any other neutral oil

In a pot filled with boiling water, blanch the leaves for about 30 seconds and strain. In a food processor, quickly mix with the oil. Pour in bowl and immediately place the first bowl in a second, larger bowl filled with ice to fix the chlorophyll. Let steep in the refrigerator for 4 hours.

Let the oil reach room temperature. Pour through a coffee filter and store.

TUB O' DUCK FAT

The idea for Tub o' Duck Fat comes for our desire to put our surplus duck fat to good use rather than throwing it out. This method ensures even cooking of the chosen meat while keeping it from drying out. Our first attempt was with leg of veal, and then everything else followed: venison, duck filet, pigeon, rib steak... Once the meat is cooked, we save the fat to roast garlic, herbs and vegetables.

SERVES 4
PREPARATION: 20 MIN

· 1.8 kg (8 cups) duck fat
· 1 tbsp neutral oil
· 1 carrot, sliced
· 1 onion, sliced
· 3 cloves garlic, crushed
· 1 green part of the leek, thinly sliced
· 3 sprigs thyme
· 1 bay leaf
· 4 sage leaves
· 60 (¼ cup) water

In a rondeau pan 30 cm (12 in) in diameter and 15 cm (6 in) high, over low heat, melt the duck fat without boiling it until the temperature reaches between 85 and 90°C (185 and 195°F). Always remain within this range when cooking with the Tub o' Duck Fat.

In a frying pan, over high heat, heat the oil and sauté the vegetables and herbs until lightly coloured.

Place the vegetables at the bottom of the rondeau pan and add the water. (There should be at least 10 cm (4 in) melted fat over the vegetables.) Cook the pieces of meat in the Tub o' Duck fat by following the instructions in the given recipe.

TIP

+ The vegetables will create a protective barrier between the meat and the heat source. When the temperature is correctly maintained in the Tub o' Duck Fat, you should regularly see small pockets of evaporating air appearing at the surface. It's possible to reuse the fat a number of times by storing it in the refrigerator between uses and filtering it well. You need to add new vegetables every time you use the Tub o' Duck Fat.

VEGETABLE GLAZE

MAKES 250 ML (1 CUP)

· ½ red pepper
· ½ onion
· ½ carrot
· ½ leek
· ½ head garlic
· 5 litres (20 cups) water
· 4 tbsp honey
· 1 tbsp soy sauce
· 1 tbsp sherry vinegar

Wash, peel and roughly chop the vegetables [TIPS]. In pot, bring the vegetables and water to a boil and reduce by half. Strain through a conical strainer [TIPS] and bring back to a boil. Add the honey. Continue boiling the liquid until you obtain a texture close to that of molasses. Remove from heat, and then add the soy sauce and sherry vinegar. Cool down in the refrigerator.

TIPS

+ You can add other vegetables. It's a great way to use those vegetables that are starting to whither, as well as trimmings and peels.

+ You can filter the liquid through a sieve. However, you'll most likely have a few floating particles left. A coffee filter or a muslin will also do the trick.

VEGETABLE STOCK

· 1 carrot
· 1 leek
· 1 bunch parsley
· 1 onion
· 4 litres (16 cups) water
· Freshly ground black pepper

In a pot, place the roughly chopped vegetables. Pour the water over the vegetables, bring to a boil and let simmer for 45 minutes. Strain and add pepper. Let cool and store in the refrigerator.

WHITE POULTRY STOCK

PREPARATION: 3 HRS

· 2 kg (4 lbs) poultry carcasses
· 500 g (1 lb) Mirepoix [P. 448]

1 bouquet garni (mixture of fresh herbs; bay leaves, parsley, thyme, etc.)

With a cleaver, break the carcasses apart, then place them in a large pot. Cover with cold water, bring to a boil, skimming the surface from time to time. Add the mirepoix and the bouquet garni. Simmer for 2 hours over medium heat. Strain, refrigerate and remove the fat that forms on the surface. The next day, reduce over medium heat until you reach the consistency of a glaze. (Only about 20% of the original liquid should be left after the liquid has been reduced.)

TECHNICAL
MATERIAL

WHIPPED CREAM DISPENSER

You can buy both hot and cold dispensers. Before you use them, it's very important that you read the manufacturer's instructions and follow them closely. Here are the basic guidelines.

Hot dispenser

You must always use a hot dispenser for preparations that are to be served hot. Heat up your preparation without letting it boil before you pour it into your hot dispenser. Make sure the cap's seal is in place before you close the lid. Put in the first gas charger, shake well, and remove. It's normal for a little gas to escape. Put in the second charger, shake again, and remove. The content is now ready.

Sometimes you have to keep the dispenser hot before using. Boil water in a saucepan, and remove it from the heat. Plunge the base of the dispenser into the hot water. The preparation will stay hot for at least 20 minutes.

Cold dispenser

Any preparation containing gelatin that you intend to use with your cold dispenser must first be cooled before you pour it in. Make sure that the cap's seal is in place before you close the lid. Put in the first gas charger, shake well, and remove. It's normal for a little gas to escape. Put in the second charger, shake again, and remove. Refrigerate the dispenser upside down for 6 hours before using it. If you're in a hurry, you can refrigerate the dispenser upside down in a tub of ice. It then takes 4 hours.

CAUTION: WHEN THE DISPENSER IS EMPTY, IT'S IMPORTANT THAT YOU LET OUT ALL THE AIR BEFORE REMOVING THE LID.

If your preparation does not contain gelatin, simply cool it before pouring it into your dispenser. Put in the gas chargers, shaking well each time. Serve immediately.

PACOJET AND ICE CREAM MAKER

At the restaurant, every ice cream and sorbet recipe is made with a Pacojet, a device with a high-speed rotating blade that gives frozen preparations a very smooth, aerated texture while keeping them light. This device is rather expensive, so in this book we recommend you use an ice cream maker.

If you use a Pacojet to make ice cream or sorbet, reduce the amount of sugar specified in every recipe by about 20 % for best results.

THERMOMIX

A Thermomix is like a food processor that heats the food while mixing it up, providing you with perfectly heated creations. We use it for preparations such as sabayon and green onion oil.

TABLE
OF CONTENTS

INDEX

This book is the result of a group effort that saw a bunch of "toqués" come together to venture into the world of publishing for a journey that would last nearly three years. First Normand and Julia, who met at the screening of *Well Done* and set the wheels in motion. Then came Dominique, capturing every moment on camera and bringing you the spirit of the artisans of the *Toqué!* family from the four corners of Quebec. There was Catherine, who immersed herself completely in the *Toqué!* universe, working out of room BS1-28 (dubbed "the bunker") to document the creative culinary process through the seasons, with Charles as her guide. The texts in this book were culled from hundreds of hours of interviews with our producers, cooks and collaborators, whom she met with throughout the project. Three scribes had a hand in writing and organizing the content: Catherine, Julia and Julie from Les éditions du passage. Helping them was Sophie, who contributed her priceless anecdotes on Normand. As for the cooking itself, Normand, Charles, Marc-Antoine and Christine collected, recreated, tested and corrected all the recipes in this book. None of this would have been possible without the involvement of each and every cook and restaurant employee who participated not only in the photo shoots but also in the writing of the recipes, which Linda meticulously revised and harmonized. Finally, Raphaël, who shaped all this content into the beautiful object you now hold in your hands.

DOMINIQUE MALATERRE

Winner of more than 100 North American prizes, Dominique Malaterre shares her time between experimental contemporary photography and advertising. For this book, she opted to zoom in on the *Toqué!* universe through interactive photography, using a pair of digital cameras with the same settings; one stayed with her, while the other was entrusted to the restaurant's crew. Her impressions of *Toqué!* as a pictorial expression of Quebec's gastronomic identity conveys how the restaurant's dazzling culinary creations echo the fundamental elements of the Lower Saint Lawrence's vast landscapes as well as the Automatists' canvases.

TEXTS
Catherine Pinto, Julia Duchastel and Julie Clade

RECIPES
Linda Nantel, Marc-Antoine Dionne
and Jean-Sébastien Giguère

RECIPE REVISION AND EDITING
Linda Nantel

INDEX
Sophie Mhun

ENGLISH TRANSLATION
Jacob Homel and Enrico Caouette

ENGLISH REVISION
Carl Angers

KITCHEN COORDINATORS
Normand Laprise, Charles-Antoine Crête,
Jean-Sébastien Giguère, Marc-Antoine Dionne
and Christine Lamarche

WITH THE HELP AND PARTICIPATION OF
Cheryl Johnson, Rahim-Bin Abdullah Abdul,
Amin Nasrallah, Valérie Roger, Fei Suet Wong,
Steve Plante, Paul-Harry Toussaint, Raphaël
Gauthier, Samuel Beaulieu-Boivin, Anthony
Santi, Gabrielle Rivard-Hiller, Gaël Vetterli,
Philippe Reeves, Julien Thomas, François Allard,
Héléna Hubert, Robert Moore, Steven Molnar,
Jérémie Aucoin, Felix N. Bacolcol, Émilie
Beaulieu, as well as Gilbert Lemieux, bartender,
and Samuel Chevalier-Savaria, sommelier

PHOTOGRAPHY
AND ARTISTIC DIRECTION
Dominique Malaterre

ADDITIONAL PHOTOGRAPHY
Charles-Antoine Crête, Catherine Pinto
and Hans Laurendeau

RETOUCHING OF PHOTOGRAPHS
Nathalie Chapdelaine

LABEL DESIGN
Marc-André Chaput and Marie-Noëlle Chouinard

DESIGN
Feed

Toqué! would like to thank all the producers who
took part in this book and who supply the restaurant daily, as well as all of the restaurant's patrons
in its nearly 20 years of existence.

Our thanks to Ivanhoe Cambridge for graciously
lending us local BS1-28.

PRINTED AT
TRANSCONTINENTAL INTERGLOBE PRESS
BEAUCEVILLE, QUEBEC, CANADA
THIRD QUARTER, 2013